"The Tools
of My Trade"

JACK LONDON

"The Tools of My Trade"

THE ANNOTATED BOOKS IN JACK LONDON'S LIBRARY

David Mike Hamilton

University of Washington Press

Seattle and London

Library of Congress Cataloging in Publication Data

Hamilton, David Mike.
  "The tools of my trade."

  Bibliography: p.
  Includes index.
  1. London, Jack, 1876–1916—Books and reading.
2. London, Jack, 1876–1916—Library—Catalogs.
I. Title.
PS3523.046Z635   1986   818'.5209   84-40323
ISBN 0-295-96157-0

Manufactured in the United States of America

124001

For Carol

Contents

Photographs

Jack London Atop Sonoma Mountain

Preface

Jack London was an avid reader from his earliest years to his death 23 November 1916. During his forty-year lifetime, he amassed a considerable knowledge of the world through his personal life experiences and through the recorded life experiences of others—in books.

The purpose of this book is to explore, through an introductory essay and annotated bibliography, London's use of books and pamphlets as source material for his fiction and reference material for his general education.

Jack London owned more than fifteen thousand books. He read most of them, and annotated a significant number of the ones he read. *"The Tools of My Trade"* is a bibliography of the books London used in his work. It is also a bibliography of the books London's friends and colleagues sent to him, complete with their inscriptions.

All the books listed in this bibliography come from London's personal library, most of which is now housed in the Henry E. Huntington Library, Art Gallery, and Botanical Gardens, San Marino, California. A tragic sale of portions of the library was made shortly after it came to the Huntington. The result of this misfortune has been the dispersal of a number of important books from London's library, including his copy of *Das Kapital* and *A Guide to the Alaskan Goldfields*. I have been able to locate only a few of the books that were sold. They are now in private hands.

The listing of London's library is alphabetical by author's surname, or, in the case of collected works, by the title. Identification of each book has been made by author's name, full title, pagination, place of publication, publisher, and date. Illustrative matter, including plates, maps, diagrams, and so forth, have been noted simply as "illus." The location of the book has also been given. Huntington Library holdings have been identified as "HL" in both the text and the notes, and followed when available by the accession number of the book.

Following the brief bibliographic description of the book, I have sketched a résumé of the book's contents, sometimes drawn from the book's introduction or preface. Fiction is noted by form, poetry simply by "poems."

If known, the name of the bookseller is also given, along with his place of business, and whatever other slogans or advertising matter the bookdealer may have included in the book.

Inscriptions, notes, and other markings have been reproduced as faithfully as possible. Editorial interjections, including punctuation, have been bracketed. For the sake of clarity, however, book titles have been italicized in all quotations, bracketed punctuation has occasionally been added to prevent ambiguity, and the length of London's dashes has been normalized. No attempt has been made to normalize capitalization and punctuation, or regularize style. Most of the markings London made in his books are casual, ephemeral jottings hurriedly marked on the rear (or front) pages of a book. I have tried to maintain and preserve the flavor of these notes by interceding editorially as infrequently as possible.

London's markings characteristically took five forms: pencil slashes, "x's" in the margin, brackets, underlinings, or marginal notes. His markings were characteristically hurried, cryptic, and succinct. In some cases, Charmian, London's second wife, also read and marked the same book. When this occurred, I made note of it, but in most cases did not attempt to characterize her annotations as well.

Differentiation between Jack's markings and Charmian's was usually quite simple. Charmian had a very light touch; her handwriting was small, faint, and more exact. Jack, however, made bold, strong lines and markings. Occasionally the two made similar marks, and when that happened, I made note of the dubious authenticity of a Jack London annotation.

The Chicago Manual of Style was used as a guide for all aspects of this book. Series titles, colophons, and inserted material have been noted when present. Signature collation and line endings were not included in the bibliography, because most of the books in London's library are not *rare* in their own right; the particular copies examined are unique because Jack London owned them. With few exceptions, the books are listed in the *National Union Catalog,* and copies are probably available at most libraries of university size.

I have researched and found as many of the books in London's library as possible in the ten years that have passed since this project began. I have gone through each book in his library page by page, and listed herein those books that were annotated, marked, or inscribed by London or one of his friends or colleagues.

London used and consulted his library on a daily basis for historical background, descriptions of local color and history, geographical information, and for ideas and motifs for his short stories and novels. If the reader has gained an appreciation and understanding of London's method of authorship after studying this book, then my purpose in compiling the bibliography will have been fulfilled. Following tradition, I disclaim perfection. These are the books I have seen, and, to the best of my ability, described. Should the reader find fault with my citations, it is my hope that I will be informed of the error, and given a chance to correct it. And should other books from Jack London's library surface, I should like to know of their existence.

Of course, it is always the bibliographer's intent to strive for perfection. If I have not succeeded in attaining that lofty height, so be it. But, as Jacob Blanck wrote in his *Bibliography of American Literature,* "it is nevertheless my sincere hope that no one will leave this Bibliography . . . with a violent attack of superiority complex." I second the notion.

Jack London

Acknowledgments

The source material for this bibliography—Jack London's personal library—is housed in the rare-book stacks of the Henry E. Huntington Library, San Marino, California. Housed there, too, are many of the manuscripts, letters, and personal papers once belonging to Jack and Charmian London, as well as the archives and personal papers of many of their contemporaries. It is from these collections that I have gathered much of the material for this work.

The principal collections examined during my research, aside from those at the Huntington, include: the Jack London material at the University of California's Bancroft Library, Berkeley, California; the Irving Stone Archive, Special Collections, University of California, Los Angeles, California; the Jack London material in the Bender Room, Stanford University, Stanford, California; and the private collections of I. Milo Shepard, Jack London Ranch, Glen Ellen, California, and Russ Kingman, Glen Ellen, California. To the librarians and owners of these collections, who generously gave of their time and permitted me access to the materials in their possession, I wish to express my thanks.

Among the many who have aided me in writing and compiling this bibliography, I am particularly indebted to Richard Weiderman, who provided me with the original idea for research, and to Milo Shepard, who responded most generously to my many requests, granted me access to the Huntington's Jack London Collection, made available all the materials at the Jack London Ranch and Jack London State Park, and granted permission to publish the quotations from Jack London's work that appear within. I am also indebted to Alan Jutzi of the Huntington Library, who spent countless hours leafing through Jack London's books, page by page, in search of annotations; to Carey Bliss, who made several pertinent suggestions regarding the scope of this work; and to the other members of the Huntington staff who were so helpful: Mary Wright, Eugene Garcia, Stephen Crosby, and Kenneth Funston.

I wish to make acknowledgment with thanks also to Robert Leitz III of Louisiana State University, Shreveport, and Charles Watson of Syracuse University. Their careful reading of the manuscript has improved the book immeasurably. And thanks are due, too, to Earle Labor of Centenary College; Andrew Horn and Diana Thomas of the University of California, Los Angeles; Andrew Sinclair of London, England; Phillip Moore of Menlo Park, California, and Howard Lachtman of the University of the Pacific. All were of tremendous help to me during various stages of completion of this book. Thanks go, too, to the staff of the University of Washington Press whose superb work vastly improved the quality of this book: Naomi Pascal, Bruce Wilcox, and Julidta Tarver.

For permission to quote from copyrighted material, acknowledgment with thanks is made to Milo Shepard, executor of the Jack London estate; James D. Clark, Bancroft Library, University of California, Berkeley; and Daniel H. Woodward, Henry E. Huntington Library, San Marino, California.

This study could not have been made without the aid and support of my family: my mother, brother, and sister, who continually sent clippings pertaining to Jack London, allowed me to drag them to symposiums, and presented me with many first editions of Jack London's work for my research.

I owe most to the late Franklin Walker, for providing me with a scholarly example to follow. And, of course, to my wife, Carol, who patiently waited out the brunt of the storm, tactfully ignored my "Londonmania" when it approached extremes, and finally helped me put it all together.

                                                                    −David Mike Hamilton
                                                                    Palo Alto, California

Introduction

Expression Is Far Easier than Invention

Many years after Jack London's death, writer Celeste Murphy visited the author's ranch in Glen Ellen to inspect his library and write a story about it for a special issue of the *Overland Monthly and Out West Magazine.*[1] Murphy was impressed not only by the sheer size of London's collection (which she estimated to contain some fifteen thousand volumes) but also by its diversity. Here were books on almost every conceivable subject: evolution, biology, psychology, economics, political economy, travel, navigation, and philosophy, as well as drama, poetry, and fiction. That diversity applied also to the age and condition of the books. London's "tools of the trade" included "rare tomes, richly bound classics, and volumes priceless because autographed by contemporaries." It included antiquarian books from the eighteenth century, used books from the nineteenth, and contemporary volumes as well. Their condition ranged from mint to dog-eared and rodent-damaged. From Murphy's examination, it was quite clear that London was not a book collector but an author with a professional library. Charmian reinforced her conclusion: "Jack was not a collector of rarities. His objective was a diversified reference library" (*Overland Monthly and Out West Magazine*, 90 [May 1932]: 12). The contemporary examination of London's library as it now exists at the Huntington Library yields a similar conclusion: the collection still contains that same diversity of subject matter, age, and condition. In 1915, London himself described the purpose of his library:

> I regard books in my library in much the same way that a sea captain regards the charts in his chart-room. It is manifestly impossible for a sea captain to carry in his head the memory of all the reefs, rocks, shoals, harbors, points, lighthouses, beacons and buoys of all the coasts of all the world; and no sea captain ever endeavors to store his head with such a

1

mass of knowledge. What he does is to know his way about in the chart-room, and when he picks up a new coast, he takes out the proper chart and has immediate access to all information about that new coast. So it should be with books. Just as the captain must have a well-equipped chart-room, so the student and thinker must have a well-equipped library, and must know his way about that library.

I, for one, never can have too many books; nor can my books cover too many subjects. I may never read them all, but they are always there, and I never know what strange coast I am going to pick up at any time in sailing the world of knowledge." [2]

Although it is beyond the scope of this introduction to provide a thorough investigation of all the source material London used in his writing—or even that used just for one book—the following pages will provide a brief sketch of the course followed in using and developing his attitudes and habits regarding books, and hopefully provide some insight into London's writing methods, his research practices, and a few sources for some of his books and short stories.

At the very beginning of his career, Jack London complained about his weak imagination: "Go it for the *Black Cat!*" he wrote to his friend and literary confidant, Cloudesley Johns (6 September 1899, HL), "I cannot even think of a suitable plot—my damnable lack of origination you see. I think I had better become an interpreter of the things which are, rather than a creator of the things which might be." And even after success had come and the magazines began purchasing London's stories with regularity, he still complained that he just couldn't will his brain to concoct the themes: "No; I'm damned if my stories just come to me. I had to work like the devil for the themes. Then, of course, it was easy to just write them down. Expression, you see—with me—is far easier than invention. It is with the latter I have the greatest trouble, and work the hardest. To find some thought worthy of being clothed with enough verbiage to make it a story, there's the rub" (to Elwyn Hoffman, 17 June 1900, Hoffman Collection, HL).

Having decided (or discovered) at the onset of his writing career that his imagination could not sustain him in the creation of plots, London turned to books, magazines, newspapers, and his own life adventures to fill the void. It was probably not even a conscious decision, so ingrained were his efforts at self-education. In 1906, responding to a query from publisher S. S. McClure that he had been guilty of borrowing material (from Augustus Bridle's and J. K. MacDonald's "Lost in the Land of the Midnight Sun,") he explained his methods of authorship (10 April 1906, HL):

It is a common practice of authors to draw material for their stories from the newspapers. Here are facts of life reported in journalistic style, waiting to be made into literature. So common is this practice that often amusing consequences are caused by several writers utilizing the same material. Some years ago, while I was in England, a story of mine was published in the *San Francisco Argonaut*. In the *Century* of the same date was published a story by Frank Norris. While these two stories were quite different in manner of treatment, they were patently the same in foundation and motive. At once the newspapers paralleled our stories. The explanation was simple: Norris and I had read the same newspaper account, and proceeded to exploit it. But the fun did not stop there. Somebody dug up a *Black Cat* published a year previous, in which was a similar story by another man who used the same foundation and motive. Then Chicago hustled around and resurrected a story that had been published some months before the *Black Cat* story, and that was the same in foundation and motive. Of course, all these different writers had chanced upon the same newspaper article. . . . So common is this practice of authors, that it is recommended by all the instructors in the art of the short story, to read the newspapers and magazines in order to get material. . . . In conclusion, I, in the course of making my living by turning journalism into literature, used material from various sources which had been collected and narrated by men who made their living by turning the facts of life into journalism.

London's lack of imagination forced him to turn not only to the newspapers for source material but to other writers as well. Franklin Walker's essay "Jack London's Use of Sinclair Lewis Plots, Together with a Printing of Three of the Plots," (*Huntington Library Quarterly*, 17 November 1953: 59–74), provides excellent evidence that London not only purchased plots from Lewis but also used them as the basis for his novelette *The Abysmal Brute*, his unfinished *The Assassination Bureau, Ltd.*, as well as his stories "When All the World Was Young" and "Winged Blackmail." From London's letters to George Sterling we can conclude that he depended on Sterling for plots as well, particularly for "The Red One." [3]

London was so used to borrowing plots from other writers that by 1907 he considered plot creation a much inferior art. When *The Editor* posed the question: which is more acceptable, a well-told story with a weak plot or a poorly told story with a strong plot, London unhesitatingly replied that the former was "vastly more acceptable" (Jack London to *The Editor*, April 1907, HL).

London's lack of faith in his own imaginative power, and his reliance on books, can be traced back to his youth. Born of intelligent parents who—like many in 1876—were beset with economic hard times, London spent his early youth on farms. He claimed to learn to read by age four or five and said that he could not remember a time when he could not read. His wife Charmian reported that his sister, Eliza, read Mother Goose stories to him, and that from there it was but a few years before he was reading John Townsend Trowbridge's works for boys, Paul Du Chillu's *Travels,* Captain Cook's *Voyages,* and *Life of Garfield,* as well as "what Seaside Library novels I could borrow from the woman folk and dime novels from the farm hands, in which the servants gloated over the adventures of poor but virtuous shopgirls."[4]

This World of Books

Although told many times before, London's story of the reading of Ouida's *Signa* at age eight deserves retelling, for it illuminates his reliance on the printed word, even at an early age, for amusement and food for thought: "I never knew the finish until I grew up, for the closing chapters were missing from my copy, so I kept on dreaming with the hero, and like him, unable to see Nemesis at the end. My work on the ranch at one time was to watch the bees, and as I sat under a tree from sunrise till late in the afternoon, waiting for the swarming, I had plenty of time to read and dream. Livermore Valley was very flat, and even the hills around were then to me devoid of interest, and the only incident to break in on my visions was when I gave the alarm of swarming and the ranch folk rushed out with pots and pans and buckets of water. I think the opening line of *Signa* was 'It was only a little lad, yet he had dreams of becoming a great musician, and having all Europe at his feet.' Well, I was only a little lad, too, but why could not I become what Signa dreamed of being?"[5]

As London's recollection indicates, he found interest, even at eight, not in the rolling hills around him but in the dreams of a fictional character traveling the courts of Europe. The impression *Signa* made on him was deep. He mentioned the book by Ouida (Marie Louise de la Ramée) in the biographical letter he wrote to his first publisher, Houghton Mifflin Company, and rewrote that letter dozens of times in his correspondence with other, would-be writers. Some thirty years after his first reading, London came across another copy of the book in a used-book stall in New York City. Taking it back to his Morningside apartment, he read it aloud to Charmian. The book was probably as significant as he claimed. Pushing back the golden brown hills of the East Bay, it showed him finery he had never before imagined, and opened up to him a world of books he would never leave.

London's first encounter with a library of any size was in Oakland: "The second wonderful thing happened to me when, nine or ten years of age, my people were compelled to leave their mortgaged ranch and come to the City of Oakland to live. There I found access to the great world by means of the free public library of the City of Oakland. At that time Ina Coolbrith was the librarian of the Oakland Free Library. It was this world of books now accessible, that practically gave me the basis of my education. Not until I began fighting for a living and making my first successes so that I was able to buy books for myself did I ever discontinue drawing many books on many library cards from out of the Oakland Free Public Library" (Jack London to Marion Humble, 11 December 1914, HL).

Ina Coolbrith, mentioned above, encouraged the ten-year old in his reading: "Do you know," London wrote her (15 December 1906, HL), "you were the first one who ever complimented me on my choice of reading matter. Nobody at home bothered their heads, over what I read. I was an eager, thirsty, hungry little kid—and one day, at the Library, I drew out a volume on Pizzaro in Peru. . . . You got the book & stamped it for me. And as you handed it to me you praised me for reading books of that nature."

It is clear from the account of London's boyhood chum, Frank Atherton ("My Boyhood Days with Jack London," pp 12–15, HL), that London spend much of his time in the library, satiating his ravenous appetite for information, education, and imagination, by reading books such as Wilkie Collins's *The New Magdalen* and Charles Dickens's *The Mystery of Edwin Drood*. Atherton recalled that London read an average of two books per week, and remembered the day London introduced him to the library: "The Oakland Free Library was then situated next to the Old City Hall. If I remember correctly, it was a frame building of unpretentious architecture, yet comparatively modern in those days. We entered quietly, and while Johnny selected other books I gazed about in utter astonishment. Never before had I seen such a vast array of books. I wondered how anybody could ever read so many books. I tried to count them by counting those on one shelf, and then multiplying the number of books by the number of shelves. But I had scarcely begun the problem when Johnny was ready to leave."

London's own account of his life during this period was exaggerated; nevertheless it does emphasize the solid foundation upon which he built not only his education but his future abilities as a writer: "I had found my way to the free public library and was reading myself into nervous prostration. . . . on the shelves of that free library I discovered all the great world beyond the skyline. Here were thousands of books as good as my four wonder-books, and some were even better. . . . I read everything, but principally history and adventure, and all the old travels and voyages. I read mornings, afternoons, and nights. I read in bed, I read at table, I read as I walked to and from school, and I read at recess while the other boys were playing."[6]

London's selection of subject matter laid a pattern for his reading which he would continue throughout his life. For while his library contains a broad range of subjects, the books he used as reference material for his stories indicate a leaning toward old travels, voyages, and historical tomes. That he, a writer of fiction, would spend much of his time reading nonfiction accounts lends credence to his claim of a lack of imagination, and sustains the notion of his use of his library as a primary source for plots, themes, and ideas for stories.

Only one book survives this very early period in London's life: Barrett Wendell's *English Composition,* accessioned to the Oakland Library's collection early in 1893, and presumably withdrawn by London sometime that same year. It is probable that London merely neglected to return the book after making numerous markings throughout the margins.

Wendell's book may have aided London in the composition of his story "Typhoon Off the Coast of Japan," for it was about this time that he returned from his adventures there and made his first attempt at writing for publication, entering (and winning) the short story contest sponsored by the San Francisco *Call.* Clearly London had not neglected his reading, even aboard the *Sophia Sutherland,* which took him to the Bering Sea. Charmian London reported that London took great pains on the voyage to improvise a saucer of slush-oil, containing a floating wick and fitted with a shade to serve as a lamp for late-night reading of books such as *A Nest of Gentlefolk* by Ivan Turgenev.

London's interests broadened during and after his trip in 1894 to the East Coast with a contingent of Coxey's Army. At one point he recalled meeting a tramp on a park bench and discussing the reconciliation of Kant and Spencer until breakfast time: "After having satisfied the material man by 'slamming gates' and 'back-door collections' we returned to the bench. Here we took in the sunshine and talked Karl Marx and the German economists, until, in a sort of bashful way, he announced the possession of antiquarian propensities."[7] Although London implies that he was capable of holding his own in such a discussion, it is more likely that his knowledge of socialism and economics came from a cursory reading of Karl Marx's *Communist Manifesto* and street-corner discussions rather than firm grounding in the subjects. Nevertheless, the tramp's discussion had some influence on him, for after his talk with the man (who had more knowledge "and culture under his rags than falls to the average man who sits in the high places") London returned to Oakland and began formal schooling once again.

As Franklin Walker notes in his *Jack London and the Klondike,*[8] London's attitude toward reading and books, especially during the mid-1890s, is probably quite accurately recorded in *Martin Eden.*[9] It is clear that at the time he had an itch to write: his publications in the Oakland High School *Aegis* confirm this propensity. We can also probably attribute London's socialist education, not to the Oakland High School, which he was then attending, but, like Martin Eden, to discussions in the Oakland City Park, the Henry Clay Debating Society (which numbered among its members several Fabian socialists), and a socialist librarian he met during the summer or fall of 1895, Frederick Irons Bamford. Through Bamford, and the socialists at the debating society, as well as those in the park, London discovered and began reading the works of Karl Marx, John Ruskin, Thomas Carlyle, Matthew Arnold, and William Morris in earnest. It is likely, too, that he began reading Herbert Spencer, as Martin Eden did.[10] Shortly after 1895, London felt comfortable enough with the works of the aforementioned authors to quote them and recommend them in the long discourses he wrote to the editors of the local newspapers.

By 1896 London had read Marx's *Das Kapital,* and Henry George's *Progress and Poverty,* and had probably begun a literary study of the Bible as well. With the mastery of Barrett Wendell's *English Composition* completed, London moved on to John Genung's *Outline of Rhetoric,* where he learned the rules of composition, Le Roy Cooley's

Natural Philosophy for Common and High Schools, especially the paragraphs on magnetism and electricity, and Herbert Spencer's *Principles of Sociology, Principles of Psychology,* and *First Principles,* probably beginning with the last volume. Also came the beginning of a thorough grounding in Kipling.

With London's entrance into the University of California came the challenge to take all the courses, read all the books, and become successful as a writer. One of London's schoolmates, Jimmy Hopper, remembered meeting London on the steps of the University of California's Berkeley North Hall: "I first met him one morning during the fall term of 1897, [*sic*] I think. He had just entered the university; under his arm were about sixteen books, and his eyes were full of a gay fever. He told me what he meant to do. He was going to take all the courses in English, all of them, nothing else. Also, of course, he meant to take most of the courses in the natural sciences, many in history, and bite a respectable chunk out of the philosophies. But as to English, this was simple: he was going to take all of the courses in English—all of them." [11]

Whether the English courses helped or not, by the time London withdrew from the university in 1897, he was conversant in Charles Darwin, Thomas Huxley, Herbert Spencer, and John Milton. He had also studied William Jevons's *Studies in Deductive Logic,* and had probably become well acquainted with pamphlets passed out in San Francisco by the Socialist Temple on Turk Street, such as George Benham's *Patriotism and Socialism.*

Klondike Gold

July 25th, 1897 Jack London boarded the *S.S Umatilla* for the Klondike. He took with him Miner Bruce's *Through the Goldfields to Alaska,* John Milton's *Paradise Lost,* and Charles Darwin's *Origin of Species.*

Naturally, books were rare commodities in the Klondike goldfields. What few books did make it into the interior were prized possessions eagerly sought by miners trying to wait out the cold winter. One of London's gold rush comrades, Emil Jensen, remembered the budding author's Klondike library ("Jack London at Stewart River," p. 4, HL): "One unwritten law of the camp was that at night all regular visitors must bring their own candles. With candles worth a dollar

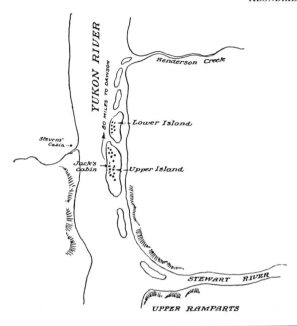

and a half each, this rule was nothing more than just. Another thing well understood was that books must be kept no longer than was absolutely necessary. Few of us had brought more than one, although some had brought as many as three. It was from Jack I borrowed my first book. Anywhere else, I would have passed that thing up without a second thought, but in the Yukon, a book was a book and I read it— [Charles] Darwin's *Origin of Species*. I confess I did not like Jack so well that week."

Jensen must have hidden his temporary dislike for London and Darwin, for London persisted in trying to educate him: "Try [Thomas] Huxley" London suggested, but Jensen only shook his head mournfully. "How about [Herbert] Spencer?" "Too serious" was the reply. " 'Well then,' remarked Jack with finality, 'here is your last bet;' saying which he resurrected from among the blankets in his bunk a book and placed it on the table before me. A book of poetry this was—portly and awe-inspiring. 'You have read every scrap of paper in camp but this,' he continued, sliding a loving hand gently over the upturned pages as though this thing beneath his fingers were the very embodiment of all that is beautiful and joygiving."

A Literary Apprenticeship

London's return from the Klondike, sans material riches but with a wealth of stories yet unwritten, marked the beginning of his apprenticeship as an author. It is interesting to note that, although fresh from the region himself, London very quickly added Harry De Windt's *Through the Gold Fields of Alaska* as well as other books about the region to his new and growing library. The Klondike was London's greatest and most important adventure and literary resource, yet even after its completion, he found it worthwhile to augment his own memories of that trip with the nonfiction accounts of others who had taken the same journey. Reliance on newspapers, magazines, and books for plots and themes would begin even as London started his literary apprenticeship in earnest. The pattern established in 1898 would carry forth until his death in 1916.

Once back in Oakland, London launched his writing career. His study was soon adorned with a clothesline, strung from one corner of the room to the other. Pinned to it were excerpts, notes, articles, and thoughts, all hastily scribbled onto scraps of paper—a quote to be worked into a fictional dialogue, a motif for a short story, a title for a novel, the beginning line of a poem, a reference to a book. The mechanics of his writing were ingrained by the long hours, days, weeks, and months spent at his craft. As the notes grew in quantity, the clothesline came down, replaced by boxes, labeled "fiction notes" or with the title of the story or project London was then working on. His reading habits, long in forming, now solidified. He read not one book but many, and not consecutively but collectively—a dozen volumes or more, arranged by their relative profundity. His bedroom was piled high with books awaiting nightly attack. Each book was open and laid face downward, one on top of the other. The weightiest of the tomes— philosophy or science—was laid on top. As he read and grew more fatigued, he would discard the top book for the next one, on a lighter subject—sociology perhaps. Then as he grew even more weary and his powers of concentration waned, he would reach for the next, proceeding down the pile until he ended with a book of poetry or a novel—the dessert of his efforts at self-education.

London's reading during these years of literary apprenticeship included not only a heavy sampling of economics and social science but also a fair amount of fiction. His letters from the period 1898–1900, particularly those to Cloudesley Johns and Anna Strunsky, are teeming with references to books he had read or had a desire to read. "Never a night (whether I have gone out or not)," he wrote to Houghton Mifflin Company (31 January 1900 HL), "but the last several hours are spent in bed with my books. All things interest me—the world is so very good. Principal studies are, scientific, sociological, and ethical—these, of course, including biology, economics, psychology, physiology, history, etc., etc., without end. And I strive, also, not to neglect literature."

Although London's library no longer contains many of the early books mentioned in his letters to Johns or Strunsky (his collection of Kipling, for instance, is extremely small relative to the influence that writer had on his style), we know from those letters[12] that London was reading Kipling quite steadily, and was deeply interested also in the works of Robert Louis Stevenson, Herbert Spencer, and Arthur Schopenhauer. Although London was introduced to the writings of Brooks Adams in 1898, and quoted the author in "The Question of the Maximum," he was still, at this point, "getting his scientific basis." Books were still largely tools of learning rather than sources for plots. A letter of 2 August 1906 to the editor of the Seattle *Post-Intelligencer,* referring to a newspaper article published in the San Francisco *Examiner* of 14 October 1900, does verify that London was scanning the newspapers for ideas for stories; nevertheless his reading for the year 1898, which included the works of William Shakespeare, Henry Wadsworth Longfellow (*Voices of the Night*), Robert Browning (*The Ring and the Book*), as well as Robert Herrick (*Hesperides*), Alfred Lord Tennyson ("The Bugle Song"), Edmond Rostand (*Cyrano de Bergerac*), and Rudyard Kipling, indicates a study of writing style rather than skimming for plots.

The year 1899 was similar to 1898 in terms of the books London read, although there seems to be some indication that he either used the books as source material for future stories then or came back to them in later years. Again, his letters to Cloudesley Johns were heavily peppered with references to Rudyard Kipling and Robert Louis Stevenson. Baruch Spinoza and Israel Zangwill joined the list, as did Ambrose Bierce, Paul Bourget, Edwin Markham, John Keats, and Thomas Malthus, and London began to feel the pressure of his reading program, complaining to Johns (27 February 1899, HL) that "there is

Reading in Oakland, ca. 1902

so much good stuff to read and so little time to do it in. It sometimes makes me sad to think of the many hours I have wasted over mediocre works, simply for want of better." Among the books he read during the year were Robert Louis Stevenson's *Ebb Time*, Frank Bullen's *Idylls of the Sea*, Grant Allen's *Miss Cayley's Adventures*, Ambrose Bierce's *Tales of Soldiers and Civilians*, Paul Bourget's *Outre-mer: Impressions of America*, Beatrice Harraden's *Fowler*, Thomas Malthus's *An Essay on the Principle of Population*, Gertrude Atherton's *A Daughter of the Vine*, Edwin Markham's *The Man with the Hoe*, James Allen's *Summer in Arcady*, and Frank Norris's *Moran of the Lady Letty* (which London liked very much). He also mentioned reading the *Rubáiyát of Omar Khayyám*, Robert Louis Stevenson's *Virginibus Puerisque*, Stephen Crane's *Black Riders*, Jean Jacques Rousseau's *Social Contract*, Thomas Carlyle's *Sartor Resartus*, and apparently had mastered Charles Dickens's *Nicholas Nickleby*, Charles Reade's *Hard Cash*, William Makepeace Thackeray's *The Snobs of England*, and Harriet Beecher

Stowe's *Uncle Tom's Cabin*, for he told Cloudesley Johns that Herbert Spencer's *First Principles* would do more for humanity than any of those four books (10 August 1899, HL).

After reading David Starr Jordan's *Care and Culture of Men*, London mentioned to Johns (29 July 1899, HL) that Jordan has become "to a certain extent, a hero of mine," an opinion he would soon alter as he learned more about Jordan's writings and politics.

Several books, however, served as milestones in this, the last year before 1900: from Otto Weisman's "Essay on the Duration of Life," Herbert Conn's *The Method of Evolution*, and Stanley Waterloo's *The Story of Ab*, all read in 1899, would eventually come the story of *Before Adam*, a novel which London probably had already planned in March when he wrote to Johns that he had "ten to twenty [novels] mapped out, but God knows when I'll ever get a chance to begin one, much less, finish it" (15 March 1899, HL). In April, he worried that his extensive reading program had got the best of him ("I grasp easily, but memorize only in a fairly average sort of way. I am sure there are thousands of books I have read, the very titles of which are forgotten"); and in May he found himself impressed by Arthur "Schopenhauer's terrific arraignment of woman, or rather his phillipic against them" (22 April and 28 May 1899, HL). The life-long problem London had in constructing plots surfaced in a later letter to Johns: "Damn plots; I don't think I could construct a decent one to save my life" (24 October 1899, HL).

During 1899 London finally came to terms with his earlier reading of the Bible, and he made his first notes for a novel about the life of Christ after reading Ernest Renan's *Anti-Christ* and *The Apostle*. Probably in exchange for some "Bull Durham" tobacco tags (which he redeemed at Smith Brothers, a bookstore and tobaccanist in Oakland), London purchased and read Arthur Schopenhauer's *The Art of Controversy*, and Oscar Wilde's *Children in Prison*, and may also have bought the first novels of Joseph Conrad.

London was still interested in obtaining his scientific basis in 1899, however, as is reflected in his reading of Paul Carus's *Primer of Philosophy* and *The Religion of Science*, and August Weismann's "Essay on the Duration of Life," which he thought to be "a wonderful piece of work," giving "food for immeasurable thought" and providing "much good to accrue from this man's labors for the welfare of humanity" (to Johns 10 July 1899, HL).

London's reading during 1899 was prodigious, as the preceding list indicates. Perhaps illustrative of the intensity with which he approached the task are a few paragraphs taken from his letter of 24 October 1899 (HL) to Cloudesley Johns: "Have been reading Jacob's *More Cargoes* [William Jacobs's *Many Cargoes*]. You have surely seen some of his magazine work, haven't you? Also have been going through Kendrick Bang's *The Dreamers* and *The Bicyclers and Other Farces*. He's clever and humourous, in a mild sort of way. Have been digging at Norman's *Eastern Question,* preparatory to a certain economic dissertative article I intend writing—Asia touches one of the phases I wish to deal with. Besides, I have gone through Curzon's similar work, and wish to take up soon Beresford's *Break-Up of China.* Am going through [Henry] Drummon[d] on evolution, Hudson on psychology, and reviewing [Thomas Babington] McCaulay and [Thomas] De Quincey in the course of English in Minto which I am giving to a friend—the photographer." From this letter, it is clear that London had directed his reading to the specific areas at which he intended to write. General study was coming to an end, and the application of his reading specifically to his writing had begun. The year 1899 ended with the purchase of a reference book: *Foster's Complete Hoyle.* Evidently there was time, in between reading, studying, and writing, to enjoy a game of cards.

First Successes

By 1900 London had become an accomplished and somewhat successful author. At the end of January he was reading proof of his first book, *The Son of the Wolf,* and hammering away at the works of Rudyard Kipling, Sir James Barrie's *Tommy and Grizel,* John Fiske, Herbert Spencer, Ernest Haeckel, and William H. Maple. His other reading that year included Maurice Hewlett's *The Forest Lovers,* Stanley Waterloo's *A Man and a Woman,* Leo Tolstoy's *The Death of Ivan Ilyich,* Thomas Hardy's *Tess of the D'Urbervilles* (which he borrowed from the then Miss Charmian Kittredge), and *Jude the Obscure,* Thomas Huxley's *Evolution and Ethics,* and Achille Loria's *The Economic Foundations of Society.* London's strong liking for Joseph Conrad's work continued in 1900, as well.

London's interest in race and race development continued in 1900 with the purchase of Herbert Conn's *The Method of Evolution* and

Josiah Strong's *Expansion Under New World Conditions,* a book that tried to substantiate superiority of Anglo-Saxon stock through scientific means.

In 1900 London married Bessie May Maddern—perhaps in part because of his reading of Israel Zangwill's *The Mantle of Elijah,* for London emulated Zangwill's theory that marriage should be for reason rather than love, and contain a scientific basis. Certainly London used Zangwill later on in his exchange of letters with Anna Strunsky, published as *The Kempton-Wace Letters.*

The Ruskin Club, formed by Frederick Irons Bamford, took up some of London's time in 1900, but, aside from *America's Economic Supremacy,* London was probably not reading books on economics to a great degree during the year. He did, however, begin to use some of the outside source material on the Klondike he had purchased, using Tappan Adney's *The Klondike Stampede* in the planning of his novel *A Daughter of the Snows* (he would begin writing it in 1902), and making notes for other potential stories such as "That Pup," which was finally developed in 1908 under the title "That Spot."

London's continued interest in the life of Christ was reflected by his reading in 1900 of Sir Walter Besant's *Jerusalem: The City of Herod and Saladin.* London had mentioned to Cloudesley Johns the prior summer that if he "could only get ahead of the game," he was "going to jump back to Jerusalem in the time of Christ, and write one giving an entirely new interpretation of the many things which occurred at that time. I think I can do it, so that while it may rattle the slats of the Christians they will still be anxious to read it." (10 August 1899, HL). The novel may have been encouraged by Bamford, a subscriber to the Christian Socialist movement, who (in 1906) made sure that London's yacht *Snark* did not want for a Bible.

In his papers, London outlined the proposed contents of the Christ novel: " 'Notes for Christ Novel[.]' Divisions of the spoils—*Numbers*—31. The Jews spoil the Egyptians. (II *Kings* XVII-27). *Genesis, Exodus*—Moses & children of Israel. *Ecclesiastes. Isaiah*[,] *Matthew*—Jesus speaking to the fishermen—mending nets." [13]

The year 1901 began much as 1900 had, except that now London was writing long letters to Anna Strunsky as well as to Cloudesley Johns. London spent the year working on socialist essays and his first novel, *A Daughter of the Snows,* and also began *The Kempton-Wace Letters* with Strunsky. High on the list of books that influenced London in 1901 must be placed Ernest Haeckel's *The Riddle of the Universe*. London had been introduced to Haeckel's work as early as 1898, but it was *The Riddle of the Universe* that had a profound effect on London, and which he would incorporate not only into his Christ novel notes and quote in *The Kempton-Wace Letters* but mention also later in *The Iron Heel* and the short story "The Strength of the Strong." Also important reading in 1901 was Emile Vandervelde's *Collectivism and Industrial Evolution*.

Other books London read during 1901 include Edward Ross's *Social Control*, Lester Ward's *Dynamic Sociology*, George Ade's *Fables in Slang*, Robert Browning's *Aurora Leigh*, William Wordsworth's *The Excursion*, Wyckoff's *A Day with a Tramp*, Josiah Flynt Willard's *Tramping with Tramps*, Maksim Gorky's *Foma Gordeev* (which London reviewed in the November 1901 issue of *Impressions*), and Frank Norris's *The Octopus* (which he also reviewed in *Impressions*).

By 1901 it was clear that London's reading had become more and more directly related to his writing. The multitude of citations to books found in his 1900 correspondence had dwindled to a mere trickle. By the end of 1901, London would already be wishing for more time to read, as he bemoaned to Anna Strunsky (18 January 1902, Walling Collection, HL): "As for my not having read Stevenson's *Letters*—my dear child! When the day comes that I have achieved a fairly fit scientific foundation and a bank account of a thousand dollars, then come and be with me when I lie on my back all day long and read and read and read and read. The temptation of the books—if you could know! And I hammer away at Spencer and hackwork and try to forget the joys of the things unread."

By 1902 London had become an established author. His *The Son of the Wolf* and *The God of His Fathers* were already in print; *Children of the Frost* was scheduled for publication in the fall, and, with the young Anna Strunsky from Stanford University, he was hard at work on *The Kempton-Wace Letters*. If not yet financially secure, he was a least tasting the first sweetness of literary success.

In February London moved his family to Piedmont, then some fifteen miles from Oakland and considered "in the country" (London to Elwyn Hoffman, 23 February 1902, Hoffman Collection, HL). The new house had "the floor space of almost four cottages": room enough to house his family and an ever-growing library too (to Johns, 23 February 1902, HL). During his residence there, he would purchase more than five hundred dollars worth of books. On a "Book Bills of Sale" he recorded some of those purchases: a ten-volume set of Sir James Barrie, ten volumes of James Whitcomb Riley, twenty-four volumes of Robert Louis Stevenson, eighteen volumes of Rudyard Kipling, ten volumes of Charlotte Smith; books by Honoré de Balzac, Charles Dickens, Victor Hugo, Sir Walter Scott, John Ruskin, Guy de Maupassant, Bret Harte, Mark Twain, William Shakespeare, and Edgar Allan Poe, as well as a *Century Dictionary, Appleton's Scientific Library,* and two sets of the Aldus Society ("Books Purchased," HL).

The London Abyss

In midyear London was invited, by the American Press Association, to interview General Christiaan De Wet about his role in the Boer War, which had recently come to an end. London accepted the assignment, read Sir James Fitzpatrick's *The Transvall From Within* for additional background on the conflict, and traveled to New York on the first leg of his journey to South Africa.

Upon arriving in New York, London learned, probably from Orlando Smith, who was then president of the American Press Association, that his assignment had been canceled. Smith must have been impressed by London, for he asked the young author to read his *Eternalism* and provide a critique of it. London accepted the new assignment and, disappointed yet determined to continue his trip anyhow, sailed to England, where he began work on his second major project of 1902: a study of the London poor entitled *The People of the Abyss.* For the next three months, he lived and worked with the poor in the city's East End slum.

As a sociological study, *The People of the Abyss* required statistics, photographs, and lots of descriptive data. This was London's first major attempt at research, and for it he compiled not only a wealth of firsthand impressions but a number of secondary sources as well. Several of these books were retained in London's library. We know, for instance, that he used Thomas Holmes's *Pictures and Problems from London Police Courts* for its description of daily living conditions among the poor; statistics on English agriculture were culled from Peter Kropotkin's *Fields, Factories and Workshops;* for descriptions of the London tenements he turned to George Haw's *No Room to Live;* and for a dis-

Jack London and George Wharton James

cussion of municipal ownership London used Haw's *Today's Work*. London relied heavily on Robert Blatchford's *Dismal England* while writing *The People of the Abyss,* as well as Edward Bowmaker's *The Housing of the Working Class*. He found the descriptions of overcrowding in *Heart of the Empire* useful as well, and began his first notes for the book—some dialect of the East Ender—in Arthur Morrison's *To London Town*. London also read Oscar Wilde's *The Soul of Man under Socialism* during the trip, and disagreed with Wilde's contention that socialism would destroy family life. Other reading included Henry Salt's *Cruelties of Civilization* and John Davidson's *The Gospel of the Poor* and *The Old Order and the New*.

London was proud of his research efforts. More than three years later he would remark on the writing of the book in a letter to Bailey Millard (18 February 1906, HL), editor of *The Cosmopolitan:* "I have tremendous confidence, based on all kinds of work I have already done, that I can deliver the goods. Anybody doubting this has but to read *The People of the Abyss* to find the graphic, reportorial way I have of handling things. (Between ourselves, and not to be passed on, I gathered every bit of the material, read hundreds of books and thousands of pamphlets, newspapers and Parliamentary Reports, composed *The People of the Abyss,* and typed it all out, took two-thirds of the photographs with my own camera, took a vacation of one week off in the country—and did it all in two months. That's going some now, isn't it?)"

A Change of Scenery

By mid-November London had finished the manuscript and returned to Piedmont. His experiences in England at an end, he was resolute not to return to his earlier Klondike fiction, and he wrote as much to his editor, George Brett, president of the Macmillan Company (21 November 1902, HL): "I have served my apprenticeship at writing in that field, and I feel that I am better fitted now to attempt a larger and more generally interesting field." Two books were mentioned in that letter to Brett: "The Flight of the Duchess," a story set in California, and an autobiographical story, "The Mercy of the Sea," about London's voyage in 1893 aboard the *Sophia Sutherland*. Probably in preparation for "The Flight of the Duchess," London began reading a number of volumes of Californiana and western Americana, such as Francis Parkman's *The Oregon Trail* and John Charles Frémont's *Memoirs of My Life*. The latter volume includes a passage about scores of wild dogs, one of which appeared to have been domesticated. London marked the passage, and abandoned "The Flight of the Duchess" for a new book: *The Call of the Wild*.

London went to his library for source material about dogs just as he had done earlier for information about London's East End. Edward Jesse's *Anecdotes of Dogs* provided him with information about canine behavior while Egerton Young's *My Dogs in the Northland* gave him accurate data about the traits of sled dogs. Upon publication of the book, a controversy arose over London's sources for the novel. Before it ended, London would acknowledge Young's contribution.

Although hard at work on *The Call of the Wild*, London also read Jacob Riis's *The Battle with the Slum* that winter. From it he resolved to write a sequel to *The People of the Abyss:* a sociological study of the poor in Boston and New York he would call "The American Abyss." Also read was Enrico Ferri's *Criminal Sociology*, which prompted the beginning of a file on "crime and criminals" that he would later use in the writing of *The Star Rover*.

After six months of extended heavy reading, London relaxed at the end of 1902 and enjoyed Arthur Symons's *Poems*—a Christmas gift from his poet friend George Sterling.

London's major efforts in 1903 were devoted to a series of essays assembled under the title *War of the Classes,* and the writing of "The

Mercy of the Sea" which he expanded and evolved into *The Sea-Wolf.*
Although records of his reading during the year are sparse, it is not
unlikely that Albert Sonnichsen's *Deep Sea Vagabonds* was used as a
source for the book. The purchase of the yacht *Spray* in May 1903 also
prompted additions to London's library. Books such as *Fore and Aft
Seamanship for Yachtsmen* and William Rosser's *The Yachtman's Handy-
Book* may have aided London not only with the sailing of the *Spray*
but with the writing of *The Sea-Wolf* as well.

Of London's socialist readings, however, we can be more definite.
In the early spring London read John Brooks's *The Social Unrest* and
William James Ghent's *Our Benevolent Feudalism,* writing reviews of
both which were published in the 1 May issue of the *International So-
cialist Review.* The two books also provided London with source material for his essay collection entitled *War of the Classes.* In addition,
Ghent's book, according to London's oldest daughter, Joan, gave London a framework for *The Iron Heel.* Socialist reading in 1903 also included *An Exposition of Socialism and Collectivism,* John Mitchell's
Organized Labor, Brooks Adams's *The New Empire* (used in "The
Question of the Maximum"), and Herbert Casson's *Organized Self-
Help* (used in "The Scab"). Austin Lewis, a prominent socialist author,
also gave London a copy of Friedrich Engels's *Feuerbach: The Roots of
the Socialist Philosophy* during the year.

London had not abandoned the four-year old Christ novel project.
His 1903 notes for the book, found in George Croly's *Tarry Thou Till I
Come* and Ernest Renan's *Life of Jesus,* were among the finest he ever
made for the planned novel, thus underscoring his acute creative abilities during the year. In Croly's book, London found the needed background information on the Roman conquest of Judea. His notes in Renan's book show that the novel was finally taking shape.

London did not neglect literature or poetry in 1903, although the
lack of extensive annotation in books from either category would indicate that his interest was recreational rather than professional. The year
began with a birthday gift of poetry from George Sterling: John Bannister Tabb's *Poems.* It ended on a similar note with Sterling's presentation of his own *The Testimony of the Suns.* Herman Scheffauer also presented London with a gift of his own poetry, *Of Both Worlds,* and Anna
Strunsky gave London a copy of William Henley's *Poems.* The extensive annotations and discussions both London and Strunsky made in
and about Henley's work later surfaced in London's story "Good-Bye,

Jack," published in June 1909.

Joseph Conrad's *Youth* made a tremendous impression on London in 1903. During a visit to the Piedmont bungalow in April, Cloudesley Johns, London's friend and literary confidant, recalled London's reading of *Youth:*

> He handed me a carbon copy of *The Call of the Wild* which had been accepted for serial publication in the *Saturday Evening Post.* I was fascinated by what I felt . . . to be Jack London's greatest long story when the author . . . came into the library . . . hurling questions at me. . . . Had I found Joseph Conrad? . . . To these questions and answers I was giving only part of my attention, as I continued to read *The Call of the Wild.* . . .
>
> "Listen to *this!*" Jack exclaimed suddenly, taking away from me the copy of his own great story and waving the book he had brought. Then, his expressive and melodic voice caressing the living sentences of the Master, he read to me Joseph Conrad's *Youth,* in boyish delight in sharing with kindred spirits his own joy of life.[14]

By July, London's marriage was breaking up. He became subject to what he eventually would call his "black moods" and his "black philosophy," which would later find its way into print as the dialogue of Wolf Larsen. London's resolve to end his marriage translated into a course of action on 27 September, as he explored the possibility of a trip to the Far East. The trip became a reality by the end of the year, when London signed a contract with William Randolph Hearst to cover the impending war between the Japanese and the Russians over Korea.

London took forty-five dollars worth of books with him when he sailed for Japan aboard the *Siberia,* 7 January 1904. Following a procedure he had established on his trip to London in 1902, he brought with him books that would explain the culture, history, and politics of the region he was visiting. For background, he read Francis Skrine's *The Expansion of Russia* and Arthur Smith's *China in Convulsion.* Walter Del Mar's *Around the World Through Japan* supplied him with statistics on the Japanese army; William Greener's *Greater Russia* examined Russian exploitation of Chinese labor, and Basil Chamberlain's *A Handbook for Travellers in Japan* and Emilii Bretschneider's *Map of China* provided him with the practical information he needed. London learned a great deal about Korea from William Griffis's *Corea: The Hermit Nation,* Alexis Krausse's *The Far East,* and Isabella Bishop's *Korea and Her Neighbors* (which he quoted extensively in "Dr. Moffett"). From John Foster's *American Diplomacy in the Orient,* London drew his essay "The

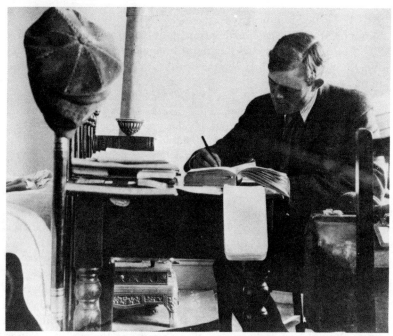

In Korea as a Newspaper Correspondent

Yellow Peril." John Hodge's *Corean Words and Phrases,* a dictionary London purchased in Seoul, enabled him to bridge the language barrier—if only slightly. While still in Moji awaiting passage to Korea (London was later arrested there for taking pictures—a forbidden activity in the fortified city) he read Hector Munro's *The Rise of the Russian Empire,* and recorded the train schedule on a page in the book.

Aside from the slight possibility that London returned to these books for information while writing "Cherry," his collection of Far East books served him only for his journalistic efforts. It was late summer before London returned to California, attended to his affairs, and began serious reading again.

During the latter part of October, George Brett sent London William Ghent's latest book, *Mass and Class: A Survey of Social Division.* It was the second of Ghent's works that London read. Together with Edwin Seligman's *The Economic Interpretation of History for Its Marxist Theory,* the books set in motion London's next ambitious novel: a projection of the future socialist struggle he would call *The Iron Heel.*

The fall was also spent in obtaining a thorough grounding in Friedrich Nietzsche. In a letter to Charmian, London made special note of the tough reading program he had laid out for himself: "Have been getting hold of some Nietzsche. I'll turn you loose first on his *Genealogy of Morals*—and after that, something you'll like—*Thus Spake Zarathustra*" (letter to Charmian Kittredge, 29 September 1904, HL). While his writing during the period was actually light (*The Game,* and a play entitled *The Scorn of Women*), London was again tackling the tough scientific and political works he had first begun some five years before. The heavy reading program (which also included Herbert Spencer's *An Autobiography* and Edward Dowden's biography of Robert Browning) would lead, finally, to the writing of *The Iron Heel.*

Among the gifts London received in 1904 were Edward Dowden's *Robert Browning* (a Christmas gift from Frederick Bamford), a presentation copy of Charles Warren Stoddard's *The Island of Tranquil Delights,* and also his *For the Pleasure of His Company,* a book of tales about San Francisco.

Glen Ellen

The year 1905 proved to be a busy one for London. In March he ran for mayor of Oakland, by fall he had a series of speaking engagements across the country, and in addition he married Clara Charmian Kittredge, the day his divorce from Bessie became final. His writing consisted of *The Game* (which he reworked in response to a request from George Brett), a revision of the play *Scorn of Women, White Fang,* and various short stories collected in *Moon-Face,* as well as essays for the socialist *Revolution.*

London's reading during the year included a number of books about socialism and the class struggle. His interest in the philosophy was augmented by books such as August Bebel's *Women Under Socialism* which gave London a better understanding of the capitalist exploitation of women; Ernest Untermann's *Science and Revolution,* the text of which may have provided the underpinnings for London's now-famous Revolution speech (Untermann became a model for the character Ernest Everhard in *The Iron Heel);* Joseph Buchanan's *The Story of a Labor Agitator* (especially for the passages dealing with the anarchist bombing of Haymarket Square); and Peter Burrowes's *Notes on the Class Struggle*. London also probably resurrected George Benham's *Patriotism and Socialism* for further information about those subjects, and used them in the notes he made for *The Iron Heel* as well as the socialist lectures he gave throughout the fall.

The winter started on a melancholy note. Disgusted with the turn of events of 1904, London wrote to Bamford, "I wish I had never opened the books at all—not only biology, but [Robert] Browning, [John] Milton, [William] Shakespeare, and all the rest, including that philosophic charlatan, [Ralph Waldo] Emerson."[15]

It was perhaps that passing distaste for his education that prompted London to discard his regular research routines and instead ask Bamford to provide the research necessary for London's new novel *White Fang*. Bamford responded with a sheet of data on dogs—straight from the *Encyclopedia Americana*. London followed the same pattern of doing little research in preparation for the writing of his expanded *Scorn of Women*, preferring instead merely to dramatize his long story of the same name from *The God of His Fathers* (recording the play on the flyleaves of Stewart White's *The Silent Places*). He did venture to use Allanson-Winn Headley's *Boxing*, however, when revamping *The Game* into novella length.

By midyear, London's attitudes had changed. He decided to purchase property in the country, began reading Oscar Wilde's *De Profundis* (which he liked very much), and, that summer, wrote to Cloudesley Johns (6 July 1905, HL) that he spent the warm days swimming and reading: "I take a book along, and read and swim, turn and turn about, until 6 PM." In midsummer he resigned from the Ruskin Club, explaining to Bamford that he was gone from Oakland for good, and started reading Maurice Maeterlinck's *Wisdom and Destiny* and a curious little nonsense book by Lewis Carroll: *The Hunting of the Snark*. London and Charmian together also read Joshua Slocum's *The Voyage of the Liberated* and *Sailing Alone Around the World* that year. After reading, "I had resolved on a voyage around the world . . . a thrilling pulse beat high in me. My step was light on deck in the crisp air. I felt that there could be no turning back, and that I was engaging in an adventure the meaning of which I thoroughly understood,"[16] London decided to take a similar trip. "It was the book that got us started planning our own trip on the *Snark*," Charmian recorded in her "Books I Have Read" (p. 26, HL). Perhaps also further encouragement came from *The Book of the Ocean,* a rare book London had purchased at Dawson's Bookstore in Los Angeles the previous winter.

Other books read in 1905 included Dorothy Richardson's *The Long Day* and Upton Sinclair's *The Jungle,* both of which London reviewed that year, May Sinclair's *Divine Fire,* Henry George's *The Menace of Privilege,* Frederick Vernon Harcourt's *Bolts and Bars,* and Leroy Scott's *The Walking Delegate.*

In her "Books I Have Read" (p.26), Charmian London recorded several other books read during the year, including Eden Phillpotts's *The Secret Woman* ("Mate & I read partly together just before our honeymoon, in Iowa"), and Robert Hunter's *Poverty* ("Splendid book. 1905").

With London's marriage to Charmian Kittredge came not only a new place to live (Glen Ellen, California) but Charmian's own library as well. Included among her books were a number of Victorian novels, as well as volumes of poetry and books reflecting her own interests, such as Ernst Gillman's *Illustrated Lectures on Horsemanship.*

In 1906, the *Snark* adventure, planned during that hot 1905 summer, was begun with the laying of the keel in mid-February. Jack and Charmian made Wake Robin Lodge (owned by Charmian's aunt Ninetta Wiley Eames) their home, and they made plans to build a home of their own. Like all of London's projects, he not only experienced it but wrote about it as well. He purchased Candace Wheeler's *Principles of Home Decoration* and in July wrote the essay "The House Beautiful." Another book purchased specifically for use on the newly begun "Beauty Ranch" (the name the London's gave to their Glen Ellen property), Anthony Bledsoe's *Business Law for Business Men,* provided London with information on labor rights and wills, and would later be useful in the 1916 water rights controversy and also for *The Iron Heel,* which was finally completed in the fall of 1906.

London's major writing consisted of *Before Adam, The Iron Heel,* and *The Road. Before Adam* had been in the planning stages for at least a few years (as had *The Iron Heel*), and when he began it, in late April, London resurrected a number of books to guide him in the task, including James Hewitt's *The Ruling Races of Prehistoric Times,* Winwood Reade's *The Martyrdom of Man,* and John Moore's *The Universal Kinship* (London also wrote a review of the latter). The publication of *Before Adam* in the October issue of *Everybody's Magazine* (the manuscript had been completed a mere forty days after he had begun it)

initiated another of what would become common charges of plagiarism. After reading the first installment, Stanley Waterloo, author
of *The Story of Ab* (which London had read in 1899), charged, "Jack
London not only starts out with the same proposition I based my
work on, but he employs in some instances practically the same language" (quoted in London's letter to Waterloo, 20 October 1906, HL).
London immediately replied, admitting his reading of the book, but
insisting that, far from being a case of outright plagiarism, *Before
Adam* was written as a reply to *The Story of Ab,* because the latter was
"unscientific." "You crammed the evolution of a thousand generations
into one generation" London wrote "—something at which I revolted
from the time I first read your story." The point of *Before Adam,* London explained in his letter to Waterloo, was to "demonstrate the excessive slowness of social evolution in the primitive world."

The result of the controversy prompted London to write some illuminating words on the subject of plagiarism, as he viewed it, in a
letter to B. W. Babcock (3 December 1906, HL), a writer for the New
York *Times:*

> You ask me for my views in general upon plagiarism. I think the
> whole subject of plagiarism is absurd. I can conceive of no more laugh-
> able spectacle than that of a human standing up on his hind legs and
> yowling plagiarism. No man with a puny imagination can continue pla-
> giarizing and make a success of it. No man with a vivid imagination, on
> the other hand, needs to plagiarize.
>
> I feel like being speculative for a moment. Let us suppose a bona fide
> case of plagiarism. Here's a man who has written something and written
> it well. Another man plagiarizes from him. Considering that the original
> is written well, how under the sun is the plagiarism going to get any-
> where. Suppose, however, the plagiarism is so eminently great that it
> outshines the original. Who has any complaint coming? The world is
> better off for the bigger creation. The original creation stands where it
> was, and it's ridiculous for the original creator to yowl because some-
> body else has made a bigger mudpie.

Making bigger mudpies was London's specialty, and he never considered his reliance on newspapers, magazines, and books as a form of
plagiarism. As for *Before Adam:* the world was a better place for its
existence, because it was a better book than *The Story of Ab.* The
charge of plagiarism, he thought, was completely unfounded.

By the end of June, London was at last ready to begin writing *The
Iron Heel.* He gathered together his box of notes and clippings on

A Lover of Horses, ca 1905

"Disappearing Class," and consulted additional books such as Henry George's *The Menace of Privilege,* Walter Mills's *The Struggle for Existence,* Robert Hunter's *Poverty,* (also used for the planned but never written "The American Abyss" study), and John Spargo's *The Bitter Cry of the Children* (also used when writing "The Apostate"). Ambrose Bierce's *The Cynic's Word Book,* first quoted in London's 1903 essay "The Terrible and Tragic in Fiction," also found a minor place in the new novel.

London had not yet abandoned his idea of a study of New York and Boston, "The American Abyss," in 1906; for besides Spargo's book on children, he continued making notes, consulting Isador Ladoff's *American Pauperism and the Abolition of Poverty.* He also continued his Christ novel project, using a December gift from Frederick Bamford, John Fiske's *Through Nature to God,* as an additional source.

London received several other gifts of books in 1906: Arthur Hornblow's *The Lion and the Mouse,* a novel about the Ruskin Club, was another present from Bamford; Fannie K. Hamilton presented London with a copy of Marcel Schwob's *Mimes;* from Caroline Severance came a copy of her *The Mother of Clubs;* Leonard Abbott sent Ivan Turgenev's *On the Eve;* and Elena Vacarescu sent her *The Bard of the Dimbovitza.* Bamford's March gift, William De Witt Hyde's *From Epicurus to Christ,* was employed not only in London's Christ novel but also in his summer letter to Bamford criticizing the Ruskin Club's lack of ethical principles (1 July 1906, HL).

Those final Glen Ellen summer days (before sailing aboard the *Snark*) were spent sitting "on the sand naked in the sun" reading "for an hour every day" and playing "a rubber of whist several times a week" (London to Fannie K. Hamilton, 15 July 1906, HL). Other books London read in 1906 include Herbert George Wells's *A Modern Utopia* (later used in *The Mutiny of the Elsinore*), Florence Maybrick's prison autobiography, and Robert Louis Stevenson's *In the South Seas* (London marked a passage on the trade winds). Charmian read a few books aloud to Jack in 1906, as recorded in her "Books I Have Read," including Eden Phillpotts's *The Portreeve,* May Sinclair's *The Divine Fire* (London's second reading), Ernest Untermann's *Science and Revolution,* Upton Sinclair's *The Jungle* (London had already read it, however), and Herbert George Wells's *Mankind in the Making.*

The Snark Adventure

The year 1907 marked a great expansion of London's library, primarily because the planned cruise around the world on board the *Snark* required stocking the boat not only with dry goods and material but books as well. London's plans for the trip were first to sail to Hawaii. "From Hawaii, he wrote to Fred Hayden Carruth (8 April 1906, HL), "we shall wander through the South Seas, Samoa, Tasmania, New Zealand, Australia, New Guinea, and up through the Philippines to Japan. Then Korea, and China, and on down to India, Red Sea, Mediterranean, Black Sea, Baltic, and on across the Atlantic to New York, and then around the Horn to San Francisco. We shall not rush ourselves, and shall have no schedule of places to visit. . . ."

Given the vast range of places London wanted to visit, and the small quarters in which he would be confined for the duration of the voyage, it is obvious that he could not take a library reflecting depth on all the places and people he wanted to see. He solved the problem by purchasing books "on location," as, for example, at Thrum's bookstore in Hawaii. It would be reasonable to assume that, once the *Snark* library was full, London would send the overflow of books back to Glen Ellen, repeating the procedure as he went along.

Nevertheless, the *Snark* needed a core library to begin with, and, in characteristic fashion, London overwhelmed the boat with books, as Martin Johnson would later write: "Then were dray-loads of the things brought from the London home, wood and coal, provisions, vegetables, blankets, and other things, and still other things, and above all, books—five hundred of them, on every conceivable topic, selected from Jack's library of ten thousand volumes. The *Snark* was fairly ballasted with books."[17]

London's selection of books included a fair number of titles on navigation, purchased from George E. Butler's store in San Francisco. Included were sailing directions for every stretch of water the *Snark* would sail, as well as elementary and advanced books on navigation. The navigation books came in handy once the London's had sailed, for London's conavigator, Roscoe Eames, subscribed to D. R. Teed's theory that we live on the inside of the earth. London had attempted to disprove this theory via several discussions with astronomer Edgar Lucien Larkin, but Eames was not to be shaken. As might be expected, Eames failed miserably as a navigator.

Included in the *Snark*'s professional library were Tyrrell Biddle's *Hints to Beginners in Amateur Yacht Designing* (used by London when designing the *Snark*); *Brown's Winds and Currents of the Northern and Southern Hemispheres;* William Henderson's *The Elements of Navigation* (by far the most important book aboard); Great Britain Hydrographic Office's *Sailing Directions* for the Philippines, Java, New Guinea, Fiji, and the west coast of Africa (as well as most of the rest of the seven seas); *The American Practical Navigator;* Thomas Day's *On Yachts and Yacht Handling* and *Cruises in Small Yachts;* Stanton King's *Dog Watches at Sea;* E. McCarrthy's *Familiar Fish;* Paul Eve Stevenson's *A Deep Water Voyage,* and *By Way of Cape Horn;* William Ferrell's *A Popular Treatise on the Winds;* Radford's *Handbook of Naval Gunnery;* Pirrie's *Technical Dictionary of Sea Terms, Phrases, and Words;* W. Clark Russell's *A Noble Haul;* Alexander Findlay's *A Directory for the Navigation of the South Pacific Ocean* (the *Snark* library boasted two copies of this book); William Rosser's *The Yachtman's Handy-Book;* the U.S. Navy's *International Code of Signals;* John Norie's *A Complete Epitome of Practical Navigation;* Edward Irving's *How to Know the Starry Heavens;* J. W. Kellogg's *Uses of Electricity on Shipboard;* Thornton Lecky's *The Danger Angle and Off-Shore Distance Tables* and *Wrinkles in Practical Navigation;* Henry Marshall's *Marshall's Navigation Made Easy;* and *Indian Ocean Pilot;* and, once the voyage had been under weigh for some time, a copy of *Lloyd's Calendar* for 1908. Richard Barry's *Port Arthur* contains notes in London's hand which substantiate his claims about learning to navigate while in the middle of the Pacific. Included also was a small medical library including Edward Keyes's *The Venereal Diseases,* John French's *Elements of Active-Principle Therapeutics,* and Kenelm Winslow's *Home Medical Library.* London noted passages on syphilis in both these books sometime during 1909.

The *Snark* sailed in April 1907. The Londons did not return to Glen Ellen until July 1909. Once on the high seas, the principal recreations, other than caring for the ship and themselves and London's customary thousand words a day, were reading, boxing, fishing, and playing cards. There are numerous examples of card game scores recorded on the flyleaves of London's books. Representative samples can be found in Alice Brown's *Margaret Warrener,* Arthur Compton-Rickett's *The Vagabond in Literature,* or Sir Anthony Hawkins's *Second String.*

London's library contains an impressive, in-depth collection of books on Hawaii and the South Seas. Unlike most of his library, the collection on Hawaii contains a number of rare titles. It is likely that the majority of this collection was purchased during the London's long stay in Hawaii during 1907. Many of the books include the bookmark of Thrum's, a bookstore in Honolulu. London confirmed his Hawaiian book-buying proclivities in a letter to George Brett, written shortly after the *Snark* had arrived in the South Seas (28 May 1907, HL): "Incidentally, I have already gathered much material for work in the future, down here in the Hawaiian Islands. Also, I have a new book in my mind which I shall write somewhere in the not too distant future, namely 'A Book of Sharks.' I have a dozen of the stories for this book already filed away."

Although London never did write his shark book, he did annotate several books for the collection, including William Bryan's *Natural History of Hawaii.* Another writing project London planned while in the Hawaiian Islands was an "Hawaiian Trilogy." It was to be a series focusing on the history of the people of Hawaii, and featuring the Hawaiian monarchy as the main characters. For the trilogy London consulted George Bate's *Sandwich Island Notes* (used in "Koolau the Leper"), George Chaney's *Aloha!* (London used this book for his 1908 story "Chun Ah Chun"), William Armstrong's *Around the World with a King* (also used in "Chun Ah Chun"), Isabella Bishop's *The Hawaiian Archipelago* (London took several descriptions of Maui from this book),

Aboard the **Roamer**

Herbert Bower's *The Paradise of the Pacific,* William Blackman's *The Making of Hawaii,* Helen Mathe's *One Summer in Hawaii* (this book had excellent descriptions of cannibalism which London borrowed for several stories), and William Westervelt's *Legends of Maui.* Although London did not write his trilogy, all these books supplied background material for his fiction based in Hawaii and the South Seas.

In addition to a collection of books on Hawaii, London also picked up several books about the South Seas during his *Snark* voyage: Charles Woodford's *A Naturalist Among the Head-Hunters* provided useful descriptions of South Sea labor trade, while Miles Smith's *Handbook of the Territory of Papua* aided the *Snark* crew during their exploration of New Guinea. William Ellis's *Polynesian Researches* was used for several South Sea settings, and George Brown's and John G. Paton's autobiographies gave London ideas for plots. Brown's book may have also provided a few ideas for London's later *Burning Daylight.* For information about head-hunting, London turned to Bradley Osbon's *A Sailor of Fortune,* William Torrey's autobiography, and Herbert Webster's *Through New Guinea and the Cannibal Countries.*

Although London was living a South Sea adventure, and collecting books about the regions he was visiting, he was nevertheless writing about some entirely different subjects. His major novel *Martin Eden* was composed during the cruise, and one of his finest short stories, "To Build a Fire," was also written. For the latter, London turned to Jeremiah Lynch's *Three Years in the Klondike*. London's interest in the sea prompted the reading of Frank Bullen's *Our Heritage the Sea*. In preparation for his visit to Australia, London read Charles Buley's *Australian Life in Town and Country*. Although the *Before Adam* controversy had blown over, London was still interested in evolution, as evidenced by his 1907 reading of Michael Fitch's *The Physical Basis of Mind and Morals*. And he kept up with his study of socialism, reading Frederich Engels's *Landmarks of Scientific Socialism*. For entertainment, London read Eden Phillpott's *The Whirlwind;* to prevent his continuing loss at cards he read Joseph Elwell's *Advanced Bridge;* and perhaps in part as a favor to Blanche Partington, who was a Christian Scientist, he read Mary Baker Eddy's *Science and Health*.

In 1908 London was impressed by Austin Lewis's *The Rise of the American Proletarian*, continued to make notes for his Christ novel by reading Walter Rauschenbusch's *Christianity and the Social Crisis*, and also continued his study of Herbert Spencer, reading Caleb Saleeby's *The Cycle of Life*. He incorporated some of Saleeby's thoughts in *Martin Eden*, the novel he finished that year.

In September 1908, London received and read Herbert George Wells's *New Worlds for Old*—a gift from Frederick Irons Bamford; he also read Herbert Spencer's *Facts and Comments*. Another gift from Bamford that year was Reginald Campbell's *Christianity and the Social Order*, a book that captured London's fancy—especially for the passages about individualism, the subject London had just dealt with in *Martin Eden*. Other books read during 1908 included George Turner's *Samoa a Hundred Years Ago* and Charles Tyler's *The Island World of the Pacific Ocean*.

In her "Books I Have Read," Charmian recorded several books read during the *Snark* voyage. Although many had been read by London prior to Charmian's reading, it is probable that she discussed the ideas in them with Jack, and likely that the ideas expressed sometimes found their way into the stories he was writing at the time. Included in her list are Herbert Spencer's *Facts and Comments* and also his *Autobiography,* read in October 1908; Joseph Conrad's *Lord Jim;* Edgar Saltus's

Imperial Purple; J. A. Mitchell's *The Silent War;* Arthur Morrison's *Slum Stories of London* ("Mate read this book aloud to me in Oakland, Jan. 29 '07"); Gustave Droz's *Monsieur;* Maxim Gorky's *Orloff and His Wife;* Austin Lewis's *The Rise of the American Proletarian* (read in Papeete, Tahiti, 1908); Herbert George Wells's *The Future in America;* Eden Phillpott's *The Whirlwind;* George Bernard Shaw's *Cashel Byron's Profession;* Robert Chambers's *The Fighting Chance* (read at Parker Ranch, Hawaii); *Confessions of a Child of the Century;* Henry Van Dyke's *The Opal Sea;* and Robert Louis Stevenson's *In the South Seas* and *Vailima Letters.*

By December 1908, London had become quite ill with several mysterious maladies. He decided to abandon the *Snark* voyage in favor of a return to the more temperate climate of the Valley of the Moon, later turning to Charles Woodruff's *The Effects of Tropical Light on White Men* for an answer to his illnesses.

The Beauty Ranch

The year 1909 was marked by London's return voyage aboard the *Tymeric* (during which time London read Hiram Bingham's *A Residence of 21 Years in the Sandwich Islands,* and used it in his writing of *Adventure*), the purchase of more land in Glen Ellen, and the reading of Rosalind Young's *Mutiny of the Bounty and Story of Pitcairn Island* for use in "The Seed of McCoy." London also found himself embroiled in another controversy, this time an attack by Frank Harris over the bishop of London passages in *The Iron Heel.*

In the 14 April 1909 issue of *Vanity Fair,* Frank Harris had written an article entitled "How Mr. Jack London Writes a Novel." In it, Harris compared portions of London's *The Iron Heel* with his own "The Bishop of London and Public Morality," published in 1901. Harris had written a piece of fiction, but a correspondent in the United States had reported it as a news item. Although London had taken the speech from a newspaper clipping and put it in the mouth of his character Bishop Morehouse, he had thought he was quoting a public document: the speech of the bishop of London. "I thought I had a human document," he replied, "and it made such a striking impression upon me that I filed it away for future use. Years afterwards, in writing *The Iron Heel,* I resurrected the clipping . . . [and] used it word for word. . . . I confess to having been fooled by Mr. Harris's canard."[18]

By the time London returned to Glen Ellen in mid-1909, and began expansion of the Beauty Ranch, his library had grown enormously. In 1910 there was little room to store all of it on the shelves in his sleeping porch or in his office. Many of the books, along with his notes and manuscripts, were boxed and stored in the barn some distance from the house. Still the books poured in. Even London could not keep up with the deluge. Just before his sailing in 1912 around the Horn aboard the *Dirigo,* a three-masted ship, London spoke (with characteristic exaggeration) to a New York reporter about his reading customs: "I read six books a day right along with my writing and everything else. I'm taking twenty thousand volumes with me on my trip around the Horn. I'm omnivorous. I read everthing I can lay my hands on. I'll read all of Marie Corelli's books up in a week and then say: 'I'm done with her for ten years.' I couldn't tell you a title of a single book I read, sometimes not the author. I couldn't quote a line; but I remember the feeling of the thing. My favorite author? I like them all. I never miss a Phillpotts book, nor a Kate Douglas Wiggins [sic]. I like Gouveneur Morris. Well, you know, I can't go down the whole line. I might forget and leave somebody out."[19]

The year 1910 saw the beginnings of the massive development of the Beauty Ranch, the purchase of the Kohler-Frohling Vineyards, and sailing trips aboard the *Roamer.* For his expansion of the ranch, London read John Streeter's *The Fat of the Land,* especially for information about the best kind of chickens to buy, the perfect hogpen, and other helpful farming hints. Aboard the *Roamer,* London took the U.S. Coast and Geodetic Survey's *Tide Tables for the Pacific Coast,* probably the only necessary book aboard the boat that London sailed all over San Francisco Bay. London had not yet abandoned his Christ novel in 1910, but the evidence of his work on it is limited to Aaron Drucker's *The Trial of Jesus.* Other books read during the year include Thomas Williams's *Fiji and the Fijians;* Otto Weininger's *Sex and Character* (London noted the information on homosexuality); Wilfred Walker's *Wandering Among South Sea Savages* (for its paragraphs on cannibalism); Josiah Willard's *My Life* (the beginnings of *John Barleycorn* were recorded in the endpapers of this book); Leroy Scott's *The Walking Delegate* (reviewed for the San Francisco *Examiner*); and, in December, Emma Goldman's *Anarchism and Other Essays,* a gift from the author.

London's description of character Swithin Hall's bungalow library in *A Son of the Sun* may give some indication of the books London read during 1911. Among the titles listed were "complete sets of [Leo] Tolstoy, [Ivan] Turgenieff, and [Maxim] Gorky; . . .[James Fenimore] Cooper and Mark Twain; . . .[Victor] Hugo and [Emile] Zola, and [Eugène] Sue; . . . and [Gustave] Flaubert, [Guy] De Maupassant, and Paul de Koch." Also listed were the works of Ilya Metchnikoff, Otto Weininger, and Arthur Schopenhaeur; Henry Havelock Ellis, Frank Lydston, Krafft-Ebing, August Forel, and Charles Woodruff's *Expansion of Races*.[20] Aside from Charles Woodruff's book, London mentioned specifically only Hudson's *Law of Psychic Phenomena*, Emile Zola's *Paris*, and Mahan's *Problems of Asia*.

"The Real Goods" was how he characterized Heinrich Heine's *Memoirs* in *The Mutiny of the Elsinore*, and it is likely that he read them first in 1911. And from the mention made in *A Son of the Sun*, it is likely that London first started reading August Forel's *The Sexual Question* in 1911 as well; he also read Robert Louis Stevenson's *Letters*, noting Stevenson's lack of belief in immortality.

London was always presenting books to people—and always receiving books as gifts. A rather humorous exchange of books occurred at the beginning of 1911, when London wrote to English novelist Elinor Glyn, proposing that he autograph and send her twelve of his own books in exchange for the eight she had written. London may have been somewhat embarrassed by his proposal when he found that he could come up with only eleven books to send; nevertheless Glyn good-naturedly responded to his request with her fictional "Elizabeth" series.

There is some indication that "The Book of Sharks" collection was still viable in 1911, as evidenced by London's annotations about sharks in Henry Hyndman's *The Record of an Adventurous Life*. And *The Star Rover* may have been born in 1911, too, with London's increasing interest in crime and criminals, as shown in his letter of 6 March to William Teichner. *The Valley of the Moon* was born in 1911, and that summer the Londons took a four-horse driving trip through northern California and Oregon, perhaps in preparation for the writing of the novel.

On the trip, he took Richard Cleveland's *In the Forecastle* and Ejnar Mikkelsen's *Conquering the Arctic Ice*, sources for his fall novel, *Smoke Bellew*. He also wrote, in response to a request from a New York publisher, a stirring introduction to Richard Dana's *Two Years Before the Mast*. His other solicited writings included a review of George Cook's *The Chasm*, written in response to a request from the then publishing editor, Harry Sinclair Lewis.

London's major writing during 1912 consisted of *The Valley of the Moon* and *The Scarlet Plague*. The former was written aboard the *Dirigo*, the ship London sailed aboard on his voyage around Cape Horn from New York to Seattle. In her diary, Charmian recorded the fifty books she (and perhaps Jack) read during the voyage. Included on her list were Gerhart Hauptmann's *The Fool in Christ*, Richard Le Gallienne's *The Quest of the Golden Girl*, Henry Stackpoole's *Fanny Lambert*, Leonard Merrick's *Cynthia, a Daughter of the Philistines* and *The Man Who Understood Women*, Simeon Ford's *A Few Remarks*, George Chester's *Get Rich Quick-Wallingford*, Ernest Renan's *Solomon's Song*, Violet Pagét's *Gospel of Anarchy*, Anatole France's *The Red Lily*, Robert William Chambers's *The Danger Mark*, George Ade's *In Babel*, Edgar Saltus's *Love and All About It* and *Daughters of the Rich*, three plays by August Strindberg, Matthew Arnold's *The Light of Asia*, Anatole France's *The Garden of Epicurus* (Charmian noted that this was read aloud), a biography of Oscar Wilde, Edward Lent's *Being Done Good*, Andre Castaigne's *The Bill-Toppers*, Friedrich Nietzche's *Ecce Homo*, Butler's *Kilb*, Robert Chambers's early short stories, Ford Madox Ford's *England and The English*, Sir James Barrie's *Peter and Wendy*, Gilbert Keith Chesterton's *What's Wrong with the World*, Richard Henry Dana's *Two Years Before the Mast*, Gelett Burgess's *The White Cat*, Kate Douglas Wiggin's *New Chronicles of Rebecca*, Bull's *Jacques Bonhomme*, three plays by Eugène Brieux, John Galsworthy's *The Island Pharisees*, Henrik Ibsen's *Letters*, Max Nordau's *The Interpretation of History*, Prince Kropotkin, Heineman's *The Physical Basis of Civilization*, the *Letters* of Robert Louis Stevenson, Ernest Renan's *Anti-Christ*, Theodore Dreiser's *Sister Carrie*, Lloyd Osbourne's *Infatuation*, Eden Phillpott's *The Good Red Earth*, and the *Trail of the Lonesome Pine* and *The New Religion*.

A Literary Rebirth

During the summer months of 1912 London spent much of his time studying Sigmund Freud's *Three Contributions to the Theory of Sex*, a pamphlet he later quoted in "The Kanaka Surf" and possibly also used in *The Little Lady of the Big House*. For his *John Barleycorn* (also written largely in 1912) London consulted both *The Light of Asia* and Paul Bourget's *Cosmopolis*, and found great examples of white logic in *Gospels of Anarchy* by Violet Pagét, as well as *Vital Lies*, William James's *The Will to Believe*, and Jacques Loeb's *The Mechanistic Conception of Life*. Two books on Charmian's list we know to have been read by London are France's *The Garden of Epicurus* and Nordau's *The Interpretation of History*. He would later return to *The Garden of Epicurus* when writing *The Mutiny of the Elsinore*. Also read on the voyage of the *Dirigo* was Walter Colton's classic of California, *Three Years in California*, Charles Brace's *The New West*, and Thomas Gregory's *History of Sonoma County* (all for London's *Valley of the Moon*), and William Waugh's *The Practice of Medicine*, which London consulted for its advice on treatment of stomach cancer, a malady the captain of the *Dirigo* suffered from.

London's Wolf House, which burned during the late summer of 1913, probably incorporated some of Edward Powell's ideas in *The Country Home Library*. And for a gang autobiography that London made notes for in 1912, he read Joseph Puffer's *The Boy and His Gang*.

For 1913 London planned and wrote his Cape Horn novel, a record in fiction of the *Dirigo* voyage. For it he consulted Carl Skottsberg's *The Wilds of Patagonia*, Arthur Symon's *Poems*, Arthur Clark's *The Clipper Ship Era*, Henri Bergson's *Creative Evolution*, and Frank Roesler's *The World's Greatest Migration*.

In March, London wrote to George Brett (1 March 1913, HL), with a request for $3,500.00, mainly for the construction of the Wolf House. His dire need for a single place to house his library was emphasized: "When I tell you that all these years we have been without a house; that I have been without space sufficient to shelve all my books, and that we have waited nine years for the completion of our house to approach, you will see that we have been very patient. As regards my library, it has been mostly stored away in boxes in the various barns on the ranch. Yet these books were my tools and are my tools. Most frequently, when I desire a reference, and look over my limited shelves, I find that the books which I need are stored away in some of the barns."

Writer and poet Henry Meade Bland described the ranch on a visit to it in 1915 (the Wolf House destroyed by fire, London was in practically the same cramped position he had been in when he wrote to Brett in 1913):

> Sunshine tempered by cool ocean breezes drifts through running vines into a broad southwest porch. By the side of a table piled high with books is a single chair, and beside the chair and table is a double couch. Songs of linnet and grosbeak drift in from time to time with the morning wind. The table is piled high with books—treatises they were, when we saw it, upon farming and agriculture, for Mr. London was gathering material for a work on scientific agriculture.
>
> But this porch is not Jack London's workshop, merely an annex, an outside reading table. Step through a door and you are in the real place, a combination of library, museum, and writing laboratory. All this is in the southwest corner of a low wooden building on the London farm at Glen Ellen, California.[21]

It was probably in 1913 that London decided to abandon his Christ novel in favor of a novel about crime and criminals, which would, in one chapter, incorporate the fifteen years worth of notes he had made on the life of Christ. A likely candidate for the germ of the idea for *The Star Rover* is *Life in Sing Sing* by "Number 1500," an autobiography which discusses prisoners isolated on the brink of madness. Other books read during the year include Walter Weyl's *The New Democracy,* Alfred Schultz's *Race or Mongrel,* Fitch Taylor's *A Voyage Round the World,* and the U.S. Public Health Service's *Studies Upon Leprosy,* Edgar Chambless's *Roadtown* (a gift from the author), Max Eastman's *Enjoyment of Poetry,* (also a gift from the author), Zoeth Eldredge's *The Beginnings of San Francisco,* and, perhaps after the burning of Wolf House, Rudolf Eucken's *The Truth of Religion.* In the flyleaves of that book London penned thoughts about nature's indifference to man's dreams. Frederick Bamford remembered London in 1913 with a birthday gift of Ferdinand Earle's *The Lyric Year.*

The beginning of 1914 found London embroiled in a lawsuit over the dramatic rights to *The Sea-Wolf.* In fighting it, London read L. C. Oldfield's *The Law of Copyright,* subscribed to the Authors' League *Bulletin,* which included numerous articles on the subject, and, on 29 January, asked Charmian to order *Playwright and Copyright in All*

Countries from the Macmillan Company. The year was also spent in part on writing *The Little Lady of the Big House,* a novel London had described in a letter to Roland Phillips the previous March (14 March 1913, HL):

> Say—I have a splendid motif for a novel. Have spent the past three days making notes and assuring myself of my grip on it. And now, I've got it in both my hands.
>
> Three characters only—a mighty trio in a mighty situation, in a magnificently beautiful environment. Each of the three is good; each of the three is big. It will be a winner.
>
> It is all sex, from start to finish—in which no sexual adventure is actually achieved or comes within a million miles of being achieved, and in which, nevertheless, is all the guts of sex, coupled with strength. Oh, my three are not pulling weaklings and moralists. They are cultured, modern, and at the same time profoundly primitive.
>
> As I go over this novel, I am almost led to believe that it is what I have been working toward all my writing life, and now I've got it in my two hands.
>
> Except for my old-time punch, which will be in it from start to finish, it will not be believed that I could write it—it is so utterly fresh, so absolutely unlike anything I have ever done.

The Little Lady of the Big House, which London so fervently described in 1913, turned out to be one of his biggest failures. Nevertheless, he characteristically took copious notes for the book, and consulted numerous books, including Edwin Carpenter's *The Intermediate Sex,* Enoch Kish's *The Sexual Life of Woman,* Laura Hannsson's *Studies in the Psychology of Women,* Frank Lydston's *Sex Hygiene for the Male,* Otto Rank's *Myth of the Birth of the Hero,* Stephen Powers's *Tribes of California,* and other books read as early as 1910, such as Otto Weininger's *Sex and Character,* August Forel's *The Sexual Question,* and, later, Edgar Saltus's *Love and All About It.*

London's major effort for 1914, *The Star Rover,* had been in the making for at least fifteen years. Nevertheless, several books read in 1914 also played a part in the novel's creation: Daniel Foss's *A Journal of the Shipwreck and Sufferings of Daniel Foss,* although impossible to date properly, was an extensive source for *The Star Rover.* Also used, first in preparation for the Christ novel, and later adapted to *The Star Rover,* was John Foxe's *Foxe's Book of Martyrs.* For the mountain meadows massacre chapter in the novel, London relied on Geronimo's autobiography and Josiah Gibbs's *The Mountain Meadows Massacre.* For

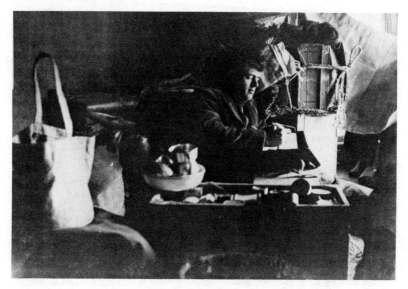

Korean War Correspondent, 1904

prison jargon, London turned to Julian Hawthorne's *The Subterranean Brotherhood*.

A minor literary effort for 1914 was London's *The Acorn-Planter*, the notes for which London recorded in Rufus Steele's *The Fall of Ug*, and information for which he obtained from Stephen Powers's *Tribes of California* (which he had used only incidentally in *The Little Lady of the Big House*).

During his April-June trip to Vera Cruz to cover the Mexican conflict, London read Phillip Terry's *Terry's Mexico* (a guidebook to the country), John Turner's *Barbarous Mexico* for it's background on Vera Cruz, and perhaps James Kilpatrick's *Tommy Atkins at War,* a description of the conflict then happening in Europe. London's other reading in 1914 included William Maxwell's *The Devil's Garden* (he wrote a review of the book as well), Francis Grierson's *The Invincible Alliance* (a gift from Frederick and Georgia Bamford), Robert Dunn's *The Youngest World* (reviewed for the *Bookman*), and Kathleen Norris's *Saturday's Child*.

The first half of 1915 for the Londons was spent in Hawaii. Just before their departure in February, London had written a play entitled *The Acorn-Planter,* which he submitted for presentation at the annual

Hi-Jinks of the Bohemian Club (it was not selected for performance by the Bohemian Club). On the passage over, London explained to his publisher that his current work consisted of two dog stories, each about seventy thousand words long: "The first will be entitled *Jerry*, the second will be entitled *And Michael*. These two dogs, Jerry and Michael, are full brothers and, after many adventures, they both come ultimately to the same happy ending, alive and in sunset middle age, as the reader parts from them. I am making fresh, vivid, new stuff, and dog psychology that will warm the hearts of dog lovers and the heads of psychologists, who usually are severe critics on dog psychology" (letter to George Brett, 18 February 1915, HL).

Although James McClintock's excellent study of London's work ably demonstrates the positive effect London's study of psychology had on his work,[22] sadly the two dog books London mentioned here were not reflections of that improvement. Both were hack work: *Jerry of the Islands* was mostly an expansion of *The Pitiful Story of the Performing Animal;* and London may have found some of his Hawaii scenes in Sheldon Dibble's *A History of the Sandwich Islands,* W. R. Castle's *Hawaii: Past and Present,* or Ferdinand Schnack's *The Aloha Guide.*

London *was* reading some exciting new scientific works in 1915, however, most important of which was Franz Ricklin's *Wish Fulfillment and Symbolism in Fairy-Tales.* Also read during the year was Bernard Talmey's *Love: A Treatise on the Science of Sex-Attraction,* Herbert George Wells's *The Research Magnificent* (for British politics) and *The Wife of Sir Isaac Harman* (London noted passages about women), Charles Woodruff's *Medical Ethnology* (for racial theory), and *Cruising the Carribean in the Wake of Pirates* (published by the United Fruit Company). By this time London had amassed a fairly large collection of clippings pertaining to the war in Europe. Adding to his information about that conflict was Edward Powell's *Fighting in Flanders* and John Chapman's *Deutschland Über Alles.* London had already made plans to journey to New York in quest of an assignment to cover the battles then raging in Europe.

Two letters London wrote in 1914 have particular significance to the study of his reading habits. The first, a response to Max Ehrmann's *Jesus: A Passion Play,* is interesting because it marks the end of London's plans to write a Christ novel. Rather than digging deeply into Ehrmann's book, as he would have done several years earlier, London sent the author a letter thanking him kindly for the book, and sounding all the while like an expert on the subject. The Christ novel had found its end in a single chapter in *The Star Rover.*

London's letter to Joseph Conrad is equally interesting, for, after reading the novelist's works for sixteen years, London finally felt that he could write to Conrad as a colleague.

London's routine in 1915 was carefully orchestrated. Up and writing by seven—five if there was a heavy workload before him—he would begin by collecting material, outlining plots, drafting plans, and, finally, working the current tale into a finished manuscript. London's cramped workroom included a desk with alphabetically arranged drawers and files where he kept important references—the clothesline of his literary apprenticeship long abandoned in favor of more expensive equipment. Shelves along one wall of the office held the extracts, plots, and notes for future stories, all fully systematized and at hand for use.

Work in London's shop went on undisturbed until noon, unless the thousand-word minimum had been reached before that hour. During working hours, London allowed no interruption. If more time was needed to write, his working day stretched on into the afternoon.

Everything London did was grist for his literary mill: his Glen Ellen life was described in *The Little Lady of the Big House;* his literary apprenticeship found itself woven into *Martin Eden;* even his endeavors in agriculture were fictionalized to some extent in *The Valley of the Moon.*

The busy life of a famous author created an even busier one for his personal servant. Sekine, who served as London's personal houseboy, remembered the author's apparently inexhaustible energy and his passion for reading as soon as his guests were gone. London also kept him busy making bookstands, since the floor of the room was usually flooded with books coming from all over the world.[23]

London's energy and passion for reading did not decline in 1916—the last year of his life. He read William Alexander's *A Brief History of the Hawaiian People,* using it as a primary source for "Shin Bones." His "Cherry" was in progress at the time of his death on 22 November 1916; for it he probably drew on Herbert Giles's *A History of Chinese Literature* and Homer Hulbert's *The Passing of Korea.* London continued his study of Sigmund Freud in 1916, devouring each issue of the *Psychoanalytic Review* as it came out. He also planned a study of insanity, perhaps after reading Stephen Smith's *Who Is Insane?*

Sir Basil Thomson's *The Diversions of a Prime Minister,* which contained a legend of Mary Butako, led to the writing in August of "When Alice Told Her Soul." And Alphonse Maeder's *The Dream Problem,* Edwin Holt's *The Freudian Wish and Its Place in Ethics,* and Henry Holt's *On the Cosmic Relations* all served to spur London's study of Freudian psychology—"the first psychology with a soul," as London called the author's theories.

London's study of psychology lead to the reading of Carl Gustav Jung's *Psychology of the Unconscious,* a book which—had London lived—might have influenced his writing more than any other. "It is big stuff" he wrote to Leo B. Mihan (24 October 1916, HL). The three hundred notations he made in the book—more than in any other book in his library—stand as evidence of just how "big" London thought the "stuff" was.

Jung's *Psychology of the Unconscious* marks the culmination of London's study of psychology—a study which had tremendous impact on London's thinking and especially on his writing. During this final stage in his writing career, London abandoned much of his hackwork and began to write stories of significant literary merit. "I tell you," he remarked to Charmian, "I am standing on the edge of a world so new, so wonderful, that I am almost afraid to look over into it" (Charmian London, *Book of Jack London,* 2:2). The effect of this and other books by Carl Jung and Sigmund Freud on London's literary output have been discussed at length in Earle Labor's *Jack London* (New York: Twayne Publishers, Inc, 1974) and James McClintock's *White Logic* (Cedar Rapids, Michigan: Wolf House Books, 1975).

The influence London's study of psychology had upon his writing only serves to underscore the importance of the magazines, newspapers, and books that came in ever increasing numbers into London's study each day. These materials were the primary sources for his fiction and nothing else. The condition of his books today also illustrates this fact. His library is not a collection of prized first editions, rare tomes, or handsome finely printed works of art, but is rather an assortment of shabby, ordinary reference books stuffed with clippings, pinned with notes, and marked with an occasional match.

The matches found in some of the books were placemarkers—a habit London had fallen into early in his career, and one he chose to write about in *The Little Lady of the Big House:* "As Forrest ate he

Jack and Charmian London and the No. 7 Remington

watched the hunting of the meat-eating yellow-jackets. Sturdy, more frost-resistant than bees, they were already on the wind and preying on the benumbed flies. . . . The last fly was gone ere Forrest had sipped his last sip of coffee, marked *Commercial Breeding of Frogs* with a match, and taken up his proofsheets."[24]

Nary a book in London's library survives today with a dust jacket. The early attempts at book jackets were drab, colorless things, and London hated the looks of them, as Charmian so explicitly stated in a letter to Mary Low (6 August 1916, HL): "This is a postscript to my longer letter of today, in which I forgot to tell you that Jack especially wishes you to take off the paper covers on his books, before you put them on your shelves. Some persons insist upon leaving these paper covers on the books, and it always makes him very much annoyed. So be a good girl, and rip them all off, and let the books show their own coats!"

London died in November 1916, leaving behind a legacy of fifty-one books and an adventurous life which still fascinates many. Naturally, after his death, the ranch operations slowed down. The shipment of books slowed to a trickle: there was no further need to satisfy an insatiable appetite for information. The books stored in the barn, left undisturbed for years, slowly disintegrated as the weather, field mice, and rats took their toll.

In 1919 Charmian set out to build herself a house on a tree-rimmed knoll overlooking the Valley of the Moon. In this House of Happy Walls, as she named it, she finally assembled London's literary archive and library.

A young girl from the Sonoma area, Beatrice Barrangon Ragnour, was hired to catalogue the books. She set upon the task with the ferver of youth. Charmian was pleased with the results, especially because Beatrice discovered a number of duplicates that could be sold. "I wonder if any one you know would be interested in buying some duplicate sets of books from Jack's library," she wrote to Hetty Gray Baker (18 March 1924, HL). "In sorting out the sets after Jack died, and putting them into the library in my new unfinished house, Beatrice found several duplicate sets, some of them never unpacked. They are as follows, and if I can sell all or some of the sets, I'll put one of Jack's bookplates in each volume of each set." The books consisted of sets of William Makepeace Thackeray, Thomas Babington Macaulay, Charles Dudley Warner, Washington Irving, and *The Immortals or: The Heroes of the Eighteenth Century*. Trading on London's name, the provenance, and the added bookplate, Charmian tried selling the books at $5.00 each— a hefty sum in days when books could be purchased new for $1.25. Still, had she succeeded (and apparently she did not, for duplicate sets still remain in the London library), she would have amassed almost four hundred dollars during a time when ranch income didn't always meet expenses.

Meanwhile the work of assembling and cataloguing the library went on. Beatrice dashed off notes to Charmian hoping that "we'll be able to get into that library together" (1924, HL), commenting on the subject arrangements she had made, or explaining where Charmian could find particular books in the newly assembled library: "In a library of such size as yours and with such a diversity of subjects represented (and frequently only one book on one subject) it just wasn't feasible to catalog the books by subject in the index. The subjects have only general divisions as History, Biography, Science, etc., represented. Each subject is located in a definite position, more or less accessible according to presumed demand. A short examination of any sections should reveal the books available on any given subject. As to Abraham Lincoln and his statesmen—I would suggest History or Biography or the Encyclopedias. History occupies the northwest corner of the room, with the Encyclopedias directly below. History then continues in the high shelves above the fiction on the north wall, clear across the east (fiction below) over the safe door merging into Biography around the southeastern window to the middle section containing Jack's books and translations. Your books on Lincoln are either around the safe door and the southeastern window or in the northwestern corner where American history centers. Sorry I can't be more definite."

In categorizing London's library, Beatrice assigned shelf numbers to each book and laboriously entered the number on the rear pastedown of each volume. It is clear that Charmian wanted the library not just for her personal use but also as a center of study of her famous husband. Even the House of Happy Walls was constructed with the public in mind. Today it fits its purpose well as a museum in the Jack London State Park.

Among Beatrice's other tasks was assisting Charmian with the organization of London's manuscripts. With the fire at Wolf House still fresh in her mind, along with the constant financial drain of the ranch, Charmian was convinced that London's manuscripts would be better housed in a rare-book library or museum.

With the aid of Willard Samuel Morse, a prominent Los Angeles book collector specializing in California authors, Charmian was able to make arrangements for Henry Edwards Huntington to purchase London's manuscripts for his newly founded library in San Marino. The purchase price was $25,000. Huntington assigned Leslie Bliss, his librarian, to the task of overseeing the new purchases in Glen Ellen, and reporting on the other London archives yet in Charmian's possession. According to Bliss: "Mrs. London was most hospitable and the material for sale was fascinating indeed. Had it not been for the fact that she had persuaded her husband to give her all his manuscripts early in her work with him they might all have been destroyed, as he had been in the habit of destroying them after publication. This fact accounts for the nonpreservation of the manuscripts of *The Call of the Wild* and *The Cruise of the Dazzler*." [25]

Bliss took advantage of his visit to the Beauty Ranch to examine London's personal correspondence files. He was impressed with the extensiveness of the collection and it's importance to future scholars. Consequently he asked Charmian to include *all* London's letters, including the ones he had received, in the negotiations. "Mrs. London agreed, asking only that any correspondence relating to current business, such as ranch affairs, be excluded at least until a later date." [26]

With the transfer of London's manuscripts and correspondence to the Huntington Library a fact, it was only a matter of time before the library would follow. In 1959, some forty-five years after London's death, Irving Shepard (London's nephew) transferred ownership of the library to the Huntington. Several more important gifts came to the Huntington in 1976 and, most recently, in 1983. The London archive was finally made accessible to scholars the world over. The bibliography of books which follows is an index to London's chartroom: a small glimpse at the many foreign coasts London visited and translated, with his pen, into the favorite stories of generations.

ANNOTATED BIBLIOGRAPHY

ADAMS, ANDY. *The Outlet*. Boston: Houghton, Mifflin and Company, 1905. x, 371 pp., illus. HL 332398

Contents: Account of the creation of a market for surplus Texas cattle at the close of the Civil War.

Marginalia: London's penciled markings (which appear on four pages) concern the destruction of the buffalo herds by the United States Army.

ADAMS, ARTHUR HENRY. *London Streets*. London: T. N. Foulis, 1906. 43 pp. HL 337660

Contents: Poems.

Inscription: "To Jack London with the author's friendship—Arthur H. Adams. Cash profits on sale to date: Nil. Cash deficit to date: £21. Does poetry pay?"

ADAMS, BROOKS. *America's Economic Supremacy*. New York: The Macmillan Company, 1900. ix, 222 pp., illus. HL 337239

Contents: Essays concerning English colonialism in the West Indies, Russian interests in China, and the Spanish War.

Bookseller: Smith Brothers, Oakland, California.

Marginalia: London's interest in this book seems to have centered on page 4, where he made a large marginal slash. On the rear endpaper he wrote: "Pig-iron statistics—4." Several other pages bear annotations in an unknown hand.

ADAMS, BROOKS. *The New Empire*. New York: The Macmillan Company, 1903. xxxvi, 243 pp., illus. HL 338659

Contents: Neither "history nor economics can be intelligently studied without a constant reference to the geographical surroundings which have affected different nations."—Prefatory Note.

Inscription: "Jack London."

Marginalia: Penciled slash next to a passage on page 211 discussing the necessity of maintaining an open mind. London wrote "Q. E. D." in the margin.

London's familiarity with Brooks Adams's work dates from 1898, as evidenced by the brief mention in "The Question of the Maximum": "Capitalistic production, in its modern significance, was born of the Industrial Revolution in England in the latter half of the eighteenth century. The great inventions of that period were both its father and its mother, while, as Mr. Brooks Adams has shown, the looted treasure of India was the potent midwife."[27]

ADAMS, EDWARD FRANCIS. *A Critique of Socialism Read Before the Ruskin Club of Oakland, California*. San Francisco: Paul Elder and Company, 1905. v, 27 pp. HL 336802

Contents: Critical essay attacking the socialist viewpoint.
Inscription: "The Joy & Strength of Life to you this happy Christmastide. Faithfully yours, Frederick I. Bamford. Christmas. 05."
The Ruskin Club, to which London belonged, consisted of a group of socialist intellectuals. The club was founded and chaired by Frederick Irons Bamford, an Oakland librarian who had helped a much younger London with his studies. When Bamford, A. A. Denison, Austin Lewis, and others formed the Ruskin Club in 1898, London joined eagerly, and remained an active participant for several years. The club disbanded in 1906.

ADNEY, TAPPAN. *The Klondike Stampede*. New York: Harper & Brothers, 1900. xii, 470 pp., illus. HL 102002

Contents: Personal account of the author's adventures in the 1897-98 Klondike gold rush.
Bookseller: Smith Brothers, Oakland, California.
Marginalia: Local color captured London's interest in this book. The passages he marked include a history of the Silver Bow strike and the exploits of Charlie Anderson and Swiftwater Bill.
London used this book as a general reference source on the gold rush. Some of the facts culled from its pages were woven into his 1902 essay "The Gold Hunters of the North" (in which Charlie Anderson appears as a Swedish miner). London also used Adney's account of Swiftwater Bill for *A Daughter of the Snows* and *Burning Daylight*. In a page of notes for a Klondike story entitled "That Pup," London made heavy use of Adney's book: "Make a splendid and humorous Klondike story. Work up the unloading first, by the two miners, getting Anderson drunk, and . . . work up the drunkedness as a man would get drunk and behave there, saloon, etc. 'See

Tappan Adney's book on this topic. . . .' " [28]

As a correspondent for *Harper's Illustrated Weekly*, Tappan Adney personally visited the goldfields, and observed and interviewed many of the miners who had journeyed there. His book was one of the first and most popular accounts of that mad rush for Canadian gold, and the information he supplied about it was generally accepted as factual, thus explaining London's reliance on *The Klondike Stampede* not only for his fiction but also for his nonfiction essay "The Gold Hunters of the North," which appeared in the *Atlantic Monthly* July 1903.

ALEXANDER, WILLIAM DE WITT. *A Brief History of the Hawaiian People.* New York: American Book Company, 1899. 357 pp., illus. HL 332659

Contents: A "simple and concise history of the Hawaiian People, which, it is hoped, may be useful to the teachers and higher classes in our schools."—Preface.

Marginalia: Although heavily annotated by Charmian London, a few of the markings in this book appear to have been made by Jack London. His interest was in Pélé, the goddess of volcanoes, and the eruption of the volcano Hualalai, and also in a few of the early battles between the white explorers and settlers and the Hawaiian natives. The conquest of Oahu, the art of distilling, the capture of Isaac Davis's schooner, *Fair American* (recounted in London's "Shin Bones"), and the wreck of the *Arthur* were also subjects in this book that London found of interest. He intended to include Alexander's account of the death of Kamehameha in a planned Hawaiian trilogy. Although London made many annotations and notes for this trio of novels, he never wrote any of them.

THE AMERICAN PRACTICAL NAVIGATOR. *Being An Epitome of Navigation and Nautical Astronomy.* Washington: Government Printing Office, 105. 652 pp., illus. HL 68554 1905 PF

Contents: Handbook of navigation, containing tables and charts and other navigational aids.

Bookseller: George E. Butler, Chronometer and Watchmaker, San Francisco, California.

Marginalia: London marked various sections of the "Difference of

Latitude and Departure" table for quick reference, and also marked passages discussing the finding of latitude by meridian altitude. *Enclosures:* Five-page typescript with the following headings: "Correction of the Sun's Declination at Sea for Longitude and for Time," "Chronometer Sight," "Latitude by Meridian Altitude," "Longitude by the Sun at Noon," "To Correct a Compass Course," "How to Use Tables I and II," "To Find Difference of Longitude." Also, one page of autograph notes: "For use in A.M. sights. G.M.T. is yesterday evening. Correct it for yesterday noon. Corr. Dec. for yesterday noon. Corr. Equat. of T. for yesterday noon. The hour angle of G.M.T. is 20 hrs. etc., of yesterday. Difference between G. hour angle & ship hr. A. is difference of longitude in time. Change time to longitude."

When London made the horrible discovery that his *Snark* captain could not navigate, he went to the ship's library of five hundred volumes and opened up the books on navigation. From *The American Practical Navigator* and other similar works, London was able to learn enough about navigation to pilot the yacht to Hawaii. His "Finding One's Way About," printed in *The Cruise of the Snark,* recounts the experience of learning to navigate while in the difficult circumstances just described.

AMSBARY, WALLACE BRUCE. *The Ballads of Bourbonnais.* Indianapolis: The Bobbs-Merrill Company, 1904. 181 pp., illus. HL 337326
Contents: Ballads "written in the hope of preserving, if possible, the dialect of the Illinois French-Canadian."—Introduction.
Inscription: "To Jack London. My compliments. H. H. Fuller. Howard City."

ANDERSON, JOHN REDWOOD. *The Mask.* London: Simpkin, Marshall & Company, Limited, 1912. 93 pp. HL 337636
Contents: Poems.
Inscription: "To Jack London with the Author's sincere appreciation. June 2nd 1912."

ARMSTRONG, WILLIAM N. *Around the World with a King.* New York: Frederick A. Stokes Company, 1904. xviii, 290 pp., illus. HL 270102

Contents: Account of the travels of King Kalakaua of Hawaii, as recorded by a member of his cabinet.

Marginalia: Local color and the affairs of the Hawaiian kings characterize the passages marked by London in this book. They deal with drunkenness, the Hawaiian kings and their destiny, a royal matrimonial alliance, and the frigate *Resolution*. King Kalakaua appears in two of London's stories: "Shin Bones" and "Chun Ah Chun."

This was another of the many books London annotated for his planned "Hawaiian Trilogy." The third book in the series was to be a biographical novel of King Kamehameha.

Around the World with a King was part of the *Snark* library.

ARNOLD, SIR EDWIN. *The Light of Asia; Or, the Great Renunciation. (Mahabhinishamana.) Being the Life and Teaching of Gautama, Prince of India and Founder of Buddhism.* New York: A. L. Burt, 1879. ix, 305 pp. HL 336829

Contents: "In the following poem I have sought, by the medium of an imaginary Buddhist votary, to depict the life and character and indicate the philosophy of that noble hero and reformer, Prince Gautama of India, the founder of Buddhism."—Preface.

Marginalia: London marked passages dealing with the mortal darkness, sorrow, the ache of birth, the "om" chant, the sick, and the ten sins. On the rear endpapers he recorded some ideas for his future book *John Barleycorn* (completed in January 1913): "Barleycorn. cheats of sense[.] snares of the flesh[.] mists out of the sensate[.] the fogs of sentiency[,] miasmas of—. destroy birth and death[.] The lies of passion[.] Fleeting sense[.] The snarls—The bitter rules, the jar of law. The paradox of being[.] Sense-struck— shadows & futilities[.] 12 41 /15[.] Our lusts and rapacity. p. 160 p. 161—Pessimism of *sentiency*[.] 162[.]"

AUTHORS' LEAGUE OF AMERICA. *The Bulletin of the Authors' League of America.* New York: Authors' League, April 1913, Number 1. 15 pp. HL

55

Barleywine

cheats of sense
snares of the flesh
mists ~~and~~ of the sensate
the fogs of sentiency
miasmas of ———
destiny birth & death
The lies of passion
        fleeting sense
The snares
The bitter rules, the jar
        of law.

The paradox of being
Sense-struck —
shadows & futilities.
our lusts & rapacity.

p. VII — Pessimism
of sentiency
§ 162 —

Contents: Articles largely concerned with copyright legislation and issues

Marginalia: Copyright was an important issue in this number of *The Bulletin,* and London's interest in it prompted two marginal slashes on page 4.

The Authors' League of America was founded as a lobbying body to protect the copyright interests of authors. London joined the group in order to protect his (and others') rights and interests in motion picture screenplays and subsidiary rights.

AUTHORS' LEAGUE OF AMERICA. *The Bulletin of the Authors' League of America.* New York: Authors' League, July 1913, Number 3. 20 pp. HL

Contents: Author's rights and copyrights.

Marginalia: London's annotations deal with the issue of American copyright and the procedures for copyrighting material in magazines.

AUTHORS' LEAGUE OF AMERICA. *The Bulletin of the Authors' League of America.* New York: Authors' League, March 1914, Number 11. 19 pp. HL

Contents: Motion picture copyrights.

Marginalia: The motion picture industry, still in infancy in 1914, was not covered under the 1909 copyright act. London marked passages in this issue explaining how authors could stop motion picture companies from pirating their works.

Enclosure: Two pages of London's handwritten notes: "I'll break the thing wide open, based (1) . . . on the law & the contracts & assignments[.] (2)on collusion & inveracity on your & Noel's part. Prove conspiracy on part of Noel & Pelton. Base my right to m[otion] p[icture] on this. To Pelton: 'I'm so mad at this double cross of Noel, & your acquiescence in it, that I am going to fight both of you—I'll pay the [$] 1100 you advanced on *The Sea-Wolf* and no more.'"

London assigned the dramatic rights to *The Sea-Wolf* to Joseph Noel some time after its publication in 1904. When motion pictures became profitable, Noel sold his dramatic rights to Henry Pelton. London was furious over the deal, and charged that Noel had no right to sell the motion picture rights. He finally agreed to reimburse Pelton for monies advanced to Noel, and take back all rights to the novel. The anger evinced in the note above came about because, as months passed, the sum Pelton had advanced mysteriously grew. London knew he was being taken advantage of, and became furious. The full story is told in the exchange of letters between Noel and London, housed in the Huntington Library. London's side of the story will be published in *The Jack London Letters* (Stanford: Stanford University Press, in press).

AUTHORS' LEAGUE OF AMERICA. *Yearbook.* New York: Authors' League, 1915. 43 pp. HL
Contents: Copyright issues.
Marginalia: London was interested in the progress being made by Hugh A. Bayne, Authors' League legal counsel, in copyright litigation.

BARBER, MARGARET FAIRLESS. *The Roadmender.* London: Duckworth & Company, 1910. 158 pp., illus. HL 330795
Contents: "The Roadmender," "Out of the Shadow," "At the White Gate."
Inscription: "Mother of Mazie to Jack London. Dec. '16th 1913."

BARING-GOULD, SABINE. *Curiosities of Olden Times.* Edinburgh: John Grant, 1896. 300 pp. HL 337226
Bookseller: Joseph McDonough, Rare Books, Albany, New York.
Contents: Essays.
Marginalia: London marked passages about strange and ludicrous wills, medieval punishments, and fines. On the rear pastedown, he recorded his findings: "p. 17—Cyphers[,] good stuff. 40-41—voice of the dead. 43—The ancient will of a pig[.] 90-91-92-93—fines for mutilation & injury. 96—shoeing humans with iron. 97—quarreling women."

BARRY, RICHARD HAYES. *Port Arthur: A Monster Heroism.* New York: Moffat, Yard & Company, 1905. 344 p., illus. HL 330688

Contents: Account of the Japanese siege of Port Arthur on 9 February 1904.
Marginalia: Penciled figures scratched onto the rear free endpaper.
Port Arthur was undoubtedly a book in the *Snark* library. The figures appear to be navigational arithmetic; London must have been charting the course while reading this book. His library contains a number of war-related volumes, most of which were used as background for his Korean-based newspaper articles. This book, however, was written by a fellow correspondent *during* the war. London probably brought it along to remember old times.

BASHKIRTSEVA, MARIE MARIIA CONSTANTINOVNA. *The Journal of a Young Artist, 1860-1884.* New York: Cassell & Company, Limited, 1899. viii, 434 pp., illus. HL 332494
Contents: "In these pages, science, art, literature, social questions, love, are treated with all the cynicism of a Machiavelli and the naïveté of an ardent and enthusiastic girl."—Translator's Preface.
Bookseller: Doxey Importer, San Francisco, California.
Marginalia: Both London and his wife Charmian read this journal. Both annotated it as well. Jack London made marks beside passages about Bashkirtseva's worries about her art, her talent, her hatred of men and love for dogs, and her fear of her teacher. Also marked are a number of passages about achievement of fame and success.

BATES, GEORGE WASHINGTON. *Sandwich Island Notes.* New York: Harper & Brothers, 1854. 493 pp., illus. HL 622
Contents: "I have endeavored to portray the condition of things as they appeared to me in 1858 [*sic*]. . . . I have taken especial pains to develop the past and present condition of the people . . . and have endeavored to specify a few reasons for the 'ANNEXATION' of that important group of islands."—Preface.
Bookseller: Dawson's Bookshop, Los Angeles, California.
Marginalia: London wrote "184—cave in Kaui" on the rear pastedown and marked a passage about the Waipio Valley. Several passages about Molokai were noted by Charmian.
London consulted *Sandwich Island Notes* while writing his 1908 story "Koolau the Leper."

BEBEL, AUGUST. *Women Under Socialism*. New York: New York Labor News Press, 1904. vi. 379 pp., illus. HL 336804

Contents: Attack on capitalist society illuminating the oppression of women, women's social inequality, and the place of prostitution in capitalist economies.

Marginalia: London was interested in the capitalist exploitation of slaves during the Civil War, women in jail, and Mary Wollstonecraft.

BECKE, LOUIS. *By Rock and Pool on an Austral Shore and Other Stories*. London: T. Fisher Unwin, 1901. vi, 250 pp. HL 330691

Contents: Sea tales of the South Pacific.

Marginalia: London marked only one passage: a description of a shark-fishing episode in which dead dogs were used as bait.

One of the many novels London planned to write but never quite managed to put down on paper was a book on sharks. His fascination with the fish probably began while sailing on the shark-infested waters of San Francisco Bay, and was strengthened by his sailing trip to the South Seas. This was but one of the many notations he made regarding sharks.

BELL, WILLIAM MARA. *The Rise of Man: An Interlude in Philosophy*. San Francisco: Published by the Author, 1906. 562 pp. HL 3367717

Contents: "On Life and Literature," "On Law and Government," "On Marriage and Morals," "On Science and Religion," "On Race, Creed and Color."

Inscription: "To Jack London Esq. With the Compliments of the Author[,] William MaraBell. Nov. 20th, '06. San Francisco, Cal[.]"

BENHAM, GEORGE B. *Patriotism and Socialism*. San Francisco: Socialist Labor Party, 1895. 15 pp. HL

Contents: Socialist tract on the exploitation of the working class by capitalists.

Marginalia: London was interested in the discussion of the exploitation of the church by capitalists, and in the fight against wage slavery.

This pamphlet was used as a source for *The Iron Heel,* and also for a number of London's socialist speeches. It is quite likely that London found it at the Socialist Temple on Turk Street in San Francisco, a place he frequently visited prior to 1905.

BERGSON, HENRI LOUIS. *Creative Evolution.* New York: Henry Holt and Company, 1911. xv, 407 pp. HL 336733

Contents: General treatise on evolution.

Marginalia: London's notes in this book are among the most copious in his entire library—even though only one quarter of the book is marked. The subjects of interest to London include Herbert Spencer, materialism, neo-Lamarckism, variation and heredity, neo-Darwinism, the meaning and nature of intelligence, intelligence and instinct, and the nature of instincts and the meaning of life. On the rear pastedown he wrote: "76 to 84—Question of inheritance of acquired characters[.] 87—original impetus of life. 99—Why not original impetus of *matter?* 102[.] 150[.] 111—vegetable consciousness. 113—theory that vegetable and animal are descended from common ancestor. 117[.] 120[.] 130[.] 135—the crux of the common ancestry of vegetative, instinctive, & rational life. 136-7-8-9-40[.] 172[.] 187—the meat of what Bergson is after. 189-90—metaphysical approach and positive approach. 194—introducing the wedge of his metaphysic."

In a letter of 25 June 1914 to his socialist friend Ralph Kasper, London admitted that he had "no patience with fly-by-night philosophers such as Bergson." Nor, he added, did he have any "patience with the metaphysical philosophers. With them, always, the wish is parent to the thought, and their wish is parent to their profoundest philosophical conclusions. I join with Haeckel in being what, in lieu of any other phrase, I am compelled to call 'a positive scientific thinker'" (*Letters,* p. 425).

London mentions Bergson several times in his fiction. In *The Mutiny of the Elsinore,* Pathurst comes to the conclusion that love is the final word: "Like Bergson in his overhanging heaven of intuition, . . . so I have trod the materialistic dictums of science underfoot, scaled the last peak of philosophy, and leaped into my heaven."[29] Paula, in *The Little Lady of the Big House* (p. 125), holds the philosopher in contempt: "I defy you, Aaron, I defy you, to get one thought out of Bergson on music that is more lucid than any thought he ever uttered in his *Philosophy of Laughter,* which is not lucid at all." But Darrell Standing makes the most concrete remark about Bergson's work in *The Star Rover:* "First of all, Bergson is right. Life cannot be explained in intellectual terms."[30]

BERKMAN, ALEXANDER. *Prison Memoirs of an Anarchist.* New York: Mother Earth Publishing Association, 1912. 512 pp., illus. HL 332490

Contents: Personal narrative of Berkman's experiences as an anarchist, and an analysis and account of his life in prison.

Inscription: "To my friend & brother Jack London, with whom I often disagree, but whose ability and revolutionary spirit I admire[.] Fraternally[,] Alexander Berkman.

Emma Goldman, editor of *Mother Earth,* introduced London to this book in a letter of 26 September 1911 (HL), noting that "as the only revolutionary American writer," he could not help but "appreciate the first revolutionary literary American book. . . . I know you are a busy man, imposed upon a grea[t] deal, yet, I make bold to ask you a favor, a very great favor. Would you read Berkman's Mss? . . . Then, too, if the book appeals to you strongly, perh[a]ps you would feel moved to write the preface."

Knowing full well that Berkman would not stand for his words, London agreed to read the manuscript and write a preface. That fall, he dashed off an impertinent attack on Berkman's foolishness. Citing love and comradeship as the basis of his intellectual disagreement with anarchy, London attacked Berkman's philosophy, and then attacked Berkman personally, calling the latter's attempted assassination of coke manufacturer Henry C. Frick foolish, and his failure, even when standing pointblank in front of the man, a stupid blunder. London claimed that no one knew why Berkman wanted to kill Frick in the first place, no one could understand how he missed when he tried, and no one could see how Berkman's subsequent suicide attempt in the police station could fail either.

Berkman did not accept London's preface ("it more than damns me with faint praise," he said in a letter to London dated 23 February 1912, HL), and found another, more complimentary one to put in its place. In 1916, London resurrected his preface, sent it to a socialist publication, and introduced the introduction with a rather maudlin paragraph claiming that the socialists had forgotten him as a fighter for the cause.

BERRY, FREDERICK FORREST. *The Torch of Reason Or Humanity's God.* Cincinnati, Ohio: The Torch of Reason, Publishers, 1912. xv, 477 pp., illus. HL 330696

Contents: "For ten years I have been trying to think of the right way by which to reach that peculiar intelligence which refuses an audience to Truth. There are enough good and scientific books on Socialism to convert the world in a day; but they are, for the most part, dry and hard to read. At least, they are hard to *get read.* In *The Torch of Reason* I have tried to come to the rescue of the prejudiced mind. I have written something that I feel will be read. It was my aim to blaze a new trail, far and away from the beaten paths of all conventional Socialistic propaganda."—Author's Apology.

Inscription: "Complimentary of our united love and Comradeship, to Charmian and Jack London, from Ray and Forrest Berry[.] 1912[.] Just because we love you."

Berry's correspondence with London began in February 1907. A St. Louis socialist, Berry was interested in London's literary efforts, Gaylord Wilshire's socialist magazine, and his own writing career. He wrote to London on 25 January 1911 (HL), begging for a reaction to his *Torch of Reason:* "I want you to read the *Reason* story of mine, Comrade, and when you have done so, I will be glad to have you . . . criticise it and tell me what you think of it. I will promise you that your words will be seized upon—greedily—as advertising material in pushing the book among the heathen." In 1913, however, London pleaded that he was too overworked to help Berry with another project. Smarting from the rejection, Berry never got in touch with London again.

BIBLE. ENGLISH. 1896? *The Holy Bible, Containing the Old and New Testaments.* London: Oxford University Press, [1896?] 1,000, 48, 239, 31 pp., illus. HL 336704

Contents: King James Bible.

Marginalia: The dimensions of Noah's ark, the story of Moses and the children of Israel, the fisherman in the Book of Matthew, the story of Jesus, building a house upon a rock, and the books of Matthew, Mark, Luke, and John all were of interest to London. This Bible contains numerous markings, most of which, however, are in an unknown hand.

BIBLE. NEW TESTAMENT. ENGLISH. 1906. *The New Testament of Our Lord and Saviour Jesus Christ. Arranged in the Order in Which Its Parts Came to Those in the First Century Who Believed in Our Lord.* New York: E. P. Dutton & Company, 1906. xxxii, 561 pp., illus. HL 336780
Contents: New Testament.
Bookseller: Paul Elder & Company, San Francisco, California.
Inscription: "To Jack with my love. Fred. Christmas, [']07."
Marginalia: The annotations made in this Bible are wholly concerned with the Christ novel London was planning to write at the time. His markings are found beside passages describing the story of Christ, from birth to crucifixion. On page 175, he made a note for the novel: "Have the Goth instrumental in catching Barabbas— & make Barabbas strong character—also, as characters, the two thieves[.]"
A devout believer in "Christian Socialism," which was popular at the time, Frederick Irons Bamford sent London this Bible as a Christmas gift. The book went with London aboard the *Snark* in 1907.
The writing of a novel about Christ had been one of London's goals for quite some time. He first indicated his intentions in a letter dated 10 August 1899 to his friend, Cloudesley Johns: "If I can only get ahead of the game, I'm going to jump back to Jerusalem in the time of Christ, and write [a novel] . . . giving an entirely new interpretation of many things which occurred at that time. I think I can do it, so that while it may rattle the slats of Christians they will still be anxious to read it" (*Letters,* p. 52).

BIBLE. OLD TESTAMENT. PROVERBS. *The Proverbs of Solomon or the Words of the Wise in Verse. Translated from the Massoretic Text*

of the Hebrew by Rev. Isidore Myers, B.A. New York: Bloch
Publishing Company, 1912. 145 pp., illus. HL 289228
Contents: Old Testament and Proverbs.
Inscription: "Mr[.] Jack London[.] With compliments[,] admiration,
and best wishes of Rabbi Isidore Myers[.] Los Angeles Cal[.] April
28th 1913.

BIDDLE, TYRREL E. *Hints to Beginners in Amateur Yacht Designing,
With Lines for a Single-Handed Cruiser, and a 5 to 10 Ton Cutter
or Yawl.* London: Norie & Wilson, 1890. 19 pp., illus. HL
336833
Contents: Handbook for the novice shipbuilder.
Marginalia: Only three pages were marked in this book. They contain information about the displacement of water, buoyancy, and
the momentum of ships.

BIERCE, AMBROSE GWINNETT. *Ashes of the Beacon. The Land Beyond the Blow. For the Ahkoond. John Smith, Liberator. Bits of Autobiography.* (The Collected Works of Ambrose Bierce, Volume I.) New York: Neale Publishing Company, 1909. 402 pp., illus. HL 338982 (v.1)

Contents: Short stories.

Marginalia: A descriptive passage in one of Bierce's stories, telling of a great mirage of monsters that appeared after a thunderstorm, caught London's eye. On the rear pastedown he wrote: "374-5—great mirage description for desert story."

London disliked Bierce personally, but read his books anyway, encouraged by George Sterling. In a letter of 31 May 1906 to Sterling, London took a characteristic dig at "bitter Bierce": "I wouldn't dare lock horns with Bierce. He stopped growing a generation ago. . . . He never reads books that aren't something like a hundred years old, and he glories in the fact" (*Letters,* p. 204). Regardless of his personal animosity toward the older writer, London knew a good story when he saw one, and was not above using Bierce's talents to his own advantage.

BIERCE, AMBROSE GWINNETT. *The Cynic's Word Book.* New York: Doubleday, Page & Company, 1906. v, 233 pp. HL 337238

Contents: Satirical dictionary of selected words.

Inscription: "Dearest Wolf: I believe you can stand for even the definition of 'Grapeshot'! Personally, I prefer that of 'Husband.' As ever, Greek. Oakland, Oct. 22nd, 1906."

Marginalia: London marked the definitions of "Husband," "Faith," and "Heaven."

George Sterling, or "Greek" as he was fondly known, was responsible for many of the books in London's library, especially the volumes of poetry. Because he was a close friend, London took Sterling's opinions quite seriously. The definition of "Grapeshot" that Sterling thought London could stand for appeared in *The Iron Heel:* "To show the tenor of thought, the following definition is quoted from *Cynic's Word Book* (1906 A.D.), written by one Ambrose Bierce, an avowed and confirmed misanthrope of the period:

Dearest Wolf :

I believe you can stand for even the definition of " Grapeshot " ! Personally , I prefer that of " Husband . "

As ever,

Greek .

Oakland , Oct. 22ⁿᵈ , 1906 .

'Grapeshot, n. An argument which the future is preparing in answer to the demands of American Socialism.'"[31]

BIERCE, AMBROSE GWINNETT. *The Monk and the Hangman's Daughter. Fantastic Fables.* (The Collected Works of Ambrose Bierce, Volume VI.) New York: Neale Publishing Company, 1911. 383 pp. HL 338982 (v.6)

Contents: Contemporary satirical fables.

Marginalia: London's interest was in the fable "Moral Principle and Material Interest." On the rear pastedown, he wrote "165—fables."

BIERCE, AMBROSE GWINNETT. *Shapes of Clay.* (The Collected Works of Ambrose Bierce, Volume IV.) New York: Neale Publishing Company, 1910. 376 pp. HL 338982 (v.4)

Contents: Poems.

Marginalia: Two poems, "Religion" and "Arthur McEwen," interested London. He marked the page number for the latter on the rear pastedown: "—87."

BIERCE, AMBROSE GWINNETT. *Tangential Views.* (The Collected Works of Ambrose Bierce, Volume IX.) New York: Neale Publishing Company, 1911. 384 pp. HL 338982 (v.9)

Contents: Essays.

Marginalia: "37—The Socialist[.] 48—George Washington[.] 58—The Moon[.]" written on the rear pastedown.

BINGHAM, HIRAM. *A Residence of Twenty-One Years in the Sandwich Islands; Or the Civil, Religious, and Political History of Those Islands, Comprising a Particular View of the Missionary Operations Connected with the Introduction and Progress of Christianity and Civilization Among the Hawaiian People.* Hartford, Connecticut: Hezekiah Huntington, 1847. xvi, 616 pp., illus. HL 384864

Contents: "I have given briefly, . . . an account of the people, for an indefinite period previous to the discovery of the Islands by Captain Cook; and . . . their history during the subsequent forty years. . . . thence onward, . . . the history of the mission and the history of the nation."—Preface.

Marginalia: London used this book extensively for its historical background, and also for its colorful incidents which he interwove into *Adventure* and a few of his other South Sea and Hawaiian tales. Specific passages that interested him include an account of the felling of a coconut tree (said to be a signal for strife); the historical characters Kaahumanu, Isaac Davis, John Young, and Kamehameha; Captain Brown's fight against Kaeo; and the English soldiers' battle with the Hawaiians. His notes on the rear endpaper demonstrate his intense interest: "Female[:] Namahana[,] Halakua[,] Lililia[.] 20—the incest motif in Hawaiian myths[.] 40—John Young & Isaac Davis[.] 47—method of maintaining a dead man's footprints. 126—Arrival of king at Honolulu, salutes, noise, slaying dogs for luau, etc. etc. 127-8-9—death & orgies of Likelike[.] 128—old-time gambling game[.] 135—a royal meeting, embraces, lifted up their voices & wept[.] 152-3-4—Written Hawaiian language[.]"

BISHOP, ISABELLA LUCY (BIRD). *The Hawaiian Archipelago: Six Months Amongst the Palm Groves, Coral Reefs, and Volcanoes of the Sandwich Islands.* London: John Murray, 1906. xv, 318 pp., illus. HL 334860

Contents: Account of the author's experiences, explorations, etc., while riding on horseback in the interior of the Hawaiian Islands.
Marginalia: Both Jack and Charmian London read this book, and it includes many markings by both. The majority of the markings were made by Charmian; however, two markings, one beside a passage describing the trees on Maui, and another beside a description of the Makawao crater, were made by Jack.

BISHOP, ISABELLA LUCY (BIRD). *Korea and Her Neighbors. A Narrative of Travel, with an Account of the Recent Vicissitudes and Present Position of the Country.* New York: Fleming H. Revell Company, 1898. 488 pp., illus. HL 332764

Contents: Account of four visits to Korea, beginning in January 1894.
Inscription: "Jack London[.]"
Marginalia: London read this book while in Korea during the Russo-Japanese War. He was interested in Bishop's description of the average Korean, the harbor at Seoul, the meaning of Korean marriage, the road from Seoul to Wonsan, and remarks about Korean coinage.

In "Dr. Moffett," London recalled reading to his servant, Man-youngi, Bishop's description of a visit she had once paid to a Korean magistrate.

13.

did not drop. He looked straight into mine, and in the look there was challenge as well as request.

I did not reply at once, but turned to Mrs. Isabella Bird Bishop's book on Korea. On page 86 therein I read her description of a visit she had once paid to a Korean magistrate and which was a sample of the treatment she received from all magistrates.

"One attendant, by no means polite, took my kwan-ja to the magistrate, and very roughly led the way to two small rooms, in the inner one of which the official was seated

BJÖRKLUND, GUSTAF. *Death and Resurrection from the Point of View of the Cell-Theory.* Chicago: The Open Court Publishing Company, 1910. xix, 205 pp., illus. HL 336762

Contents: "death is not a finality, and . . . the purpose of life is not limited to the span of our days between the cradle and the grave, but . . . has a further and fuller significance."—Publisher's Preface.

Inscription: "'Brass Tack' information for Comrade Jack London from Comrade J. C. Fries[.]"

Fries was one of London's many socialist acquaintances.

BLACKMAN, WILLIAM FREMONT. *The Making of Hawaii: A Study in Social Evolution.* New York: The Macmillan Company, 1899. xii, 266 pp., illus. HL 332491

Contents: "This work does not purport to be a history of the Hawaiian people, but a study of their social, political, and moral development."—Preface.

Bookseller: Brentano's, New York, New York.

Marginalia: London's library contains two copies of this book. Both were read and annotated by Charmian London, but only this copy was annotated by Jack London. He was interested in Hawaiian kings: their divine lineage and absolute power, the reverence the people felt for high rank, and the names Hawaiian people used to identify generations. On the rear pastedown London wrote: "22-3-4—respect ceremonial of commoners toward chiefs. 47— peculiar custom of calling all of his own generation his brothers & sisters etc."

London's copy was a July 1906 reprint of the 1899 edition.

BLAND, HENRY MEADE. . . . *A . . . Song of Autumn . . . And . . . Other Poems.* San Jose, California: The Pacific Short Story Club, 1907. 96 pp. HL 338634

Contents: Poems.

Inscription: "For dear Jack London, With pleasant memories of one afternoon with the books at College Park, and white [vivid] recollections of another among the hills at Glen Ellen. from his friend the author of these vague mists. Henry Meade Bland, San Jose, Cal., Dec. 28, 1907[.]"

For dear Jack London,

With pleasant memories of our afternoon with the books at College Park, and white recollections of another among the hills at Glen Ellen.

from his friend the author of these vague mists.

Henry Meade Bland,

San Jose, Cal.,

Dec. 28, 1907

A member of the Pacific Short Story Club (London later joined), Bland was one of London's good friends. He often reviewed London's fiction for the newspapers and later wrote several articles about him. In his spare time Bland was a poet of local prominence (he later became California's poet laureate), but earned his living teaching English at the college in San Jose.

BLATCHFORD, ROBERT. *Dismal England*. London: Clarion Press, [1902?] 240 pp. HL 332485

Contents: Sociological articles discussing the English poor.

Marginalia: An invaluable reference source for *The People of the Abyss, Dismal England* gave London many ideas for his study of the

London slum. The passages he marked concerned the problems of the sick, starvation, unemployment, the plight of a peat worker, injuries caused by improper working conditions, and the hard statistics of the London poor.

BLEDSOE, ANTHONY JENNINGS. *Business Law for Business Men: A Reference Book Showing the Laws of California for Daily Use in Business Affairs*. Oakland, California: Printed for the Author by R. S. Kitchener, 1904. xxxiii, 574 pp., illus. HL 336734
Contents: Popularized law reference book.
Marginalia: London bought this book for use on the ranch. He was interested in passages that tell how to fire an employee, how to discharge a servant, how to record a contract, and how to make a will and revoke an old one. When the water rights issue arose on the ranch, London went back to the book and marked a passage concerning riparian rights. Portions of this book were used in *The Iron Heel*.

THE BOOK OF THE OCEAN, AND LIFE ON THE SEA. *Containing Thrilling Narratives and Adventures of Ocean Life in All Countries, from the Earliest Period to the Present Time*. Auburn: Alden, Beardsley & Company, 1853. 2 volumes in 1, viii, 335, 335 pp., illus. HL 336828
Contents: "To record some impressive examples of calamity, or unlooked for deliverance, is the object of these pages. . . ."—Preface.
Bookseller: Dawson's Bookstore, Los Angeles, California.
Marginalia: The wreck of the *Frances Mary* and the loss of the whaling ship *Essex* were two episodes in this volume capturing London's eye. Other calamities London found interesting include the sinking of the *Lady of the Lake* following a collision with an iceberg; a young boy's sudden rise to ship's captain when all is presumed lost; the desertion of an admiral; the story of shipwrecked sailors; dying of thirst; smelling an empty cologne bottle; and sucking wine through quills. On the endpapers, London summarized his findings: "p. 20—good wreck sketch. 262—good short story idea[.] 293—good for story when almost driven to cannabalism[.] 335—Good idea—wrecked men in boat[,] pull to a ship that's just sink-

ing[.] 2 vol. 142—dandy note for suffering—smelling the empty cologne bottle[.]"

BOURGET, PAUL. *Cosmopolis: A Novel*. New York: Tait, Sons & Company, 1893. 343 pp. HL 330699
Contents: Novel.
Marginalia: London jotted down some notes for *John Barleycorn* on the endpapers of this book: "Barleycorn says 'I am the anaesthesia of the absolute truth. Absolute truth does not hurt.—(enlarge)[.]' The book also served as a place to record the results of a *Snark* card game":

3	8
11	11
15	22
	26

BOWMAKER, EDWARD. *The Housing of the Working Classes*. London: Methuen & Company, 1895. ii, 186 pp., illus. HL 336225
Contents: "The present volume is an attempt to present the whole case" of conditions under which the working class live.—Preface.
Marginalia: London used many statistics in the *People of the Abyss*. In this book he found an account of the average weekly earnings of dock laborers, and the hardships they faced such as high rents and meager salaries.

BRACE, CHARLES LORING. *The New West: Or, California in 1867–1868*. New York: G. P. Putnam & Son, 1869. 373 pp. HL 1768
Contents: Account of a journey in California.
Marginalia: London's interest was in California life and local color. He marked passages about Montgomery Street in San Francisco, trees in San Francisco, the death rate in California, San Francisco's climate, hotel life, and fog, the Calistoga hotsprings, California's labor class and society, the Sierra foothills, Yosemite, and a hand-organ exhibitor.

BRALEY, BERTON. *Sonnets of a Suffragette*. Chicago: Browne & Howell Company, 1913. 99 leaves. HL 337666

Contents: Poems.

Inscription: "My Dear Jack London—Here's my first book—a poor thing, perhaps—but mine own.

"I'm sending it to you with my best wishes in return for your bully tale, *Adventure*.

"Sincerely yours[,] Berton Brawley[.] 103 E. 16th St.[,] New York[.] Jan[.] 1914[.]"

Enclosure: Newspaper clipping pasted onto front cover: "Jack London: An Appreciation" by Berton Braley.

Braley was a New York poet who occasionally wrote to London. Some of his verses were published in the *Saturday Evening Post*.

BRANDES, GEORGE MORRIS COHEN. *Anatole France*. New York: The McClure Company, 1908. 127 pp., illus. HL 337330

Contents: Biography of Anatole France.

Bookseller: Book Department. The White House. Raphael Weill & Company Incorporated. San Francisco, California.

Inscription: "To Jack London: There are only a few times in the space of one's life-time when the meeting with another personality is indeed a living sonnet, and, as in the words of Rossetti: 'a monument, memorial to the soul's eternity of one dead deathless hour.' Edith De Long Jarmuth[.] Sept[.] 21—1910. While at Wake-Robin Lodge[.]"

BRETSCHNEIDER, EMILII VASIL'EVICH. *Map of China and the Surrounding Regions*. Shanghai: Kelly & Walsh, Limited, 1900. 1 sheet. HL 334774

Contents: Folded map.

Marginalia: London traced the route of his 1904 trip to Korea on this map.

BRIDGE, NORMAN. *House Health and Other Papers*. New York: Duffield & Company, 1907. v, 204 pp. HL 68504

Contents: "House Health," "Human Talk," "The Blind Side of the Average Parent," "Some Commencement Ideals," "A Domestic

Clearing House," "The True Gospel of Sleep," "Some Unconceded Rights of Parents and Children," "The Trained Nurse and the Larger Life."
Inscription: "To Jack London in the hope that he may never be sick til he is a hundred years old. N[orman] B[ridge.]"

BRIDGE, NORMAN. *The Penalties of Taste and Other Essays.* New York: Duffield & Company, 1908. 164 pp. HL 336743
Contents: "The Penalties of Taste," "Two Kinds of Conscience," "Bashfulness," "The Nerves of the Modern Child," "Some Lessons of Heredity," "Our Poorly Educated Educators."
Inscription: "To Jack London, the friend of book-lovers & book writers from Norman Bridge[.]"

Dearest Adolf :
You and I will not, I imagine, get to be old in years. Should we do so, it is my hope that we have somewhat of Uncle George's success in the undertaking, for "undertaking" it is likely to be.
Greek.

BRIDGE, NORMAN. *The Rewards of Taste and Other Essays.* Chicago: Herbert Stone & Company, 1902. 270 pp. HL 63727

Contents: "Some Tangents of the Ego," "The Mind for a Remedy," "The Etiology of Lying," "Man as an Air-Eating Animal," "The Rewards of Taste," "The Psychology of the Corset," "The Physical Basis of Expertness," "The Discordant Children."

Inscription: "To Jack London in the hope he may become a Governor. N. B."

BROMLEY, GEORGE TISDALE. *The Long Ago and the Later On, Or Recollections of Eighty Years.* San Francisco: A. M. Robertson, 1904. xiii, 289 pp., illus. HL 336820
Contents: Autobiography.
Inscription: "Dearest Wolf: You and I will not, I imagine, get to be old in years. Should we do so, it is my hope that we have somewhat of Uncle George's success in the undertaking, for 'undertaking' it is likely to be. Greek."
"Uncle George" Bromley was one of the more distinguished members of the Bohemian Club, a gentlemen's club consisting mostly of wealthy businessmen. London and Sterling were both honorary members.

BROOKS, JOHN GRAHAM. *The Social Unrest: Studies in Labor and Socialist Movements.* New York: The Macmillan Company, 1903. 394 pp. HL 336815
Contents: Scholarly study of the rise of socialism.
Marginalia: London marked passages about the use of blacks to weaken trade unions, the lowering of standards and legislation for labor protection, the destruction of unions and its beneficial effect on socialist movements, the beginnings of socialism, and the founding of Parti-Ouvrier.
London reviewed this book in early 1903, intending to publish the review in the Hearst papers. When Hearst declined the piece, London published the review in the *International Socialist Review,* 1 May 1903.

BROWN, ALICE. *Margaret Warrener.* Boston: Houghton, Mifflin and Company, 1901. vi, 501 pp. HL 332385
Contents: Novel.
Marginalia: Paper was in short supply aboard the *Snark,* and was to be used for London's manuscripts, not for score-keeping. Thus the flyleaf of a book usually sufficed in this regard: "Oct. 6. I owe Mate .30[.] I owe Martin .30[.]" In addition to the promissary note, London recorded the scores of four card games. He won only one.
The handiest book usually suffered the indignities recorded above; thus it is not surprising to note that, in her "Books I Have Read,"

Charmian wrote: "*Alice Brown* read aboard *Snark,* Solomons, Oct. '08"(p. 32, HL).

BROWN, GEORGE. *George Brown, D. D. Pioneer Missionary and Explorer.* London: Hodder and Stoughton, 1908. xii, 536 pp., illus. HL 332489

Contents: Autobiography.

Marginalia: The death of Captain Alexander Ferguson, a South Sea Island trader, was the subject of a passage that London marked for future reference. On the rear pastedown, he wrote: "356—to 370— poor colonists in New Ireland[.] 370—Solomons Islands[,] murder of a captain. 377—grief of native at death of one cared for.[.]"

Ferguson appears briefly as a character in *Burning Daylight.*

BROWN'S WINDS AND CURRENTS OF THE NORTHERN AND SOUTH-ERN HEMISPHERES. Glasgow: James Brown & Son, 1905. vi, 100 pp., illus. HL 336824

Contents: Handbook for sailors, showing the principal trade winds and currents.

Marginalia: This book was quite useful to London in his journey to the South Seas. He was particularly interested in the currents near the west coast of North America, the rules to follow for tropical storms, the chart of hurricanes in the North Pacific and also in Australia, and the directions for sailors trying to avoid being caught in a storm track.

BRYAN, WILLIAM ALANSON. *Natural History of Hawaii: Being an Account of the Hawaiian People, the Geology and Geography of the Islands, and the Native and Introduced Plants and Animals of the Group.* Honolulu: The Hawaiian Gazette Company, 1915. 596 pp., illus. HL 332492

Contents: Travel guide and history of Hawaii.

Marginalia: Only two pages interested London enough to merit a characteristic scrawling slash in the margin; the subject of interest was sharks. Charmian also enjoyed this book and made numerous markings in the margin. Some time after London's death, she wrote to Bryan about Hawaii and received a cordial reply.

Buchanan, Joseph Ray. *The Story of a Labor Agitator.* New York: The Outlook Company, 1903. xi, 460 pp., illus. HL 332442

Contents: Buchanan's memoirs of labor wars, strikes, and struggles. *Marginalia:* Buchanan's recollections of the Haymarket Square bombing, in which eight policemen died, prompted London to make a number of annotations. He was interested primarily in the story of the condemned anarchists, Samuel Fielden, Michel Schwab, and August Spies; their futile attempts to obtain clemency; and their subsequent execution. London also had Charmian copy a three-page passage from the book concerning the myth of an independent press in America.

The Haymarket Square bombing was especially interesting to London. In a letter of 18 September 1901 to Elwyn Hoffman (HL), he had commented on the controversy: "Do you remember the Haymarket affair? Without the slightest unmanufactured evidence, seven strong men were selected out of the anarchists of Chicago in order that the blood-cry of society might be satisfied. I know a woman in San Francisco, one of the sweetest truest women ever made. She knew the Haymarket prisoners as I knew Morton, and not only that, she was rounded up and a prisoner herself. An experience for a delicate, sensitive woman sufficient to wreck her, and wrecked she was. You will remember Governor Altgeld afterward pardoned the two anarchists serving life sentences, for he had examined the evidence and seen that these friendless ones, as well as those executed, had been convicted without the slightest relevant evidence—blood-lust as low as that of the reddest Red. Furthermore, it was a deed of revenge, vengeance, while the deeds of the Reds, mistaken though they be, are prompted by the highest motives. By the way, Altgeld, because he did pardon the life-timers, was killed politically and has since been damned by the name, 'anarchist'. . . ."

Buley, Ernest Charles. *Australian Life in Town and Country.* New York: G. P. Putnam's Sons, 1905. x, 288 pp., illus. HL 334399

Contents: History and description of Australia and her people.

Marginalia: "Chapt. I good" London wrote at the end of this book. It describes the geographical features and climate of Australia.

BULLEN, FRANK THOMAS. *Our Heritage the Sea.* New York: E. P. Dutton and Company, 1907. xxiii, 338 pp., illus. HL 330726

Contents: Popular scientific treatise on the ocean.

Marginalia: London was interested in the controversy over Whewell's assertion that a 5,000-fathom tidal wave could move at speeds of up to 500 miles per hour.

London was compared to Bullen in an article in the London *Times* (23 June 1900): "His school days were few, but everywhere he went he read everything he could lay his hands on, and he forgot nothing that he read. His education seems to have been much like that of Frank T. Bullen, who wrote *The Cruise of the Cachelot* and *Idylls of the Sea.* The forecastle student isn't common, but when you find a boy absorbing good literature in the ample leisure of a long voyage, you may be sure that the culture he received will not be lost."

BULLEN, FRANK THOMAS. *A Sack of Shakings.* London: C. Arthur Pearson, Ltd., 1901. viii, 388 pp. HL 330725

Contents: Essays, reprinted in great part, from the *Spectator.*

Marginalia: The chapter on ocean winds and the description of a ship sailing serenely through the water were of interest to London.

BURGESS, JAMES J. HALDANE. *Tang: A Shetland Story.* Lerwick: Johnson & Grieg, 1898. 239 pp. HL 330715

Contents: Novel.

Inscription: "To Comrade Jack London[,] With Best Wishes. J. J. Haldane Burgess, U. A. Lerwick, Shetland, Scotland."

BURNETT, FRANK. *Through Tropic Seas.* London: Francis Griffiths, 1910. xvi, 173 pp., illus. HL 332637

Contents: Tales, legends, and romances.

Marginalia: London was interested in three anecdotes: the landing of a boat near the treacherous coral reef at Manihiki; the innocent question of a native who, after being told of the uses of the coconut tree by a missionary, asked why God didn't put a fish in the coconut too, since He was supposedly being so helpful; and the ungrateful attitude of a native who had been treated by a doctor. He took the following notes: "35—Dandy South Sea Stuff—in whaleboat running the gut into Manihiki. 96—good anecdote of the fish in each coconut[.] 98—comic illustration of ingratitude[.]"

BURNS, THOMAS. *Eleven Indictments of the Bible*. Portland, Oregon: Free Thinkers Library, 1915. 15 pp. HL.
Contents: Atheistic pamphlet.
Inscription: "Jack London[,] compliments of Tom Burns[.]"

BURROWES, PETER E. *Notes on the Class Struggle*. New York: Collectivist Society, 1904. 44 pp. HL.
Contents: Socialist anthology.
Marginalia: London's markings indicate his interest in the Civil War and the actions of the masses; he also marked several poems for copying. On the front cover, he wrote: "Debate with Owen. I do not deny ethical factor, I insist upon underlying factor[.]"
William C. Owen, author of *The Coming Solidarity,* was scheduled to debate London in Los Angeles in February or March, 1906.

BUTLER, GEORGE FRANK. *Echoes of Petrarch: Sonnets of Love and Interludes*. Chicago: Ralph Fletcher Seymour Company, 1911. 67 pp. HL 337662
Contents: Poems.
Inscription: "To Mr. and Mrs. Jack London from Geo. F. Butler[.]"
Butler was an Indiana doctor and friend of Edward Simpson Goodhue, doctor for the Molokai Leper Colony. He occasionally sent London books of his poetry. London probably enjoyed the poems, for, after reading one of Butler's earlier books, he wrote an extremely complimentary letter to him (19 October 1915, HL): "By some mischance, *The Travail of a Soul* had been put on a shelf of *finished* books, so that only just now have I discovered and read it, which reading has given me memorable and profound pleasure. "It is *true* poetry, *pure* poetry, and its beauty is holy. It has the pitch and elevation of beauty that is holy. . . ."

CALIFORNIA. SECRETARY OF STATE. *California Blue Book or State Roster: 1911.* Sacramento: State Printing Office, 1913. xii, 934 pp., illus. HL 44882

Contents: Social register.

Inscription: "With Compliments of Henry Ward Broedon[.] M[ar]ch 31, 1914."

CAMPBELL, REGINALD JOHN. *Christianity and the Social Order.* New York: The Macmillan Company, 1907. xiii, 284 pp. HL 336701

Contents: An "attempt to show the correspondence between the principles of Christianity and those of modern Socialism."—Introduction.

Inscription: "F. I. Bamford, Oakland, California. To Jack with my love. Fred. Jan. 31, [']08."

Marginalia: This book belonged to Bamford and bears many of his markings. London did mark one passage, however, concerning the absurdity of the development of individuality when so many are starving.

CANTON, WILLIAM. *The Invisible Playmate: A Story of the Unseen.* New York: Duffield & Company, 1906. 95 pp. HL 337682

Contents: "The Invisible Playmate," "Rhymes About a Little Woman," "An Unknown Child-Poem," "At a Wayside Station."

Marginalia: London marked two passages. Both discuss the meaning of love.

CARPENTER, EDWARD. *The Intermediate Sex: A Study of Some Transitional Types of Men and Women.* London: George Allen & Company, Ltd., 1912. 175 pp. HL 336712

Contents: "Introductory," "The Intermediate Sex," "The Homogenic Attachment," "Affection in Education," "The Place of the Uranian in Society."

Inscription: "Jack London[:] hearty greetings from Ed. Carpenter[.] April[,] 1914[.]"

Enclosures: Clipping entitled "A Letter from Edward Carpenter Regarding Homosexuality;" publisher's flyer: "*The Intermediate Sex:*

Extracts from the Press;" and a letter of 2 March 1914 from London to Carpenter: "I do not need to tell you that I have read you and followed you for years. Incidentally, I may mention that I have for years specialized on sex, but that, because of my wandering life, mostly off in the South Seas and in Alaska, and in all manner of out-of-the-way places, I have always been unable to get your book *The Intermediate Sex. . . .*"

Carpenter replied on 12 April 1914 with a copy of the book and a cover letter in which he asked London to accept the book "as a token from me of the pleasure I have had in reading your books."

CARUS, PAUL. *Primer of Philosophy*. Chicago: The Open Court Publishing Company, 1899. vi, 242 pp. HL 336721

Contents: "*The Primer of Philosophy* is not expressly designed to give instruction to beginners in philosophy, but it is, nevertheless, eminently available for that purpose."—Preface.

Marginalia: London was interested in the definition of meliorism, a discussion of subjectivity versus objectivity, duality and monism, materialism, a definition of experience and of truth, and explanations of the theories of John Locke, René Descartes, and John Stuart Mill.

CARUS, PAUL. *The Religion of Science*. Chicago: The Open Court Publishing Company, 1899. vi, 145 pp. HL 336155

Contents: "Principles, Faith, and Doctrines," "The Authority for Conduct," "Ethics of the Religion of Science," "The Soul," "Immortality," "Mythology and Religion," "Christ and the Christians: A Contrast," "The Catholicity of the Religious Spirit," "In Reply to a Freethinker," "In Reply to a Presbyterian."

Marginalia: Science, God, a definition of truth, and the influence of the concept of Christ on the modern man were the subjects London found of interest.

CASSON, HERBERT NEWTON. *Organized Self-Help. A History and Defence of the American Labor Movement*. New York: Peter Eckler, Publisher, 1901. x, 211 pp. HL 336783

Contents: Socialist's view of the American labor movement.

Inscription: "To My Comrade, Jack London, with Socialist greetings. Herbert N. Casson[.] 111 West 115 Street, New York City."

Marginalia: The danger of forbidding free speech, the destruction of civilization by the rich and powerful, statistics on unemployment, working conditions of nonunion miners, scabs, and the fight against powerful businesses were subjects of interest to London in Casson's book. London's notes include: "Coal Miner of Throop—p[.] 25[.] Surplus labor statistics by Carrol D. Wright—p[.] 33[.] Abraham Lincoln on strikes—p[.] 45[.] Mayor Swift & Henry Lloyd on capitalists—p[.] 60[.] New York *Journal* on the forbidding of free speech—p[.] 66[.] Low wages in the United States one hundred years ago—p[.] 73-4-5[.]"

In "The Scab," published in *War of the Classes* (pp. 124–25), London briefly recounts the story, as told by Casson, of one capitalist scab: "Mr. Casson tells of a New York capitalist who withdrew from the Sugar Union several years ago and became a scab. He was worth something like twenty millions of dollars. But the Sugar Union, standing shoulder to shoulder with the Railroad Union and several other unions, beat him to his knees till he cried 'Enough.' So frightfully did they beat him that he was obliged to turn over to his creditors his home, his chickens, and his gold watch. In point of fact, he was as thoroughly bludgeoned by the Federation of Capitalist Unions as ever scab workman was bludgeoned by a labor union. The intent in either case is the same,—to destroy the scab's producing power. The labor scab with concussion of the brain is put out of business, and so is the capitalist scab who has lost all his dollars down to his chickens and his watch."

CASTLE, WILLIAM RICHARDS. *Hawaii: Past and Present.* New York: Dodd, Mead and Company, 1914. xii, 230 pp., illus. HL 332596 PF

Contents: Travel guide and popular history of Hawaii.

Bookseller: Thrum's, Honolulu, Hawaii.

Inscription: "Mr[.] & Mrs[.] Jack London with regards of Mr[.] and Mrs[.] W. R. Castle—March 1915[.]"

Marginalia: London marked passages about the general background of Hawaii: descriptions of its geography, rainfall, flora, fauna, and population. He also marked a few pages that explain the ancient

feudal system of the islands, the old taboos and gods, early criminals, leprosy, and specific details about the Pelekunu and Wailau
valleys.

CHAFIN, EUGENE WILDER. *The Master Method of the Great Reform:
Speeches. . . .* Chicago: Lincoln Temperance Press, 1913. 159
pp., illus. HL 336776
Contents: Speeches made in favor of prohibition.
Inscription: "To Jack London & wife with compliments of the author, Eugene W. Chafin. Feb. 27, 1914[.]"
The prohibition candidate for president in 1908, Chafin was involved in the management of the Jack London Grape Juice Company, a largely unsuccessful enterprise to which London had lent
his name.

CHAMBERLAIN, BASIL HALL. *A Handbook for Travellers in Japan
Including the Whole Empire from Yezo to Formosa.* London: John
Murray, 1901. ix, 579 pp., illus. HL 334812 PF
Contents: Travel guide to Japan.
Inscription: "Jack London[.]"
Enclosures: Newspaper and magazine clippings: "Russia's Internal
Weakness," December, 1903. "The Eastern Puzzle." "St. Petersburg
Angry," 1904. These articles were torn from San Francisco news-
papers. Also: *The Outlook,* volume 76, 2 January 1904, pages 1-2,
and 26 December 1903, pages 977-78; *The Pacific Commercial Adver-
tiser,* 14 January 1904; *The Independent,* pages 3093–94; and two reviews of Albert J. Beveridge's *The Russian Advance.*
When London sailed for Japan aboard the *S.S. Siberia,* 7 January
1904, he took a trunkful of books to inform him of the political situation in Korea. In that trunk was Basil Chamberlain's *Handbook.*
London complained to Charmian in one of his letters, written
while still aboard the *Siberia,* that he had not been "left alone long
enough to read a line." [32] But he had evidently had time before sailing to stuff a few clippings into this book which would help him
understand the Korean situation, and also found time to add to that
collection while the *Siberia* was in Honolulu harbor on 14 January.

CHAMBLESS, EDGAR. *Roadtown*. New York: Roadtown Press, 1910. 172 pp., illus. HL 332402 PF

Contents: Roadtown was Chambless's version of a utopia.
Inscription: "The Eddie Bible on Continuousness by Ed Chambless. Loaned for life to Jack and Charmian By Daddy Longhouse.

"Interest on this loan always due; the kind you can take and radiate.

"Roadtown is efficiency; efficiency is truth; truth is beauty; beauty is goodness; goodness is God; God is goodness; goodness is beauty; beauty is truth; truth is efficiency; efficiency is *Roadtown.*"
Enclosure: Publisher's flyer: "Roadtown Progress."

Chambless sent London this book in February 1913, "as a loan, hoping to interest [him] . . . in the city of the future," and also hoping to persuade London to fictionalize the book (Chambless to London, 11 February 1913, HL). London replied that he could not see how the book could be fictionalized, but invited Chambless up to the ranch to discusss the matter. Evidently they could not come to terms, for nothing came of the proposal.

CHANEY, GEORGE LEONARD. *"Aloha!" A Hawaiian Salutation.* Boston: Roberts Brothers, 1880. ix, 299 pp., illus. HL 334797

Contents: "A book of grateful recollections of a winter's residence in the Hawaiian Islands."—Preface.
Bookseller: Thrum's, Honolulu, Hawaii.
Marginalia: The Austrian Consul to Hawaii, Mr. Afong, and a rich description of a tropical forest were the subjects of interest to London. His notes include: "12—Ah Fong[.] 86-87—description of ferns & Hilo forest[.]"
Ah Fong became Ah Chun in London's "Chun Ah Chun."

CHAPMAN, JOHN JAY. *Deutschland Über Alles or Germany Speaks: A Collection of the Utterances of Representative Germans—Statesmen, Military Leaders, Scholars, and Poets—In Defence of the War Policies of the Fatherland.* New York: G. P. Putnam's Sons, 1914. v, 102 pp. HL 334831

Contents: German propaganda defending World War I policies.
Marginalia: The "Great War" was of vast interest to London: he col-

lected boxes of articles, clippings, and books on the subject, probably in preparation for a book he planned to write about the subject.
In this book, he marked passages concerning the German propensity for war, German militarism and barbarism, including the suicide rate among young German boys, the culture of war, the speech
of Imperial Chancellor Bethmann-Hollweg, the Boxer Rebellion,
and German relations with France.

Cheney, Warren. *The Challenge*. New York: A. L. Burt Company, 1906. 386 pp., illus. HL 330743
Contents: Novel.
Marginalia: "Cheney—I have a quarrel [*sic*] with you. A Bidarka
(main holes)—describe—not the large vessel you describe. An
oomiak is larger—a big open boat."

Cheney, Warren. *The Flight of Helen and Other Poems*. San
Francisco: Elder & Shepard, 1901. 64 pp. HL 266971
Contents: Poems.
Inscription: "Sincerely Yours. Warren Cheney[.] Berkeley. July.
1903."

Citizen's Alliance. Bureau of Publicity. *Socialism: How to
Get Something for Nothing*. San Francisco: Citizen's Alliance,
1915. 24 pp. HL
Contents: Antisocialistic pamphlet.
Marginalia: London marked a passage asserting that capitalism was
served best by a large labor pool—the more menial laborers, the
better. He also wrote a note to his secretary, Jack Byrne: "File
properly[.]"

Clark, Arthur Hamilton. *The Clippr Ship Era: An Epitome of
Famous American and British Clipper Ships, Their Owners,
Builders, Commanders and Crews: 1843-1869*. New York: G. P.
Putnam's Sons, 1911. xii, 404 pp., illus. HL 337288
Contents: Personal account of the author's experiences and research
"of the most exciting portion of" the clipper ship era.—Preface.
Marginalia: This book was used as source material for Mr. Pike's

discussion of the *Flying Cloud* found in *The Mutiny of the Elsinore.* The passages marked include a description of sailing aboard a California clipper, the rivalry between clipper ships, the record of the 1859 ninety-seven-day passage around the Horn by the *Sierra Nevada,* and an account of the voyage of the *Challenge* in which the points of the sailor's knives were broken off by the officers of the ship. At the end of the book, London wrote: "p[.] 111—Getting ship under way [*sic*]."

CLEVELAND, RICHARD. *In the Forecastle, Or, Twenty-Five Years a Sailor.* New York: Hurst & Company, [187?] 407 pp., illus. HL 330744

Contents: Collection of journals, letters, and accounts of life at sea. *Marginalia:* London marked passages about ship worms, a young captain less than twenty years old, the first horse in Hawaii, a landing in Hawaii during which Cleveland met Isaac Davis, a tale about an Hawaiian king who asks a missionary trying to convert him to jump from a high cliff ("Give me proof, by going and throwing yourself from yonder precipice, and, while falling, call on your God to shield you, and if you escape unharmed, I will then embrace the worship of your God."); and noted these passages on the rear flyleaf: "31—worms boring into ship[.] 35—extreme youth of officers[.] 208—First horses landed in Hawaii, even barring Captain Cook. First horses in Hawaii. 208. Kamehameha—an early appearance in history. 210—naïve pronunciation of Oahowhoo & Waikiki. 211—motif for short story—dandy—one good short story[.] 212—short story motif—the long swim. 212—motifs for early Pacific a vast Klondike stories. 291—on to 299 & still on, for data of a revolution swing by Smoke & Shorty."

The source material for *Smoke Bellew* was drawn from passages describing a revolt aboard a ship sailing through Chilean waters.

COLL, JAMES ALOYSIUS. *The Dust of Dreams.* Cincinnati: The Editor Publishing Company, 1899. 100 pp., illus. HL 337687
Contents: Poems.
Inscription: "To Jack London:
You went into the land of gold—
  I know not what to dare or do,—

> To Jack London:
>
> You went into the land of gold—
> I know not what to dare or do,
> But if you found no gold, the field
> of letters found the gold in you!
>
> Aloysius Coll
> Connellaville, Pa.
> June 21-1901.

But if you found no gold, the field
 of letters found the *gold* in *you!*
Aloysius Coll[.] Convellaville, Pa. June 21—1901."

COLTON, WALTER. *Three Years in California.* New York: A. S. Barnes & Co., 1851. 456 pp., illus. HL 332664

Contents: Description of the author's travels in California during the gold rush.

Marginalia: London was interested in the description of California fog on page 66, Captain Gillespie on page 64, and the foreigner's good fortunes on page 61.

COMPTON-RICKETT, ARTHUR. *The Vagabond in Literature.* London: J. M. Dent & Company, [1906?] xv, 206 pp., illus. HL 334789

Contents: Essays by various authors describing the vagabond element in modern literature.

Marginalia: Dummy whist was the card game of the day, and the score card was this book: "Aboard *Snark*[.] Russells to Guadalcanal, Solomons. October 15 '08[.] Dummy whist aboard *Snark* October 15, 1908. Paoubru (Russell Group, Solomons), back to Penduff-ryn, Guadalcanal, Solomons after trip to Lord Hour & Tasman. Out 15/08. Mate owes me .30[.] Martin owes me .30[.] Hell!"

CONN, HERBERT WILLIAM. *The Method of Evolution: A Review of the Present Attitude of Science Toward the Question of the Laws and Forces Which Have Brought About the Origin of Species.* New York: G. P. Putnam's Sons, 1900. ix, 408 pp., illus. HL 337049

Contents: Review of the literature of evolution.
Bookseller: Smith Brothers, Oakland, California.
Marginalia: Weismann's theory of heredity was the subject of the three pages of markings in this book.

London discussed Weismann's theories in a letter of 24 August 1899 (HL) to Johns: ". . . Have you read anything of Weismann's. He has struck a heavy blow to the accepted idea of acquired characters being inherited, and as yet his opponents have not proved conclusively one case in which such a character has been inherited. Another idea he advances well, is that death is not the indispensable correlative of life, as hitherto it has been supposed to be. In fact, his researches in the germ-plasm have proven quite the contrary. Read him up, you will find him interesting. But it's heavy. If you have not studied evolution well, I would not advise you to tackle him. He takes a thorough grounding in the subject for granted."

CONNOLLY, JAMES BRENDAN. *The Deep Sea's Toll.* New York: Charles Scribner's Sons, 1905. 315 pp., illus. HL 330756

Contents: "The Sail Carriers," "The Wicked *Celestine*," "The Truth of the *Oliver Cromwell*," "Strategy and Seamanship," "Dory-Mates," "The Salving of the Bark *Fuller*," "On George's Shoals," "Patsie Oddie's Black Night."
Inscription: "What's t'y a comin' in from sea
    Like a ghost from o'er the dawn!
And who was Tom O'Donnell
    And his flying Colleen Bawm.

To Jack London[.] From James B. Connolly. At his home[,] December 23[,] 1905."

James Connolly was a well-known American writer of sea stories. His vast knowledge of sea-fishermen and the ways of the sea attracted London when they first met in Boston. Both Connolly and London were together in Vera Cruz, Mexico, in 1914, where they entertained the wounded troops.

CONNOLLY, JAMES BRENDAN. *The Seiners.* New York: Charles Scribner's Sons, 1905. vi, 314 pp., illus. HL 330757
Contents: Sea novel.
Inscription: "And here's to it that once again
   He'll travel and sail and race again
Here's to us that's living and to
   them that's gone before:
"And when to us the Lord says 'Come'
   He'll bow our heads—'His will be Done'
And all together we shall be
   Beneath the ocean's roar
To Jack London[.] James B. Connolly, At his flat[,] December 23 1905[.]"

CONRAD, JOSEPH. *The Children of the Sea: A Tale of the Forecastle.* New York: Dodd, Mead and Company, 1898. 217 pp. HL 330759
Contents: Sea novel.
Bookseller: M. S. Smith & Sons, Oakland, California.
Marginalia: Although largely annotated by Charmian London, one mark on page 167 can be attributed to Jack London. It is beside a passage about loving simple words.

CONRAD, JOSEPH. *Falk. Amy Foster. To-Morrow: Three Stories.* New York: McClure, Phillips and Company, 1903. 271 pp. HL 330760
Contents: Short stories.
Marginalia: London marked a description of Amy Foster on page 157: "the penetrating power of his mind."

CONRAD, JOSEPH. *Lord Jim: A Romance.* New York: Doubleday & McClure Company, 1900. 392 pp. HL 330761 PF
Contents: Novel.
Bookseller: Smith Brothers, Oakland, California.
Marginalia: Most of the annotations appear to have been made by Charmian during her reading of this book in Glen Ellen, 1907.
   "It is an Epic," Charmian wrote in her "Books I Have Read"

(p.8, HL) "this *Lord Jim.* It reminded me, as soon as I had read a little way, of *The Ring and the Book,* of Robert Browning's—from the way Conrad handled his idea."

Conrad was one of London's favorite authors. When, in *Martin Eden* (p. 318), Martin becomes fully conscious of the "great stuff he was writing," he immediately likens his work to Conrad: "He compared the tale, as yet unwritten, with the tales of the sea-writers, and he felt it to be immeasurably superior. 'There's only one man who could touch it,' he murmered aloud, 'and that's Conrad. And it ought to make even him sit up and shake hands with me, and say, 'Well done, Martin, my boy.'"

CONRAD, JOSEPH. *The Mirror of the Sea.* New York: Harper & Brothers, 1906. 328 pp. HL 330763 PF

Contents: Short stories about seafaring life.

Bookseller: Smith Brothers, Oakland, California.

Marginalia: London was especially interested in "The Fine Art," "Cobwebs and Gossamer," and "Rulers of East and West."

In *The Mutiny of the Elsinore* (p. 259), London decided to put this book in the hands of Mr. Pathurst: "I fell asleep quickly and awoke at midnight, my lamp still burning, Conrad's *Mirror of the Sea* on my breast where it had dropped from my hands. . . . At twelve-fifteen, in the midst of Conrad's delightful chapter, 'The Weight of the Burden,' I heard Mr. Pike come along the hall."

CONRAD, JOSEPH. *Romance: A Novel.* New York: McClure, Phillips & Company, 1904. 428 pp., illus. HL 330764

Contents: Novel.

Marginalia: London wrote a few notes for *The Game* on the back flyleaves of *Romance:* "gas jets in dim lighted hall[,] a cluster with patent burners over ring. The bass rumble of masculine voices—in the front row she recognizes some pre-eminently respectable old man—also recognizes the Jew her employer—had heard him telling his wife the lie which enabled him to be there—prepare, in opening, when she asks that night off from the shop, & only Jew's wife is left. row of reporters who sat on stage, just room for them between ring & wall. one of the reporters chewing gum. Now again her gaze returned to him and she experienced an ever new relief at sight of the moving jaws. She noticed the bandages on Joe's hands & thought at first he had been injured then saw other man the same. Referee (describe)—introduced—cheers for her man—all come together in center, seconds as well, with heads together[.] Both men nodded, & went back to their corners[.] Maybe wind-up, the Jew speaks kindly to her & she leaves the hall with him." *Enclosure:* Photograph of Joseph Conrad.

It is beyond question that Conrad's work strongly influenced London; at one point, shortly after finishing *The Call of the Wild*, London wasn't sure whether he wanted his friend Cloudesley Johns to read his own masterpiece, or listen to him read Conrad. Johns later remembered the episode in his own autobiography: "[Jack], with no more than 300 words done as his morning's work, came into the library with a chessboard and box of pieces under one arm and a book in the other hand, hurling questions at me. Had I been playing much chess while I was in New York? Had I found Joseph Conrad? I had played some chess at the Press Club; I had not really found Conrad, having read with delight only some excerpts of his work in book reviews. . . . 'Listen to this!' Jack exclaimed suddenly, . . . waving the book he had brought. Then, his expressive and melodic voice caressing the living sentences of the Master, he read to me Joseph Conrad's *Youth* in boyish delight in sharing with kindred spirits his own joy of life. With the reading of *Youth* completed, followed by a lively discussion of the heartwarming and heartrending story and Jack's insistence that I must read *Lord Jim* and other Conrad works before leaving for Los Angeles, my host jumped up, turning from the neglected chessboard. . . ."[33]

CONRAD, JOSEPH. *Tales of Unrest.* New York: Charles Scribner's Sons, 1898. 348 pp. HL 330766.

Contents: Novel.

Inscription: "Fannie K. Hamilton. June, 1898. To Jack London, with grateful appreciation. F. K. H. August 3, 1903. East Dedham, Massachusetts."

Newspaper writer Fannie K. Hamilton had interviewed London for a feature article published in the August 1903 issue of *The Reader.* London thanked her for the book on 14 August, claiming that his

Conrad collection was now complete.

CONRAD, JOSEPH. *Victory: An Island Tale*. Garden City, New York: Doubleday, Page & Company, 1915. 462 pp. HL
Contents: Novel.
Marginalia: London made numerous markings in this book. Sailing the Sacramento River delta region in 1915 aboard the *Spray* with Cloudesley Johns, he read many passages aloud, writing, "I'll read from here on" at one point in the book. An accident marred one of the pages of the book, and Johns recorded the event in blue pencil: "Possum, without warning, leaped into my lap as I was reading this page. His feet were not clean. Cloudesley Johns."
London did not often write to other novelists in praise of their work. The effect *Victory* had upon him, however, warranted an exception to this rule (*Letters*, pp. 451-52): "The mynah birds are waking the hot dawn about me. The surf is thundering in my ears where it falls on the white sand of the beach, here at Waikiki, where the green grass at the roots of the coconut palms insists to the lip of the wave-wash. This night has been yours—and mine.

"I had just begun to write when I read your first early work. I have merely madly appreciated you and communicated my appreciation to my friends through all these years. I never wrote to you. I never dreamed to write you. But *Victory* has swept me off my feet, and I am enclosing herewith a carbon copy of a letter written to a friend at the end of this lost night's sleep.

"Perhaps you will appreciate this lost night's sleep when I tell you that it was immediately preceded by a day's sail in a Japanese sampan of sixty miles from the Leper Settlement of Molokai (where Mrs. London and I had been revisiting old friends) to Honolulu.

"On your head be it. Aloha (which is a sweet word of greeting, the Hawaiian greeting, meaning 'My love be with you').

In a letter to Johns, written the day before, (a copy of which was enclosed in the letter to Conrad), London praised *Victory* even more boldly (3 June 1915, HL): "In reply to yours of May 15. First of all, whatever you do, read Conrad's latest— *Victory*. Read it, if you have to pawn your watch to buy it. Conrad has exceeded himself. He must have deliberately set himself the challenge, and it is victory for him, because he has skinned *Ebb Tide*.

"He has made a woman out of nothing—out of sweepings of life, and he has made her woman glorious. He has painted love with all love's illusion—himself, Conrad, devoid of illusion.

"Lena goes without saying. She is Woman. But it is possible, absolutely possible, for the several such men as Mr. Jones, Ricardo, Pedro, Heyst, Schomberg, Morrison, Davidson, and Wang and his Alfuro woman to exist. I know them all. I have met them all. I swear it.

"As regards the love of this book, the sex of this book—all the love and the sex of it is correct, cursedly correct, spendidly, magnificently correct, with every curse of it and every splendid magnificence of it duly placed, shaded and balanced. Yes, and the very love of Ricardo is tremendous and correct.

"In brief, I am glad that I am alive, if, for no other reason, because of the joy of reading this book."

Possum, without warning, leaped into my lap as I was reading this page. His feet were not clean.

blondedly John

COOK, GEORGE CRAM. *The Chasm: A Novel.* New York: Frederick A. Stokes Company, 1911. 379 pp. HL 330772

Contents: Novel.

Inscription: "Jack London—Chasm-Bridger! from Sinclair Lewis and the Stokes Co."

Marginalia: London reviewed this book for his friend Sinclair Lewis. The notes containing his reactions to the volume were hurriedly scrawled onto the endpapers: "A story told in a new vocabulary, which the world is coming to know, & which will be recorded by future historians; a story told in a new psychology, which the world is coming to know, & which, some day, will be known by all, and which, in a later day, will be known by antiquarians as the psychology of society at the time it was in the process of emerging from the Dark Ages of Capitalism.

"An intellectual novel, keen with the life of to-day—*and quick with the life of tomorrow.* And more power to the elbow of Frederick A. Stokes Company for publishing such a live wire, up-to-date, 1911 book. Ca Ira! Ca Ira!"

London first learned of *The Chasm* from a letter of 1 December 1910 letter from Sinclair Lewis, who was exuberant about the prospects of the book; Cook, it seems, was not only a "good 'red,'" he had even quoted Jack London! When the book was finally published, Lewis sent him this copy, 21 January 1911. In his letter he noted that London's name had been quoted on pages 138 and 139 "as a matter of controversy," and begged for a few words about the novel which could be "of decided commercial advantage" (1 December 1910, HL). The notes London took were typed into a letter to Lewis, dated 15 February 1911.

COOLEY, LE ROY CLARK. *Natural Philosophy for Common and High Schools.* New York: Ivison, Blakeman & Company, 1871. 246 pp., illus. HL 337048

Contents: "The great aim of this little book is to present the most elementary facts of Natural Philosophy, in such a way as to exercise the child continually in observing phenomena and in drawing inferences from what he observes."—Preface.

Bookseller: M. S. Smith & Company, Oakland, California.

Marginalia: Magnetism and the creation of electricity by means of friction were two ideas that interested London in this book, one of the earliest additions to his library. There are many other annotations, made in an unknown hand. London's copy was printed in 1881.

CORTEZ, DOLORES. *Mary of Magdala or the Magdalene of Old.* Los Angeles: Privately printed, 1905. 26 pp. HL 28245

Contents: Fable.

Inscription: "To Jack London. May this little volume be a talisman to soothe the cares that the feverish activity of civilization brings and a chord of harmony from the greensward and running brooks of fair nature. Dolores Cortez. 87 E. Walnut[,] Pasadena. Ca. April 18—1905[.]"

Although London did not use this book for his Christ novel, the story of Mary of Magdala was to play an important part in it. Worrying that the reader's interest might peak too soon and "reach the climax at the Crucifixion;" London decided to work "in Mary Magdalen before her conversion and bathing of Christ's feet; so that the Goth becomes acquainted with her and thus marvels the more at her penitence. At least he may know of her by common repute" ("Christ Novel," HL).

CRILE, GEORGE W. *A Mechanistic View of War and Peace.* New York: The Macmillan Company, 1915. xii, 104 pp., illus. HL 336798

Contents: "Introduction," "The Phenomena of War," "A Biological Interpretation of War," "A Mechanistic View of German Kultur," "A Mechanistic View of the Vivisection of Belgium," "Evolution Toward Peace."

Marginalia: London was a student of human nature. In this book, he underlined and marked passages that helped him understand the forces at work during war: reasons for marching and singing during mobilization; the effects on the body of waiting under fire; facing death—the last struggle; the physical consequences of a people at war; and the brute in man.

Enclosure: Letter from Dr. I. Katsuki to Jack and Charmian London, dated Honolulu, 19 February 1916, thanking them for lending him the book, and noting that Crile was "the one who discovered the ariociassociation method of anaesthesia by which we can now prevent the shock after surgical operation."

CROLY, GEORGE. *Tarry Thou Till I Come, Or Salathiel, the Wandering Jew.* New York: Funk & Wagnalls Company, 1902. xxxv, 587 pp., illus. HL 330777

Contents: Historical romance.
Bookseller: Smith Brothers, Oakland, California.
Marginalia: This was another of the sources London consulted for his planned Christ novel. His notes concerned the Roman conquest of Judea, the treatment of women in Judea, Salathiel's discontent, and reaching the summit of Sanaria: "26—Roman order in Judea[.] 39—Jewish women (freedom)[.] 41—Landscape descriptive of Judea[.]" His note on the last page of the Appendix was: "The blasts

of the Roman Trumpets[.]"
After reading the book, Charmian wrote "annotations best of all" on the rear endpaper.

DANA, RICHARD HENRY. *Two Years Before the Mast: A Personal Narrative of Life at Sea.* Boston: Estes & Lauriat, 1895. 362 pp.
Contents: Sea novel.
It is unfortunate that London's copy of this sea tale has presumably been lost, for few books stirred the author as much as Dana's classic. In response to repeated requests from a New York publisher, London wrote an "Introduction to *Two Years Before the Mast*," citing its importance as a classic of the sea. The piece was published in *The Human Drift* (1917).

D'ANNUNZIO, GABRIELE. *Francesca Da Rimini.* New York: Frederick A. Stokes Company, 1902. xiv, 223 pp., illus. HL
Contents: Play written in blank verse.
Inscription: "To Herself from Constance Skinner and from Herself thence to Jack London."
Marginalia: Both Jack and Charmian London read this book. Most of the marginal markings belong to Charmian; a few may be ascribed to Jack. Many of the markings are beside passages about love. Both Jack and Charmian London were familiar with D'Annunzio's work. *"Flame of Life,"* Jack London wrote in a letter of 17 September 1905 to Ida Winship (Russ Kingman Collection, Glen Ellen, California), "is a youthful attempt of D'Annunzio's. Read his *Gioconda,* (a play) if you want to enjoy some of the very best he has ever done. It is magnificent. And in her "Books I Have Read" (HL), Charmian London also praised D'Annunzio's writings: *"Gioconda . . .* Exquisite—beautiful. In form, a play. Particularly remember his— Settala's—raptures over a piece block of Carrera marble, seeing also in it her form that he will create. The wife's lost hands, broken by fall of the mistress's statue." *The Child of Pleasure,* however, was not well liked by either of the Londons. "Amateurish in its effort to show everything he knew," wrote Charmian.

Poet and historian Constance L. Skinner was a member of Cloudesley Johns's household in Los Angeles, and it was through Johns that she met London. In January 1905 Skinner was writing for the Los Angeles *Examiner*. As a reporter for that paper, she attended London's "Scab" lecture at the Simpson auditorium. Her favorable comments eventually led to friendship, manifested in small part through presentation of this book.

DAVIDSON, JOHN MORRISON. *The Book of Lords*. London: William Reeves, [1907?] 102 pp. HL 336153

Contents: "The Origin of the Lords," "Blue Blood," "Our Oldest Nobility at Work," "Runnymede and Magna Charta," "Creeping Things," "Burrowing Animals," "Temporary Rejectors," "Bright Examples," "Summary."

Marginalia: The increase in the value of labor following the bubonic plague (or black death) epidemic in England, 1348–49, was the subject that interested London in this book.

DAVIDSON, JOHN MORRISON. *The Gospel of the Poor*. London: William Reeves, 1902. 162 pp. HL

Contents: Book extolling the merits of socialism and condemning the conditions of the poor under capitalism.

Marginalia: London underlined several quotations, including several by Algernon Charles Swineburne.

DAVIDSON, JOHN MORRISON. *The Old Order and the New*. London: Francis Riddell Henderson, 1902. 174 pp. HL 336806

Contents: Treatise on socialism.

Marginalia: This book, which London probably bought (along with the two preceding ones) in London in 1902, is heavily annotated. The marked passages include a quotation from Thomas Carlyle, a description of living conditions of the poor in London, landlordism, British steel production, the GNP of England, the poor's portion of the national income, statistics on life expectancy broken down by class, and quotations from John Stuart Mill, Karl Marx, Jean Jacques Rousseau, Ferdinand Lassalle, Lord Byron, Henry Wadsworth Longfellow, and Frederic Harrison. London's notes at the end of the book consisted of the following: "59—annual income[.] 60-61—annual rent—64—more swag (rent)[.] 65—more interest[.] 69—Profit (annually[).] 73—what workers get[.] 80—

war debt[.] Quotations: 11–29–35–72–74–75–79–86–104–110–
113–143[.]"

DAVIS, JOHN E. *Sun's True Bearing or Azimuth Tables*. London:
J. D. Potter, 1900. xxv, 255 pp., illus. HL 336795
Contents: Book of tables.
Marginalia: London wanted to know how to use Sumner's method
of finding the position of a ship at sea, and marked the latitude table
for 6°. The flyleaves of the book were used as a scratch pad for navigational arithmetic, and for a few cryptic notes: "7 ft. outside[,]
III[,] 21[.] IIII[,] 8 ft[.] 2 ft. inside [.]"

DAY, THOMAS FLEMING. *On Yachts and Yacht Handling*. New
York: The Rudder Publishing Company, 1901. 191 pp., illus.
HL 338127
Contents: General handbook of the various types of yachts and how
to handle them at sea.
Marginalia: After reading this book, London marked several other
titles listed in the publisher's advertisements, including: *A Deep
Water Voyage* and *By Way of Cape Horn* by Paul Eve Stevenson, *A
Noble Haul* by W. Clark Russell, *Cruises in Small Yachts, Handbook
of Naval Gunnery* by Radford, *Technical Dictionary of Sea Terms,
Phrases, and Words* by Pirrie, *Dog Watches at Sea* by Stanton H. King,
and *Familiar Fish* by E. McCarthy. They were ordered for him 12
June 1906.

DEFOE, DANIEL. *A Journal of the Plague Year Written by a Citizen
Who Continued All the While in London*. London: J. M. Dent &
Company, 1908. 303 pp. HL 331168
Contents: Fiction.
Marginalia: Markings beside passages on page 3 detailing the increase in burials in St. Giles-in-the-Fields and St. Andrew, Holborn.

DEL MAR, WALTER. *Around the World Through Japan*. New York:
The Macmillan Company, 1902. xvii, 435 pp., illus. HL
334783

Contents: Notes and impressions of a tour through Japan and the world.

Marginalia: Undoubtedly this was one of the many books London carried with him on his way to the Korean front in 1904. The annotation he made within the book concerns a description of the size and strength of the Japanese army: "201—Japanese Army statistics[.]"

DIBBLE, SHELDON. *A History of the Sandwich Islands.* Honolulu: Thomas G. Thrum, 1909. v, 428 pp., illus.   HL 332498

Contents: General history of the Hawaiian islands, from their earliest recorded history through the introduction of Christianity, and the beginnings of the decline of the Hawaiian monarchy.

Marginalia: Both Jack and Charmian read and annotated this book fairly heavily. London marked passages about high priest worship, the system of taboos, a visit from Captain Vancouver, descriptions of the islands at the time of Captain Cook's visit, Kamehameha and his reign, and the missionaries: "12—origin of the first tabus[.] 35—John Young, Isaac Davis[.] 39—ruling chiefs at time of Captain Cook's arrival. 43-44—hand to hand fighting in old days[.] 54—first haole vessels in Honolulu[.] 65–70—Death & burial of Kamehameha. 71—Chapter III[,] Feudal System of Hawaii[.] 89— Their ancient astronomy[.] 94–97–102—Good stuff for missionary psychology 'old school.' 102–3–4—personal ornament, execution & burial[.] 199–203—list & brief history of Chiefs in 1825[.] 232–34—'telling one's thought'—simple-minded idea of conversion[.] 236–7—old time missionary preaching tour."

DICKINSON, GOLDSWORTHY LOWES. *A Modern Symposium.* New York: McClure, Phillips & Company, 1906. 159 pp.   HL 336813

Contents: Treatise on socialism.

Inscription: "To Jack London—'Ave, et Vale[.]' Everett Lloyd[,] The Vagabond[.] April[,] 1907[.]"

Marginalia: London read this book carefully. He was interested in a warning of the danger of bureaucracy, the argument that religion should not be established in a state, the incapacity of government, a notion that history is one gigantic error, the corruption of the

United States government, discussions of Christ and Christianity, and, near the end of the book, Dickinson's definition of the artist.

DODSON, CHARLES LUTWIDGE (*pseudonym* Lewis Carroll). *The Hunting of the Snark and Other Poems and Verses.* . . . New York: Harper & Brothers, 1903. xiii, 248 pp., illus. HL 337614
Contents: Poems.
Bookseller: Charles E. Lauriat Company, Boston, Massachusetts.
"We are going to call her the *Snark,*" London wrote, "for the beautiful elliptical stern." As Charmian later recalled (*Book of Jack London,* 2:149-50), Jack's reason for this name was that "he could think of no other name that suited, and his friends, with bright suggestions of *The Call of the Wild, The Sea-Wolf,* and eke *The Game* had worn him out. He even put it as a threat to one and all, that if nothing less silly were forthcoming *Snark* she should be—this snappy title being chosen from Lewis Carroll's *The Hunting of the Snark.*"

It was fitting that London's yacht should be named after a book; in fact the entire voyage had been precipitated by one. After reading Joshua Slocum's *The Voyage of the Liberated,* a tale "of sailing up from South America in canoe with wife & children after his barque was wrecked" (Charmian London, "Books I Have Read," p. 26), the Londons turned to Slocum's *Sailing Alone Around the World* and *Voyage of the Spray,* which they read at Glen Ellen in 1905. "I had resolved on a voyage around the world," Slocum wrote (p. 11), "a thrilling pulse beat high in me. My step was light on deck in the crisp air. I felt that there could be no turning back, and that I was engaging in an adventure the meaning of which I thoroughly understood." No wonder, then, with such words to incite him, that London decided to sail around the world on a *Spray* of his own.[34]

DOUBLEDAY, RUSSELL. *A Year in a Yawl: A True Tale of the Adventures of Four Boys in a Thirty-Foot Yawl.* New York: Doubleday, Page & Company, 1901. vii, 365 pp., illus. HL 336890
Contents: Narrative of a seafaring adventure.
Inscription: "Christmas 1901—From Santa & Wife[.]"
Although Santa & Wife remain unidentified, Russell Doubleday

was a man not unknown to London. As publisher for Doubleday, Page & Company, and a loyal admirer of London's work, he tried more than once to persuade London to sign with the Doubleday firm. His persistence paid off. In 1912 London gave the company *A Son of the Sun*.

DOWDEN, EDWARD. *Robert Browning*. London: J. M. Dent & Company, 1904. xvi, 404 pp., illus. HL 334792

Contents: Biography of Browning.

Inscription: "To my Friend, Jack London, whose cheer strengthens my Ruskin work; whose sympathy invigorates my intellectual life; and whose literary style is one of my great delights. Affectionately, Frederick I. Bamford. Christmastide, 1904."

Robert Browning was London's favorite poet. The influence Browning's poetry had on London's work cannot be discounted: he is quoted or mentioned in much of London's fiction, including *A Daughter of the Snows, The Kempton-Wace Letters, The Road, Burning Daylight, Adventure, The Abysmal Brute, The People of the Abyss, The Sea-Wolf, The Red One*, and *The Mutiny of the Elsinore*.

In a letter to Albert Mordell (2 October 1916, HL), London discusses his love for books, and his particular fondness for Browning: "I have enjoyed reading your *Dante and Other Waning Classics*, especially so because I agree with every word you have uttered therein.

"Honestly, I have never been able to complete that reading of the *Inferno*, much less the rest of Dante's provincial creed. The foregoing is likewise true of the *Imitation of Christ* and the *Confessions of St. Augustine*.

"I can still fall for the rolling wonder of the music of *Paradise Lost*. Intellectually, it has always affected me as would affect me the reading of a sort of modernized version of an ancient sun myth. I never had the courage to attempt to read *Paradise Regained*.

"Of course, the *Odyssey* and the *Illiad* are human folk epics.

"My best choice of all epics, however, is Browning's *The Ring and the Book*. Were I wrecked on a desert island, and were I permitted to have with me in my prized shelf of books one epic only, I should select *The Ring and the Book*. . . ."

In *A Daughter of the Snows*, London gives further praise to Browning: "Why, I have stolen away, at night, with your Browning, and

> To my friend, Jack London, whose cheer strength and my Ruskin work; whose sympathy invigorates my intellectual life; and whose literary ... is one of my great delights.
>
> Affectionately,
> Frederick I. ......
> Christmas-tide,
> 1904.

locked myself in like a thief in fear. The text was senseless. . . . I, who am strong and dominant, who have played large with destiny, who could buy body and soul a thousand painters and versifiers, was baffled by a few paltry cents' worth of printed paper! . . . But I intend to sell out,—mines, Company, everything,—and study Browning."[35] London, too, wanted to study Browning, as he explained in a letter of 19 December 1899 to Anna Strunsky: "Seems as if I have known you for an age—you and your Mr. Browning. I shall certainly have to re-read him, in the hope after all these years of obtaining a fuller understanding" (*Letters*, p. 74).

Dowell, Charles L. *Rhymes of Revolt*. Iola, Kansas: Socialist Cooperative Publishing Company, 1913. 22 pp., illus. HL
Contents: Poems.
Inscription: "From the author."
Marginalia: A recollection of past correspondence prompted London to jot this note: "Had a hot interchange of letters with him I think."

Doyen, E. Grattan. *Satan of the Modern World*. New York: Broadway Publishing Company, 1904. vi, 291 pp. HL 331709
Contents: Novel.
Inscription: "With Compliments of E Grattan Doyen[.]"

Drucker, Aaron Phinias. *The Trial of Jesus, From Jewish Sources*. New York: Bloch Publishing Company, 1907. 64 pp. HL 336703
Contents: Historical investigation into Jesus' conviction, exonerating the Jews.
Marginalia: This volume was yet another important source for London's planned Christ novel. He marked passages describing the night-time trial, an accusation that Jesus spoke blasphemy, the claim of Tacitus that Jesus was crucified for promoting rebellion, the refusal of the Romans to fight a defenseless crowd, the Roman spy Caiaphas, the conspiracy of the high priest, and the betrayal of Jesus.

Dumont, Henry. *The Vision of a City and Other Poems*. San Francisco: The Whitaker and Ray Company, 1907. 115 pp. HL 326956
Contents: Poems.
Inscription: "To Jack London with Compliments of Henry Dumont[.] Oct.—7, 1907[.]"
Dumont was one of George Sterling's friends, and dedicated this book of poems to him.

DUNBAR, ROBIN ERNEST. *Arthur Sonten: A Comedy in Three Acts.* South Bend, Indiana: Published by the Author, 1913. HL 337674

Contents: Drama.

Inscription: "To Jack London[.] Presentation copy from R. E. Dunbar[.] Aug[.] 5/13[.]"

Enclosing *Arthur Sonten,* Dunbar asked London to critique it for him and, if London liked the book, to collaborate with him on another which he was writing. London acquiesced in the first request, but graciously declined the second.

DUNHAM, SAMUEL CLARKE. *The Goldsmith of Nome and Other Verse.* Washington, D.C.: The Neale Publishing Company, 1901. vii, 80 pp. HL 255444

Contents: Poems.

Inscription: "To Jack London, With the compliments of Sam C. Dunham. 1528 Q St., N. W., Washington, D.C., March 27, 1901."

Dunham moved to San Francisco after publication of this volume, and later wrote to London (21 August 1913, HL) for a job: "Can't you utilize me in your work? I am an expert stenographer and a good typewriter. . . ." But Jack had no openings. He did have praise for Dunham's work, however, and gave it freely in a letter of 21 June 1913 letter (HL) to Barse and Hopkins: "I have just finished reading my good friend Sam Dunham's *The Men Who Blaze the Trail.* Sam certainly knows the Great Northland from the grassroots up, from the aurora borealis down through all the frozen muck to the uttermost bedrock. I swear by his poems; and I love them for the words of a man who is a man and who knows the work of men." To Dunham (21 June 1913, HL) London wrote: "Long ago I read your Klondike report in the *Bulletin of the Department of Labor,* and later your report on Nome. Then from the San Francisco *Examiner* I clipped your 'Lament of the Old Sour Dough,' which same I read to all the sour doughs I ran across. So you see we are not unacquainted. And now I have read *The Goldsmith of Nome.* I cannot express to you how I have enjoyed it, but I can say this: your verse has struck the truest note of the Northland. I do not believe, because of that very fact, that it will strike a responsive chord in the heart of anyone who has not lived the Northland life. 'Just

Back from Dawson,' 'Sence I Come Back from Dawson,' and 'I'm Goin' Back to Dawson'—the huge delight I have experienced in reading and rereading those three poems I know it would be impossible for me to share with anyone save an old Sour Dough. My own feelings down here, when I think of the Northland, is that nobody understands. How does it strike you? Ah, I take it back. It has struck you, and struck you hard; for do I not read: 'For the folks down here don't hanker for the things I have to say,' and 'As when first you blazed the pathway to the white and silent land, and I know that when you read them you will feel and understand?'"

Dunn, Joseph Allan. *Care-Free San Francisco.* San Francisco: A. M. Robertson, 1913. 83 pp., illus. HL 261141

Contents: Guidebook to San Francisco.
Inscription: "Jack[,] with the
compliments of the author[,] Allan Dunn[,] to one who cares[.] Jan[.] 10[,] 1913[.] Belvedere [California.]"

Dunn, Robert. *The Youngest World.* New York: Dodd, Mead and Company, 1914. 492 pp. HL 330790

Contents: Novel of the northland.
Marginalia: London wrote his reactions to this book on the rear endpapers: "(2) A man-size book for men. by the same token Women who like men will like it[.] As big as Alaska, as young as Alaska, as old as the human race. (1) A fine achievement. My congratulations Robert Dunn. I knew you of old. I knew you had it in you. And now you've got it out of you, more power to your elbow[.]"

Robert L. Dunn was the only American correspondent in Korea who could keep up with London during the 1904 Russo-Japanese War. The two men became good friends at the time, and when, ten years later, Dunn's publishers asked London for a review of *The Youngest World,* he was happy to oblige them. His comments were published in *The Bookman.*

Durland, Kellogg. *The Red Reign: The True Story of an Adventurous Year in Russia.* New York: The Century Company, 1908. xxv, 533 pp., illus. HL 334772

Contents: Author's experiences in Russia.
Inscription: "Adams[.] Red Page of the *Bulletin*[.] Dear Adams:— Please return to me when I get back from Tasmania[.] Jack London[.]"

EAMES, ROSCOE LORENZO. *Eames' Light-Line Short-Hand. A Practical, Phonetic System, Without Shading. For Schools, Business and Reporting.* San Francisco: Roscoe L. Eames, Publisher, 1887. viii, 122 pp., illus. HL 336117
Contents: Handbook of shorthand.
Inscription: "Compliments of the Author."
Roscoe Eames, who had married Charmian's aunt, Ninetta (Wiley), was the ill-equipped conavigator of the *Snark* during her initial journey to Hawaii.

EARLE, FERDINAND. *The Lyric Year: One Hundred Poems.* New York: Mitchell Kennerley, 1912. viii, 316 pp. HL 296571
Contents: Poems.
Inscription: "To Jack with my love. Fred[.] Birthday[,] 1913."
This book was given to London on his thirty-seventh birthday, 12 January 1913, by his friend Frederick Irons Bamford.

EASTMAN, MAX. *Enjoyment of Poetry.* New York: Charles Scribner's Sons, 1913. xi, 224 pp. HL 339870
Contents: "The purpose of this book is to increase enjoyment [of poetry]."—Preface and Summary.
Inscription: "Compliments of Max Eastman."
Marginalia: London underlined passage explaining the practical value of poetry, the absence of poetical rules, the increasing aristocracy of poetry, and a paragraph explaining that literature courses are worthless. There are also numerous annotations by George Sterling.
As editor of *The Masses,* a "revolutionary and not a reform magazine," Eastman often called upon London to contribute socialist essays. In 1913, he requested that London join the staff as a contributing editor, but London declined. Shortly after London's death, *The Masses* was suppressed by the government.
London was not without praise for this book, and on 31 May

1913 he wrote to Eastman, declaring his admiration (*Letters*, p. 386): "Just a few lines of appreciation of your *Enjoyment of Poetry*.

"It is a splendid presentation of the poet's case, especially so in view of the fact that the book is as full of common sense as it is of delicacy and distinction. In all of the book is none nonsense, none of the absurd notions about poetry that have set most persons treating it in critique—notably Mr. Hudson Maxim. You are, moreover, fully sensitized to the poetic atmosphere, and show unerring taste in your convictions and likes (in my judgment likes and convictions being one and the same thing).

"It seems to me that you reach your high-water mark on pages 116, 117, and 118. It would be hard to find elsewhere in literature a finer insight into matters that elude ordinary terms and dissections."

EDDY, MARY BAKER. *Science and Health With Key to the Scriptures.* Boston: Joseph Armstrong, 1907. xii, 700 pp. HL 336697

Contents: Christian Science writings.

Inscription: "With what of love I have learned, to Jack & Charmian, From Blanche. April 18th, 1907."

Marginalia: Eleven pages of biblical quotations and references are written in Blanche Partington's hand on the front endpapers of the book, evidently as selections to "send off" the crew of the *Snark.*

A member of the "Crowd," Blanche Partington was a poet who also worked as a drama and music critic for the San Francisco *Call.* Partington lived in Berkeley, and had an affair with London shortly before his marriage to Charmian. When she found Christian Science, she began sending information about it to her friends. London ignored it (and her) for the most part, but George Sterling was annoyed by her religious propaganda, and complained bitterly in a letter to London (1906, HL) about the "x-science material Blanche" was sending.

EHRMANN, MAX. *Jesus: A Passion Play.* New York: The Baker & Taylor Company, 1915. 282 pp. HL 336706

Contents: Drama.

Inscription: "My dear London, Please accept this book with my sincere regards—Max Ehrmann[.]"

London received this book from Ehrmann in March 1915. The

Jack London

dramatist, claiming that because London had been for a long time one of his favorite authors he owed him many hours of pleasure, sent him the book hoping "it might show, if only in some small way, my great appreciation of your work" (28 June 1915, HL).

London read the book quickly, and replied (19 October 1915, HL): "This is to tell you that down here in Hawaii I have just taken up and finished your *Jesus Passion Play*. More than anything else, what I like about it is its unrelenting reality and brass tackism. From beginning to end it is *real*. It is what surely might have happened."

ELDREDGE, ZOETH SKINNER. *The Beginnings of San Francisco from the Expedition of Anza, 1774 to the City Charter of April 15, 1850.* San Francisco: Zoeth S. Eldredge, 1912. Two volumes, 837 pp., illus. HL 334848

Contents: History of San Francisco.
Bookseller: Smith Brothers, Oakland, California.
Marginalia: London only marked the first fifty pages of volume 1. He was interested in early Spanish names for the San Francisco Bay vicinity, the first ship anchored in San Francisco Bay, early sailors on San Pablo Bay, and the founding of Stanford University.

ELLIS, WILLIAM. *Polynesian Researches, During a Residence of Nearly Six Years in the South Sea Islands; Including Descriptions of the Natural History and Scenery of the Islands—With Remarks on the History, Mythology, Traditions, Government, Arts, Manners, and Customs of the Inhabitants.* London: Fisher, Son, & Jackson, 1829. 2 volumes, xvi, 536, viii, 576 pp., illus. HL 332798

Contents: Travel history of Polynesian Islands.
Marginalia: Infanticide, a royal marriage, descriptions of the trade winds and the tides, the royalty of the region, and a description of the building of a new settlement are the subjects London found interesting. There are also several annotations by Charmian in the book.

ELWELL, JOSEPH BOWNE. *Advanced Bridge: The Higher Principles of the Game Analysed and Explained, and Their Application Illustrated, By Hands Taken from Actual Play.* New York: Charles

Scribner's Sons, 1906. xvi, 297 pp., illus. HL 336844

Contents: "This volume is intended to aid the bridge student in acquiring a practical acquaintance with the various forms of attack and defense as outlined by the best players. Particular attention is given to the dealer's play, of the dummy hand, and the underlying principles are fully illustrated by complete play of selected hands."—Preface.

Bookseller: Smith Brothers, Oakland, California.

Marginalia: An avid card player, London used this book to learn the fundamental rules and etiquette of bridge, as well as to learn the strategy of declaring "no trump."

There were several books about card games in London's library. Presumably this volume found its way into the *Snark* library, where it received heavy use.

ENGELS, FRIEDRICH. *Feurbach: The Roots of the Socialist Philosophy.* Chicago: Charles H. Kerr & Company, 1903. 133 pp. HL 336968

Contents: "Full recognition of the influence which Feuerbach, more than all the other post-Heglian philosophers, had over us, during the period of our youthful enthusiasm. . . ."—Author's Preface.

Inscription: "To Jack London, a token of appreciation and sincere regard. Austin Lewis[.] 1903[.]"

English-born Austin Lewis came to California in the late 1890s. He founded the first Far-West branch of the Socialist Labor Party and began practicing law as an attorney for organized labor. Lewis was an indefatigable proselytizer for the socialist cause, and, well versed in both German and French, translated many of the early works on Marxism (such as this book) into English. London first met Lewis sometime before 1900. It was Lewis, among others such as Frank Strawn-Hamilton and George Speed, who taught him much of what he learned about Marxism, philosophy, and economic theory.

ENGELS, FRIEDRICH. *Landmarks of Scientific Socialism.* "*Anti-Duehring.*"Chicago: Charles H. Kerr & Company, 1907. 266 pp. HL 336769

Contents: "Natural Philosophy," "Moral and Law," "The Dialectic,"

FEUERBACH
THE ROOTS OF THE
SOCIALIST PHILOSOPHY

BY

FREDERICK ENGELS

TRANSLATED WITH CRITICAL INTRODUCTION

BY

AUSTIN LEWIS

CHICAGO
CHARLES H. KERR & COMPANY
1903

"Political Economy," "Socialism."
Inscription: "To Dear Jack with my love. Fred[.]"
Although Bamford lacked the intellect of Austin Lewis (who translated this book), he was the donor of many of the more philosophical works in London's library.

AN EXPOSITION OF SOCIALISM AND COLLECTIVISM. New York: The Collectivist Society, 1902. 45 pp. HL

Contents: Socialist tract.

Marginalia: London circled a paragraph dealing with the need for legislation to shield the interests of wage earners.

EUCKEN, RUDOLF CHRISTOF. *The Truth of Religion.* New York: G. P. Putnam's Sons, 1911. xiv, 622 pp. HL 336755

Contents: "The most important task seems to be to present with the utmost possible clearness the solid nucleus of religion, and, along with this, to show its main rights."—Author's Preface.

Marginalia: London recorded a few notes on the rear flyleaf: "the evanescent kingdoms of semblance and deception[.] The mutable show[.] Nature, brazen with indifference for man & his dreams[.] transcendental over-worlds[.] Superrational sanctions & obsessions[.] immaterial & super-sensuous realms. domain of flux, of appearances that ebb & flow, transfuse, are, & are not,—that always pass."

FELDMAN, KONSTANTIN ISIDOROVICH. *The Revolt of the "Potemkin."* London: William Heinemann, 1908. 299 pp. HL 334403

Contents: Historical account of the Potemkin revolt.

Marginalia: London was interested in the mutiny, sketches of the main characters, and local-color descriptions of the revolt.

FERNALD, JAMES CHAMPLIN. *Connectives of English Speech: The Correct Usage of Prepositions, Conjunctions, Relative Pronouns and Adverbs Explained and Illustrated.* New York: Funk & Wagnalls Company, 1904. x, 324 pp. HL 336763 PF

Contents: Grammar text.

Bookseller: Smith Brothers, Oakland, California.

Marginalia: London noted the correct usage of the words "not," "nor," "or," "that," "which," "who," and "whom."

Enclosure: Manuscript discussing Fernald's rules of grammar and two-page rebuttal. Neither appears to have been written by London. Below the critique London wrote: "Give him some of the opposite examples."

116

the evanescent kingdom of semblance
and deception
the mutable show
nature; brazen with indifference
for man & his dreams

transcendental over-worlds

supernatural sanctions &
obsessions

immaterial & super-sensuous realms;
domain of flux, appearances
that ebb & flow, transfuse.
are, & are not — that always pass.

FERRELL, WILLIAM. *A Popular Treatise on the Winds: Comprising the General Motions of the Atmosphere, Monsoons, Cyclones, Tornadoes, Waterspouts, Hail-Storms, Etc. Etc.* New York: John Wiley & Sons, 1904. vii, 505 pp., illus. HL 337023

Contents: "The Constitution and Nature of the Atmosphere," "The Motions of Bodies Relative to the Earth's Surface," "The General Circulation of the Atmosphere," "Climatic Influences of the General Circulation," "Monsoons and Land- and Sea-Breezes," "Cyclones," "Tornadoes," "Thunderstorms."

Marginalia: London planned to use the chapter on monsoons in this book as the basis for a fictional weather scene. Presumably, however, the volume was purchased as a reference book for use aboard the *Snark.*

FERRI, ENRICO. *Criminal Sociology.* New York: D. Appleton and Company, 1898. xx, 284 pp. HL 336698

Contents: "The following pages are a translation of that portion of Professor Ferri's volume on *Criminal Sociology* which is immediately concerned with practical problems of criminality."—Preface.

Bookseller: D. P. Elder and Morgan Shepard, San Francisco, California.

Marginalia: "Crime and Criminals" was the heading for a large and bulky file of clippings and notes that London amassed over the years. Always interested in criminal types, London read many books on the subject and wrote quite a few short stories (such as "Just Meat") with criminal protagonists. In this volume, the author's classification of five different kinds of criminals and his views on the criminal instinct, the tendency to crime in normal persons, and the uselessness of the notion of the deterrent effects of capital punishment were of special interest to London. He recorded his reactions on the rear endpapers: "25—five kinds of criminals[.] 26—Responsibility to society[.] 28—Born criminals. 35—Inborn tendencies & acquired tendencies[.] Question raised—is he, or is he not, a free agent. Is he a born criminal, or is he a criminal by contracted habits? A criminal he must be, for responsibility to society enters in. He is guilty of crimes against society, and society must protect itself. p. 30—apply this especially to the *boy.* 35—precocity accompanied by relapse. 43—Normal men are tempted, *but* resist[.] 224—attitude of the state. Responsibility—either keep Edgar in prison, let him go & indemnify individuals for the depredations he commits, or cure him. Does society concern itself sufficiently with the curing of criminals. 242—Diderot—extinguish, not punish, the man who does harm. 251—moral disease contagious, epidemic, & hereditary[.]"

FINDLAY, ALEXANDER GEORGE. *A Directory for the Navigation of the South Pacific Ocean; With Descriptions of Its Coasts, Islands, Etc., From the Strait of Magalhaens to Panama, and Those of New Zealand, Australia, Etc.; Its Winds, Currents, and Passages.* London: Richard Holmes Laurie, 1900. 3 volumes, lvi, 1252 pp., illus. HL 340094
Contents: Sailing directions.
Marginalia: So important was this work to the crew of the *Snark* that the ship's library boasted two complete copies. London only marked this copy however. He was interested in Fakarava Island, Papeete Harbor, Tanna Island, Erromanga, Efate, Ambrym, the Port Sandwich Islands, Pitcairn Island, the Society Islands, the Marquesas, the Torres Strait, San Cristoval, Santa Catalina, the Solomon Islands, the New Hebrides, Hivaoa, and Nuku Hiva. London also marked passages describing the current and winds at Cape Horn, the equatorial countercurrent, the southeast trade winds, and hurricanes.

FISKE, JOHN. *Through Nature to God.* Boston: Houghton, Mifflin and Company, 1899. xv, 194 pp. HL 337236
Contents: "The Mystery of Evil," "The Cosmic Roots of Love and Self-Sacrifice," "The Everlasting Reality of Religion." Philosophical essays rebutting theories expounded by Thomas Henry Huxley and Herbert Spencer.
Inscription: "This book & my love to you, my dear friend Jack. Always faithfully yours, Fred. Dec. 13, [']06."
Although London disagreed with Fiske's interpretation and support of the new doctrine of evolution, he nevertheless found much use for the historian's essays. For a segment of the Christ novel London was planning at the time ("Christ Novel," HL), Fiske's essays be-

came quite useful: "Christ Novel. John Fiske's Essays: 'The Jesus of History.' 'The Christ of Dogma.'"

For the most part, however, London had little praise for Fiske's work. In a letter of 1 March 1900 to Cloudesley Johns, he commented quite characteristically on Fiske's shortcomings: "Spencer was not openly, that is, didactically favorable to a material basis for thought, mind, soul, etc., but John Fiske has done many queer gymnastics in order to reconcile Spencer, whose work he worships, to his own beliefs in immortality and God. But he doesn't succeed very well. He jumps on Haeckel, with both feet, but in my modest opinion, Haeckel's position is as yet unassailable (*Letters,* p. 96).

Parts of Fiske's philosophy were attractive to London. Fiske's definition of philosophical materialism, for instance, was quoted (albeit completely out of context) by London in a letter of 6 January 1902 to Cloudesley Johns (*Letters,* p. 128): " 'Philosophical materialism holds that matter and the motion of matter make up the sum total of existence, and that what we know as physical phenomena in man and other animals are to be interpreted in an ultimate analysis as simply the peculiar aspect which is assumed by certain enormously complicated motions of matter.' That is what we are, and we move along the line of least resistance. Whatever we do, we do because it is easier to than not to. No man ever lived who didn't do the easiest thing (for him)." Not out of context, however, was Fiske's discussion of the Anglo-Saxon, which London quoted heavily in his essay "The Salt of the Earth."

FITCH, MICHAEL HENDRICK. *The Physical Basis of Mind and Morals.* Chicago: Charles H. Kerr &Company, 1906. 266 pp. HL 366741

Contents: "A Short Outline of The Principle of Evolution." "Charles R. Darwin—The Exponent of Evolution," "Herbert Spencer and His Mistaken Disciples," "The Rhythm of Motion," "Human Knowledge and Its Limitations," "The Phenomenal Ego," "The Essence of Phenomenism," "A Natural Code of Ethics," "Limitations and Impediments," "Summary."

Marginalia: London underlined an anecdote about Charles Darwin and passages dealing with Herbert Spencer's definition of phenomena and evolution. Organic evolution and a rejection, on anatomical grounds, of the theory of a special creation were also subjects that London found interesting in the book.

FITZPATRICK, SIR JAMES PERCY. *The Transvall From Within: A Private Record of Public Affairs.* New York: Frederick A. Stokes Company, 1900. xxvi, 364 pp. HL 332765

Contents: "In Earlier Days," "After the War," "The Origin of the Movement," "The Reform Committee," "The Committee's Dilemma," "The Invasion," "After Doornkop," "Arrest and Trial of the Reformers," "Life in Gaol," "Three Years' Grace," "The Beginning of the End."

Bookseller: Smith Brothers, Oakland, California.

Marginalia: The Boer War was a subject of some interest to London, and from this book he made notations which he later planned to enlarge into an essay on the subject: "The Boers, like the Mormons, fleeing before civilisation into the wilderness, & like the Mormons, being overtaken by civilisation in the wilderness. It was as inevitable for them as it was for the Mormons. Isolation to cultivate certain peculiarities & prejudices—etc. enlarge. The Rake[.] The Boer dream—quite old—."

London had written to Cloudesley Johns about a year earlier, commenting on the Boer question: "So the poor little Boers have risen in their might. God bless them! I can admire their pluck, while at the same time laughing at their absurdity. . . . when a detached, antiquated fragment of a race attempts to buck that race, a spectacle is presented at once pitiful and impotent. Fools, to think that a man is the object of his own volition, inasmuch that a few of him may oppose the many in a movement which does not spring from the individual but from the race, and which received its inception before even they had differentiated from the parent branch!" (*Letters,* p. 64).

FITZSIMMONS, ORLANDO KELLOGG. *Metamorphose. Involving Regeneration of Individual and Race, and also the Solution of the Great Problem of Poverty.* Chicago: Progress Publishing Company, 1906. 253 pp., illus. HL 336775

The Boers, like the Mormons, fleeing before civilisation into the wilderness, & like the Mormons, being overtaken by civilisation in the wilderness. It was as inevitable for them as it was for the Mormons. Isolation to cultivate [their] peculiarities & prejudices — etc. enlarge.
The Race.
The Boer dream — quite fled.

THE END

Contents: "The sole purpose of this work is to set forth clearly the existing evils, their causes and their purpose, and then to point out an inviting method whereby Evil can be replaced with Good." —Foreword.
Inscription: "To One of the Foremost Workers for World Betterment, Mr. Jack London, With the author's compliments, Orlando K. Fitzsimmons. Buffalo N.Y. Nov. 2—'06."

FLAGG, JAMES MORGEON. *Psychological Autobiographeries . . . Poems & Tales.*New York: Published by the Literati, 1916. 175 pp., illus. HL 332599

Contents: Selected poetry and prose.
Inscription: "To Mr. J. London—Compliments of the Author[.]"

FORBES, KATE MARCIA. *The Volcano Kilauea.* Honolulu: Star-Bulletin Press, 1915. 31 pp., illus. HL 332574

Contents: Description of the history and legend surrounding the Kilauea volcano.
Inscription: "To Mr. and Mrs. Jack London from Kate Marcia Forbes."

In a cover letter of 19 January 1916 to the Londons (HL), Kate Marcia Forbes asked them for their "unqualified opinion of the book. . . . Beyond some unpublished short stories and some children's stories, it is my first attempt."

FORD, FORD MADOX. *England and the English: An Interpretation.* New York: McClure, Phillips & Company, 1907. 354 pp., illus. HL 334785

Contents: "In this book, I have tried to make [the American] understand as well as I could the Spirit of England—of the English people; of the English great town; of the English countryside."—Preface.
Marginalia: London made the following notes on the endpapers: "in order to escape the pessimism consequent upon the grim, & honest exercise of reason. The great-swarm of the living, piping its thin plaint of troubled air—I dabble in Wm. James—Here is a man of health. Here, no philosopher's stone, but, at least, a few robus true[?] things to tie to. What to [*sic*] I find? Rationality gelded to sentimentality. The ripest fruit of reason, to cease reasoning & have faith—in the vital lies. The old, ole, [sic] ancient old, somersalt of the philosophers whereby they reason reason quite utterly away."

FORE AND AFT SEAMANSHIP FOR YACHTSMEN, *With Names of Ropes, Spars and Sails of a Cutter, Yawl and Schooner.* London: Norie & Wilson, [1900?] 16 pp., illus. HL 336873

Learning to Navigate

Contents: Textbook on seamanship, in a question-and-answer format.
Marginalia: London marked a paragraph explaining what canvas to show when faced with a heavy sea and gale-force winds.

FOREL, AUGUST HENRI. *The Sexual Question: A Scientific, Psychological, Hygienic and Sociological Study for the Cultured Classes.* New York: Rebman Company, 1908. xv, 536 pp., illus. HL 336711

Contents: "This book is the fruit of long experience and reflection. It has two fundamental ideas—the study of nature, and the study of psychology of man in health and disease."—Preface to the First Edition.
Marginalia: The restriction of marriage of retarded persons, rights of the embryo, and the concept of free will are subjects London marked in this book.

According to Irving Shepard, Eliza London Shepard's son, London kept this book and others dealing with sex, venereal disease, and medicine in a locked cabinet in his study. Although he had admitted to Edward Carpenter that he, too, had specialized in sex for quite some time, he was fearful lest some of the younger residents of the Jack London Ranch learn about the subject before their time.
Forel is briefly mentioned in *A Son of the Sun.*

FOSS, DANIEL. *A Journal of the Shipwreck and Sufferings of Daniel Foss.* Boston: N. Coverly Jr., 1816. 24 pp. HL 283404

Contents: Account of the foundering of the brig *Negociator* off an island in the Pacific, 26 November 1809, and the survival of Daniel Foss, who lived on the island for five years, subsisting on a diet of seals.
Marginalia: The first twenty-three pages of this book were marked by London. The passages marked include a description of abandoning the *Negociator;* surviving on the small barren island; eating seals; writing a journal; surviving a tremendous storm; finding a beached whale; and sighting a sail.
London relied heavily on this book in writing one of *The Star Rover* episodes.

FOSTER, JOHN WATSON. *American Diplomacy in the Orient.* Boston: Houghton, Mifflin and Company, 1903. xiv, 498 pp. HL 339677

Contents: A "brief history of the diplomatic intercourse of this government with the Orient, in order to form a correct estimate of the policy which has controlled the American people in their contact with the countries in that quarter of the globe."—Preface.

Marginalia: London underlined paragraphs citing the first British visit to China, the Terranova affair of 1821, the first Chinese treaties, the independence of Hawaii, and the effects of race hatred. His notes at the back of the book include: "5—The way the British first opened up trade with China. 41—China's early high and mighty manner toward foreigners[.] 43—*ditto*[.] 59—*ditto*[.] 434—The *Yellow* Peril[.]"

London read a number of books in preparation for his journey to Korea as a war correspondent. This volume provided him with an adequate knowledge of American interests in Asia, and also aided him in writing "The Yellow Peril."

FOSTER, ROBERT FREDERICK. *Foster's Complete Hoyle: An Encyclopedia of All the Indoor Games Played at the Present Day.* New York: Frederick A Stokes Company, 1897. 625 pp., illus. HL 336943

Contents: Rulebook of card games.

Marginalia: London was interested in the rules for poker, bezique, binocle (pinochle), three-handed binocle, and piquet.

Aboard the *Snark,* the card game after dinner was a social event that the crew looked forward to with great relish. London's favorite games included whist, casino, poker, various forms of rummy, and California Jack.

FOX, JOHN. *Christmas Eve On Lonesome and Other Stories.* New York: Charles Scribner's Sons, 1904. 234 pp., illus. HL 326206

Contents: Short Stories.

Inscription: "New York. Dec. 22, 1904. Dear Jack London: If I had your experience, your equipment and a few other things, I could write more like you. I wish I could. Good luck & God bless you always[.] yours[,] John Fox, Jr."

FOXE, JOHN. *Foxe's Book of Martyrs.* London: Simpkin, Marshall, Hamilton, Kent & Company, [190-?] 454 pp., illus. HL 336716

Contents: History of religious persecution and the Reformation in England.

Marginalia: London marked paragraphs describing the rise and progress of the Inquisition and the martyrdom of John Huss: "138–39–40—Inquisition[.] 212—great description of medieval council."

Originally a source for his Christ novel, *Foxe's Book of Martyrs* was used by London in *The Star Rover.*

FRANCE, ANATOLE. *The Garden of Epicurus.* London: John Lane, The Bodley Head, 1908. 240 pp., illus. HL 330807

Contents: "The Garden of Epicurus," "On Nunneries," "How I Discoursed One Night with an Apparition on the First Origins of the Alphabet," "Careers for Women," "Miracle," "Card Houses," "In the Elysian Fields," "Aristos and Polyphilos on the Language of Metaphysics," "The Priory."

Bookseller: Hochschild, Kohn & Company.

Marginalia: Ignorance, death, and thinking were subjects that interested London, along with France's "In the Elysian Fields." His notes were written on the rear flyleaves: "32[,] 26[,] 44[—]Noseless One[,] 58[,] 69[,] 72[,] 196[,] 197[,] 200[.] The phantasmagoria of living[;] intoxicated with the show of things[.] The world, called by Compte, the 'Great Fetish.'"

London put a volume of Anatole France's work in the library belonging to the character Mulligan Jacobs in *The Mutiny of the Elsinore* (p. 95): "His library, he told me, among other things included, first and foremost, a complete Byron. Next was a complete Shakespeare; also, a complete Browning in one volume. A full half dozen he had in the forecastle of Renan, a stray volume of Lecky, Winwood Reade's *Martyrdom of Man,* several of Carlyle, and eight or ten of Zola. Zola he swore by, though Anatole France was a prime favorite."

London first read *The Garden of Epicurus* while sailing around Cape Horn aboard the *Dirigo.*

FREEMAN, ALDEN. . . . *A Year in Politics: A Record with Suggestions to Civic Workers.* East Orange, New Jersey: Alden Freeman[?] [1906?] viii, 136 pp., illus. HL 336535

Contents: Account of the Colby campaigns of 1905 and 1906.

Inscription: "Jack London with sincere regard[.] Yours for the Revolution[.] Alden Freeman[.] September, 1906[.] See page 108."

Marginalia: London noted the exorbitant costs of goods charged to seamen, and other tales of the exploitation of the men of the sea.

FRÉMONT, JOHN CHARLES. *Memoirs of My Life, . . . Including in the Narrative Five Journeys of Western Exploration, During the Years 1842, 1843–4, 1845–6–7, 1848–9, 1853–4. Together with a Sketch of the Life of Senator Benton, in Connection with Western Expansion . . . A Retrospect of Fifty Years, Covering the Most Eventful Periods of Modern American History.* Chicago: Belford, Clarke & Company, 1887. xix, 655 pp., illus. HL 334819

Contents: Memoirs.

Marginalia: London was most interested in this history of westward expansion. His markings in this book serve to illustrate that interest. He annotated passages describing the Lewis and Clark expedition, the beginning of Frémont's own expedition, the Rocky Mountains, wagon trains, buffalo herds, the plains, the Great Salt Lake, accounts of Indian wars, a sword fight, the rising of the California flag at Monterey and the ensuing battle for control of California, a tracker, a wagon train and Nebraska pioneers, and, finally, fire-ravaged Sonoma.

Bought and read early in the century, this book provided London with the probable impetus for *The Call of the Wild.* On page 98, London marked the following sentences: "Scores of wild dogs followed, looking like troops of wolves, and having, in fact, but very little of the dog in their composition. Some of them remained with us, and I checked one of the men, whom I found aiming at one, which he was about to kill for a wolf."

FRENCH, JOHN MARSHALL. *Elements of Active-Principle Therapeutics.* Chicago: The Abbott Press, 1916. 128 pp. HL 336731

Contents: Medical textbook advancing the cause of active principle therapeutics, with special emphasis on pneumonia, typhoid fever, and acute and chronic maladies.

Marginalia: London marked passages dealing with the treatment of typhoid, the desirability of small but frequent dosages, desimetric medicine, the need for early treatment of disease, and the treatment of pneumonia. He was also interested in the following drugs: calcium sulphite, digitalin, aconitine, veratrine, and strychnine (for fever), saline laxative, atropine (for relief of irritability), echinacea and calcium sulphite (as antiseptics), coniine, codeine, and morphine. On the rear pastedown he wrote: "51—how to give doses[.]"

As ship's doctor aboard the *Snark,* London built up quite a reputation as an amateur M.D. His methods were not always in accordance with skilled medical practice, but his sources were always the same: the most up-to-date, scientific works on a given subject.

Started around the time of the sailing of the *Snark,* London's medical library grew into a reference source of respectable size. From the volumes he had collected, London sought advice and remedies for some of the illnesses that plagued him later in his life.

FRENCH, NORA MAY. *Poems.* San Francisco: The Strange Company, 1910. 91 pp., illus. HL 334643

Contents: Poems.

Inscription: "Dear Fannie K. Hamilton. Read here what George Sterling calls the 'crystalline verse of our dead sister.' Affectionately, Jack London. July 27, 1910."

The daughter of a Latin professor at Wells College, Nora May French came to live in California with her sister, Helen, finding work as a designer in an art store. At age twenty-five, she joined George Sterling in his bohemian colony of Carmel. Instantly accepted by Sterling and the other writers in the town, she settled down to work on her poetry, only to become involved in a love affair with Harry Anderson Lafler. The strain of the affair proved too much for her spirit, however, and in 1907, she committed suicide.

Apparently London never gave this book to newspaper writer Fannie K. Hamilton, for it remained in his library. Eventually, London's bookplate was pasted inside the front cover.

FRENSSEN, GUSTAV. *Jörn Uhl*. Boston: Dana Estes & Company, 1905. vii, 416 pp., illus. HL 330817

Contents: "this book has sprung from the deep consciousness of modern Germany and utters the longings, thoughts, and aspirations of the German heart. . . ."—Prefatory note.

Inscription: "Jack London with love from Johannes Brimus. 'Gossamer and spider-webs go flying all over the land, and thistledown and scent of flowers are carved into every neighbor's garden.— Fate, great and beautiful and terrible, is sitting upon the everlasting stone—tracing in the sand that labyrinth of lines and confusion of paths that we mortals have then to tread.' Jan. 24—1907."

FREUD, SIGMUND. *Selected Papers on Hysteria and Other Psychoneuroses*. New York: The Journal of Nervous and Mental Disease Publishing Company, 1912. ix, 215 pp. HL

Contents: Case studies of hysteria, anxiety neuroses, and bisexuality.

Marginalia: London marked paragraphs dealing with memory, trauma, the sufferings of the hysteric, concealment of sexual ideas, and neuroses.

London's reading of Freud began around the time of publication of this pamphlet. The impact of Freud's ideas was substantial, but it was not until 1914 that he began fully to integrate Freudian analysis into his literary notes.

FREUD, SIGMUND. *Three Contributions to the Theory of Sex*. New York: Nervous and Mental Disease Publishing Company, 1916. xi, 117 pp., HL

Contents: "The Sexual Aberrations," "The Infantile Sexuality," "The Transformation of Puberty."

Marginalia: Marginal markings are found beside paragraphs discussing perversions, the erogenous zones, infantile object selection, and the differentiation between men and women.

London used this book in "The Kanaka Surf": "Ida Barton was the cause of their perturbration and disapproval. They disapproved, seriously so, at the first instant's glimpse of her. They thought—such ardent self-deceivers were they—that they were shocked by her swimming suit. But Freud has pointed out how persons, where sex

Clara Charmian Kittredge London

is involved, are prone sincerely to substitute one thing for another thing, and to agonize over the substituted thing as strenuously as if it were the real thing."[36]

FRIEDMAN, ISAAC KAHN. *The Radical*. New York: D. Appleton and Company, 1907. viii, 362 pp., illus. HL 330816

Contents: Novel.

Marginalia: London was interested in Friedman's description of the capitol building and Senate chambers in Washington, D.C. On the endpapers of the book he wrote his notes for "The Cause": "Belasco—Scorn of Women.

"Play (Write freedom to use letter episode in play). Flight of Duchesses idea.

"First act—English Embassy, Washington. She starts as he goes by. 'Who is he?' She asks. — Long-haired crank from Oklahoma (or California.[)] an anarchist (She remembered him) So he. Both looked at same moment—as they had looked in long ago. (Bring in, sooner or later, when they talk together how they recall that look).

"Before she brings about introduction, she is told who he is. Also, she speaks cynically of politics—throws hands up—cries 'It is stifling'—business man thinks she means room is warm. She says no, people, politics all everything. Her sister, tells another a man—that Duchess high ideals, reform society, etc. That's why she married husband, speaker of the House, & held same for twenty years."

"She was disappointed would play no clean part. Only rotten intrigue.

"Introduce her husband first act.

"Her father a great magnate."

"Letters on child-labor[.] Letters on Parcels delivery bribery bill affecting Post Office[.]"

"Letters episode.

"His stolen letters—from a stenographer—are stolen. He is finished. Bill comes in next day, etc. & letter series stolen."

"Her chance to steal letters—24 Wall St. all superheated. She forms desk.

"She is known to have taken them[.]

"Scene after scene—father, husband, brother, etc. try to get letters. Then father and husband have her searched by three maids— off stage. not find. She had hidden on top of *Lincoln's* portrait."

"Her husband was directly responsible for robbing hero of letters, etc.

"She had been rumored cold—by husband, father, brother—sister—women friends, etc. She proves otherwise. Comedy characters. Foxy, slippery Congressman. A newspaper man, socialist at heart, but has to keep it hidden. Stenographer or secretary who steals letters, is a socialist & loses position.

"Title—The Cause.

"Motive—Cause greater than love—[.]

"His idealism greater than hers. He will not sacrifice Cause for her (-big scene). Woman's love more immoral than man's[.] At end He tells of all the little children, the aged & broken toilers—very quietly, etc. She—you are sexless—a eunich [sic]. He, in a passion, grips her, crushes her in embrace, etc. etc. I'm man, all man—my man complement your woman—meet your woman—every step. I could take your husband by the throat & choke life out of him for sake of you. But I am more than man. I a no longer a man. I am here, sole representative of my party, the only mouth to speak in the House of Have for the millions that fester in the house of Want. It is not what I consider right. (I am the Cause.) If I fail, scandal, laughter—my power to work for Cause is shattered. etc. etc.

"He says: 'Remember Gorky & how he was given to Russian Cause.

"Husband comes in on them. Asks what is the matter.

"She says: 'I have grovelled in the dirt before that impeccable etc[.]—have offered to go away with him, etc. and he shoves me aside. etc.'

"'Were I anxious, I'd be very angry with you. Really, it is interesting to see my wife refused by a gutter sweep such as you.' (Begins to warm up. She stops him saying. 'Now you are getting rhetorical & piling up points. etc.')

"Husband: 'Why don't you accept the lady's generous offer of herself etc?' Is she not pleasing to you. Or perhaps your heart is engaged elsewhere:—some factory girl or sales lady. Perhaps too high strive you?'

"Hero: 'No woman too high for any man who fills her heart's desire.'

"Wife[:] 'He does love me. He has crushed me in his arms tonight & told me so.'

"Husband inspects him like some strange animal.

"Husband: 'Oh, Paragon of virtuous manhood!'—to wife—'And him? Does he fit your heart's desire?' Then scene in which each man offers what he has to her? etc.

"Then the wind-up.

"When two men offer.

"Husband: 'respectability. The aegis of my name.' She snaps fingers, or merely smiles: She: 'You offer me what you have already given me. And what else have you given me?[She exposes rottenness of corporative control of him, etc. etc. When she young girl, he listened to her hopes of good, etc., and left her retain impression that together they would work for good. Hero interrupts: 'I shall have you. but we must wait. He does not count. His heart is bad. He cannot live long. Look at that trembling hand. And look at this—(holds up his own hand, steady as a rock) Too many strong cigars, old man. How long do the doctor's give you?' I do not use that phrase in a familiar sense.

FROM MILTON TO TENNYSON: MASTERPIECES OF ENGLISH PO-ETRY. Boston: Allyn and Bacon, 1895. 161 pp. HL 337895
Contents: Poems.
Marginalia: London marked a passage about Keats on page 107.

FROUDE, JAMES ANTHONY. *Julius Caesar.* New York: D. Appleton and Company, 1912. xxxiii, 450 pp. HL 332593
Contents: Biography of Caesar.
Marginalia: The effect of revolution on history is the subject of a passage on page xi that interested London.

GARNER, RICHARD LYNCH. *Apes and Monkeys: Their Life and Language.* Boston: Ginn & Company, 1900. xiii, 297 pp., illus. HL 330824 PF
Contents: Anthropological study.
Enclosure: Clipping from *Brain and Brawn,* pages 273–74.

GARNETT, PORTER. *The Bohemian Jinks: A Treatise.* San Francisco: Bohemian Club, 1908. xvi, 137 pp., illus. HL 273

Contents: Short history of the beginnings of the Bohemian Club's annual "High Jinks," held in the Bohemian Grove on the Russian River.

Inscription: "Dear Jack: The Bohemian Club, working rather blindly it is true, and with many steps that are false and some that are backward—is nevertheless, giving to art a *forward movement*. It is for this reason that I am interested in it; for this reason that I think it is worth while. Faithfully yours, Porter Garnett. Berkeley, Oct. 4, 1909."

GAY, A. E. *England's Duty to Her Merchant Seamen.* Adelaide: Sands & McDougall, 1907. 207 pp., illus. HL 336880

Contents: "to show that the British sailor is not treated as he should be . . . [and] is being squeezed off the high seas . . . by the alien." —Preface.

Marginalia: London noted the exorbitant costs of good charged to seamen, and other tales of the exploitation of the men of the sea.

GEORGE, HENRY. *The Menace of Privilege: A Study of the Dangers to the Republic from the Existence of a Favored Class.* New York: The Macmillan Company, 1905. xii, 421 pp. HL 336782

Contents: "This volume strives to show in a brief, suggestive way how privileges granted or sanctioned by government underlie the social and political, mental and moral manifestations that appear so ominous in the Republic."—Preface.

Marginalia: This book was heavily annotated by London, and was probably used extensively in *The Iron Heel*. Among the subjects that caught his attention were a description of American class structure, crime, fear of poverty, the condition of the poor immigrants, the "will of heaven," Thomas Jefferson's statement on property rights, the tombs of the rich, J. P. Morgan's exploits, the wastefulness of the rich, a quotation by Benjamin Franklin on the aristocracy, conditions of the public schools, the link between poverty and insanity, unemployment, the control of the church, the press, and the university by the rich, and biographical sketches of the railroad kings and John D. Rockefeller. His notes on the rear endpapers include: "Man—68[.] Man—78-79[.] Franklin on the dignity of Labor[—]90-91[.] President Wheeler on the too-rich—93[.] 108—

Quotation. 135—what drives people crazy. Quotation[.] 139—
Quote from Mill[.] 140—Longfellow—quotation[.] 143—Quote[.]
148—Quote[.] 154—Quote[.] 165-6—Quote for Future novel[.]
237—control of legislation—quote[.] 281—Persistence[—quote.]
286[—]Persistence[—quote.] 312[—]Persistence[—]quote[.]"
George Platt Brett, president of the Macmillan Company and publisher of most of London's books, sent this volume to him in 1905,
suggesting that he read it. On 2 December 1905, London replied: "I
have just glanced at the preface of Henry George's book which you
so kindly sent me, and I know I shall enjoy reading it, agreeing
with his destructive criticism while disagreeing with his constructive theorizing"(*Letters*, p. 192).

GERONIMO. *Geronimo's Story of His Life.* New York: Duffield &
Company, 1907. xxvii, 216 pp., illus. HL 339680
Contents: Autobiography.
Marginalia: A student of the American West, and the Indian, London was quite interested in Geronimo's account of an attack of
a grizzly bear, Indian medicine, and revenge on the white man:
"22–3–4—making medicine[.]—a song & dance number[.] 54—
religion of war[.]"

GHENT, WILLIAM JAMES. *Mass and Class: A Survey of Social Division.* New York: The Macmillan Company, 1904. ix, 260 pp.
HL 336779
Contents: "In my present work I have sought to analyze the social
mass into its component classes; to describe these classes, not as
they may be imagined in some projected benevolent feudalism, but
as they are to be found here and now in the industrial life of the
nation; and to indicate the current of social progress which, in spite
of the blindness of the workers, the rapacity of the master, and the
subservience of the retainers, makes ever for an ultimate of social
justice."—Preface.
Marginalia: John Stuart Mill on the ascendant class, a discussion of
the professional class and the trader class, class conscience, child labor, class ethics, class functions, class hatred, class instinct, the ethics of fellowship, free labor, and the sacredness of private possessions are the subjects that interested London in *Mass and Class,*

although his note at the rear of the volume indicates only one page: "234—more yearly railroad deaths than Gettysburg—precariousness of life."

When George Brett presented London with a copy of *Mass and Class* in October 1904, it immediately became an important book in London's library and a primary source for London's social fiction. In his notes for *The Iron Heel*, London referred to Ghent's book: "For the retainers (divisions of the castes), see *Mass & Class*, p. 85. See *Mass & Class*, Index, for ethics of businessmen, private property, etc." ("Iron Heel: Notes," HL).

William James Ghent was a socialist affiliated with the Rand School of Social Science in New York City. He later moved west to Los Angeles and joined Gaylord Wilshire's socialist movement. Although London and Ghent shared obvious socialist sympathies, the two writers corresponded only infrequently.

GHENT, WILLIAM JAMES. *Our Benevolent Feudalism*. New York: The Macmillan Company, 1902. vii, 202 pp., illus. HL 336781

Contents: "Utopias and Other Forecasts," "Combination Coalescence," "Our Magnates," "Our Farmers and Wage-Earners," "Our Makers of Law," "Our Interpreters of Law," "Our Molders of Opinion," "General Social Changes," "Transition and Fulfillment."

Marginalia: A description of the class struggle and account of the abyss: defenseless labor, tenants and the rise of salaried management, the freedom of the economic system, and, finally, the rising of a new form of feudalism are subjects that London saw fit to mark in this book. London's review of *Our Benevolent Feudalism* appeared in the 1 May 1903 issue of the *International Socialist Review*.

Joan London claimed that "Jack had been tremendously impressed by Ghent's book when it first appeared. Now, disillusioned with the American socialist movement, contemptuous of the pacifism, cowardice and essential insincerity of its leaders, and with Ghent's prognosis of the integration of capital not only verified but exposed on every hand by the blazing torches of the muckrakers, he took Ghent's thesis of the emergence of a new feudalism and reared upon it the brilliant superstructure of *The Iron Heel*."[37] Although Franklin Walker discounts the importance of the role ("this book, rather a slight thing, hardly lives up to the prominence given it by Joan as the germinal idea of *The Iron Heel*"),[38] there is no question that London relied heavily on the book for his novel. In a series of notes entitled "Disappearing Class" (HL) London refers again and again to *Our Benevolent Feudalism:*

"Disappearing Class." "Introduction, pithy, on the disappearance of classes in history and on the outlook for the disappearance and rise of other classes in the immediate present. Disappearance of the slave farmers of Rome, of the serf farmers or feudal lords rather of Middle ages (Fr. Revolution), etc.

"Define the middle class of to-day.

"Give space to the farmer—see pages selected in back leaf of Simon's *American Farmer.*

"See Bamford, or N.Y. People, for figures of disappearing middle class. also look up and verify reports of the meeting of the International at The Hague, 1848, where Carl Marx was genius of convention and where following definitions were made:

"Proletaire—one who obtains living entirely by the labor of his hands.

"Middle Class—who obtain living partly by own labor and partly by labor of others.

"Capitalist—who gains living wholly b[y] the labor of others. *Benevolent Feudalism*—tenant farmers, p. 52.

"Show the old contention of the German socialists, that the middle class would actually disappear (See Brooks's *Social Unrest,* chapter entitled, Revolution to Reform) and show change this contention has undergone, but be careful about it for fear of socialist criticism. As an independent class, sharing in the bi-partition of the revenues, it is disappearing. Make this point clear and definite[.]"

"As the workers broke the machine on introduction, so small capitalists would break the trust machines to-day. As the worker passed from the comparative freedom of domestic production to the slavery of factory production, so the small capitalist to-day is passing from the comparative freedom of pre-trust competitive industry to slavery of post-trust industry (better)—incidentally point out, that there is a class struggle even within the capitalist class, between the small and large capitalists.

London also refers to *Our Benevolent Feudalism* twice in his notes for *The Iron Heel,* and also once to Ghent without specifying the title of the book. The continual use of feudal analogies in *The Iron Heel* further suggests that *Our Benevolent Feudalism* was a shaping force in London's *The Iron Heel.*

Gibbs, Josiah Francis. *The Mountain Meadows Massacre.* Salt Lake City, Utah: Salt Lake Tribune Publishing Company, 1910. 59 pp., illus. HL 334803

Contents: History of the Mountain Meadows massacre.

Marginalia: London marked passages describing the route of the emigrants through Mountain Meadows, an account of the battle, the assembling of Mormons, and the massacre of the Arkansas Company.

London had many books about the Mormons in his library. From this pamphlet and several other books describing the Mountain Meadows massacre, London pieced together a fictional account of the tragedy for inclusion in *The Star Rover.*

Giles, Herbert Allen. *A History of Chinese Literature.* New York: D. Appleton and Company, 1909. viii, 448 pp. HL 336757

Contents: "I have devoted a large portion of this book to translation, thus enabling the Chinese author, so far as translation will allow, to speak for himself. I have also added, here and there, remarks by native critics, that the reader may be able to form an idea of the point of view from which the Chinese judge their own productions."—Preface.

Inscription: "To Jack London—this one best book is offered by Bob Davis[.] 1912[.]"

Marginalia: The story of Confucius, Lao Tzu, and several quotations of Chinese poetry interested London. He made an inventory of his findings on the rear pastedown: "63—idealism of Tao. 101— Omar Kayam note[.] 125—Seven Sages of the Bamboo Grove[.] 235–36–37—poetry[.]"

Gilman, Stella C. *Driven Back: A Story of the American Indians.* London: George Routledge & Sons Limited, [1900?] viii, 246 pp., illus. HL 330829

Contents: Novel about an Indian youth who loved the old ways of life.

Inscription: "To Mr. and Mrs. Jack London from the author[,] S. C. Gilman[.] Hoopa Indian Mission[,] Hoopa, Cal."

London sent Gilman a copy of *Before Adam* in 1911. With her letter of thanks, she enclosed this copy of her own book, *Driven Back.*

GILMAN, STELLA LUCILE. *A Gumbo Lily and Other Tales.* New York: The Abbey Press, 1901. 176 pp., illus. HL 330828

Contents: Short stories.

Inscription: "To Mr. Jack London—Compliments of Stella Gilman."

GLYN, ELINOR SUTHERLAND. *Beyond the Rocks: A Love Story.* London: Duckworth & Company, 1906. 319 pp. HL 331806

Contents: Novel.

Inscription: "To Jack London from Elinor Glyn[.] I like this book of mine about the best of any of them. Jan[.] 1911[.]"

The gift of this and the following seven books from Elinor Glyn was prompted by a letter of 26 December 1910 from London to the English novelist (HL): "After wandering around on the edge of the world for some several years, I am at last home. I like your books so well that I have a proposition to make. I see by the leaflet issued by Duffield Company, that you have eight (8) books on the market. I'll tell you what I'll do. I'll autograph any dozen of mine that you may select, and will exchange them for your eight—autographed by you, of course.

"If you're ever out here in California, and can stand roughing it, Mrs. London and I should be delighted to have you visit us on our ranch."

GLYN, ELINOR SUTHERLAND. *The Damsel and the Sage: A Woman's Whimsies.* London : Duckworth & Company, 1903. 77 pp., illus. HL 331801

Contents: Moral tales and proverbs about women.

Inscription: "To Jack London from Elinor Glyn[.] Jan[.] 1911[.]"

GLYN, ELINOR SUTHERLAND. *Elizabeth Visits America.* London: Duckworth & Company, 1909. 283 pp., illus. HL 331805

Contents: Novel.
Inscription: "To Jack London from Elinor Glyn[.] Here is Elizabeth again[.] And you who can see into the heart of things will understand how Elizabeth appreciated all that is fine & true in your country & only laughed at what you laugh at yourselves. Jan[.] 1911[.]"

GLYN, ELINOR SUTHERLAND. *His Hour.* London: Duckworth & Company, 1910. 326 pp., illus. HL 11607

Contents: Novel.
Inscription: "To Jack London from Elinor Glyn[.] The portrait of 'Gritzko' is drawn from life & the real man was exactly so character & appearance[.] he is dead. Killed in a duel. 1911."

GLYN, ELINOR SUTHERLAND. *Reflections of Ambrosine.* London: Duckworth & Company, 1902. 328 pp., illus. HL 331802

Contents: Novel.
Inscription: "To Jack London from Elinor Glyn[.] The portrait of the Grandmother was taken from my own Grandmother. Jan[.] 1911[.]"

GLYN, ELINOR SUTHERLAND. *Three Weeks.* London: Duckworth & Company, 1910. 318 pp., illus. HL 330832

Contents: Novel.
Inscription: "To Jack London from Elinor Glyn[.] Jan[.] 1911[.]"

GLYN, ELINOR SUTHERLAND. *The Vicissitudes of Evangeline.* London: Duckworth & Company, 1905. 279 pp., illus. HL 331804

Contents: Novel.
Inscription: "To Jack London from Elinor Glyn[.] Jan[.] 1911[.]"

GLYN, ELINOR SUTHERLAND. *The Visits of Elizabeth.* London: Duckworth & Company, 1909. 308 pp., illus. HL 331803

Contents: Novel.
Inscription: "To Jack London from Elinor Glyn[.] Jan[.] 1911. This was my first book[;] the first of anything I ever wrote!"

London was quite pleased when the package containing Elinor Glyn's eight books arrived in Glen Ellen, but when he began assem-

To my friend & brother
Jack London; with
whom I often disagree,
but whose ability
& revolutionary
spirit I admire

Fraternally

Alexander Berkman

bling a dozen of his own books to send to her, he ran into problems. He wrote to her (January 1911, HL): "I have just got back to the ranch after a many weeks' absence. Of course, it is too late for me to send the books to New York, but they are off this mail to you addressed to the Ritz Hotel, Piccadilly, London.

"To save my life, remembering your disinclination for sociological studies and novels, I have been hard-put to find enough of my books on the ranch to send you. I have managed to dig up eleven. Please tell me how you like some of them.

"When I tell you that this is the first time I ever exchanged books, or offered to exchange books with anybody, you will appreciate the almost maidenly embarrassment with which I awaited an answer from you. Don't forget where our ranch is located, where we shall be very glad to receive you and show you some pretty country."

GOLDMAN, EMMA. *Anarchism and Other Essays*. New York: Mother Earth Publishing Association, 1910. 277 pp., illus. HL 336773

Contents: Political essays.
Inscription: "To Jack London and Charmian his mate of adventure. In memory of my visit to their chosen spot, so close to the liaison of Mother Earth[.] Emma Goldman[.] New York[,] Dec[.] 20[,] 1910[.]"
Enclosure: Mother Earth advertising broadside.

London had many encounters with Emma Goldman, especially while he was writing the introduction to Alexander Berkman's *Prison Memoirs of an Anarchist*. He had little regard for her anarchist ideas, however. In 1909, Goldman and Ben Reitman, a fellow anarchist, visited the ranch in an attempt "to divert Jack from his socialism, which they derided, toward their unconstructive anarchism, at which he jeered, while not depreciating their martyr-sincerity and courageous, if (to him) misguided sacrifices. Of these and some others he later said: 'The anarchists whom I know are dear, big souls whom I like and admire immensely. But they are dreamers, idealists. I believe in law . . . you can see it in my books—all down in black and white'"(Charmian London, *Book of Jack London,* 2:184).

GOODHUE, EDWARD SOLON. *Songs of the Western Sea*. San Francisco: Blair-Murdock Company, 1911. 93 pp., illus. HL 337686

Contents: Poems.
Inscription: "To dear Mr. and Mrs. Jack from their long-time beneficiary, One of the 'Minor Poets[.]' Dec[.] 22[,] 1911[.] The Doctor-age[,] Hawaii."

Goodhue, the physician for the Molokai leper colony, first corresponded with London through the *Kona Pickel Jar* which Goodhue published. When London visited Hawaii in 1907 he and Goodhue became friends, trading books and correspondence until London's death in 1916.

GOODHUE, EDWARD SOLON. *Verses from the Valley*. Oakland: Pacific Press Publishing Company, 1888. vii, 211 pp., illus. HL 20852

Contents: Poems.
Inscription: "Dear Jack London,"
"I think you have not seen this book of mine, penned the most of
it over thirty years ago. 'Each Pieces' were better skipped. Some of
'Love First,' 'My Choice,' 'Sunnyside,' 'Ebb & Flow,' 'Providence,'
etc. are as good as any I write today. 'The Clock and the Owl'—
'The Throne,' 'Psyche' [. . .] are [. . .] socialism and for the rest
accept them from a friend. E. S. Goodhue[.] March 31[,] 1914[.]"
Enclosures: "A Critic Criticized," an article about E. S. Goodhue.
Also: Three page Ms.s. poem dated 3 March 1914, and written in
Glen Ellen: "Evening in the Valley of the Moon."

GORDON, Irwin LESLIE. *The Log of the Ark by Noah.* New York:
E. P. Dutton & Company, 1915. viii, 147 pp., illus. HL 331813
Contents: Humorous fictional account of the voyage of the ark.
Bookseller: Thrum's, Honolulu, Hawaii.
Inscription: "To Jack & Charmian from Bruce[.]"

GOWEN, HERBERT HENRY. *The Paradise of the Pacific: Sketches of
Hawaiian Scenery and Life.* London: Skeffington & Son, 1892.
180 pp., illus. HL 332496
Contents: Hawaiian travel book.
Bookseller: Thrum's, Honolulu, Hawaii.
Marginalia: This book served as yet another source for London's
unwritten Hawaiian trilogy. He marked passages describing Honolulu's Chinatown and the city in general, a royal Hawaiian islands.
His notes include: "35—proper names[.] 42—Honolulu from
Punchbowl in the Eighties[.] 87–8–9—Royal Procession[.] 94–5–
6–7–8—Death & Burial of an Alii. 129—distinction between husband of the wife and father of the child[.] 136—good Pace story of
chinese (60 yrs[.]) always beaten by his mother (90 yrs[.]) for the
first time crying. 138—Chinese worship[.]"

GOWERS, WILLIAM RICHARD. *Diagnosis of Diseases of the Brain and
of the Spinal Cord.* New York: William Wood & Company,
1885. viii, 293 pp., illus. HL 336817 PF
Contents: Medical textbook.

Marginalia: London marked pages dealing with the diagnosis of syphilitic tumors.

GRAHAME, KENNETH. *The Wind in the Willows.* New York: Charles Scribner's Sons, 1913. 350 pp., illus. HL 331809
Contents: Story.
Inscription: "To Jack London with very best wishes—from Paul Bransom[.] Christmas 1913[.]"
Enclosure: Photograph of Bransom and his wife tipped in.
Paul Bransom was the illustrator of a few of London's books, including the 1912 edition of *The Call of the Wild.*

GRAND, SARAH. *(Pseudonym.) Babs the Impossible.* London: Hutchinson & Company, 1901. 387 pp., illus. HL 331807
Contents: Novel.
Marginalia: London sketched the floor plan of the *Snark* on the rear flyleaf of this book.

GREAT BRITAIN. HYDROGRAPHIC OFFICE. *Eastern Archipelago, Part I. (Eastern Part.) Comprising the Philippines, Sulu Sea, Sulu Archipelago, N. E. Coast of Borneo, Celebes Sea, N.E. Coast of Celebes, Molucca and Gillolo Passages, Banoa and Arafura Seas, N. W. and West Coasts of New Guinea, and North Coast of Australia.* London: J. D. Potter, 1890. xxvi, 584 pp., illus. HL 336909 (Pt. 1)
Contents: Sailing directions.
Bookseller: George E. Butler, Chronometer & Watchmaker. San Francisco, California.
Marginalia: London marked a passage dealing with the Banda Isles and was interested in the information about winds and typhoons.

GREAT BRITAIN. HYDROGRAPHIC OFFICE. *Eastern Archipelago, Part II. (Western Part.) Comprising the South-East Coast of Sumatra, Java, The Islands East of Java, the South and East Coasts of Borneo, and Celebes Island.* London: J. D. Potter, 1893. xxii, 421 pp., illus. HL 336909 (Pt. 2)
Contents: Sailing directions.

Marginalia: Kompang bay, Celebes Island, steamer connections between Europe and Batavia, and communications with Europe are subjects that London researched in this volume.

GREAT BRITAIN. HYDROGRAPHIC OFFICE. *Pacific Islands, Volume I. (Western Groups.) Sailing Directions for the South East, North East and North Coasts of New Guinea, Also for the Louisiade and Solomon Islands, the Bismark Archipelago, and the Caroline and Mariana Islands.* London: J. D. Potter, 1900. xxvi, 516 pp., illus. HL 336823 (v.1)
Contents: Sailing directions.
Marginalia: London marked paragraphs discussing the Solomon Islands, Santa Catalina Island, Florida Island, the Utuha passage, Tulagi harbor, Indispensable Strait, Savo Island, Guadalcanal, Pavuvu Island, and Thousand Ships Bay.

GREAT BRITAIN. HYDROGRAPHIC OFFICE. *Pacific Islands, Volume II. (Central and Eastern Groups.) Containing Former Vols. II, III, and Fiji Islands. Sailing Directions for Fiji, Kermadec, Tonga, Samoa, Union, Phoenix, Ellice, Gilbert, and Marshall Islands, Tubua, Cook and Society Islands; Paumotu, Or Low Archipelago, Marquesas; Theline Islands or Scattered Islands Near the Equator, and the Sandwich Islands.* London: Darling & Son, 1891. 516 pp., illus. HL 336823
Contents: Sailing directions.
Marginalia: London relied heavily on this and the other volumes of the *Sailing Directions.* In this book, he found information about quarantine, Tasman strait, the Society Islands, hurricanes, Tahiti, Papeete, and Murea and Wallis Islands.

GREENER, WILLIAM OLIVER. *Greater Russia: The Continental Empire of the Old World.* New York: The Macmillan Company, 1903. xiii, 337 pp., illus. HL 334771
Contents: Assessment of Russian society, industry, and politics, following a trip across the empire in 1901.
Marginalia: Undoubtedly this was one of the many books London took aboard the *Siberia,* bound for Japan in 1904. London's specific

interest in the book centered on discussions of Russian exploitation of Chinese labor, Russian unrest, and Vladivostok: "203—Inefficiency of Russian laborers at Vladivostok. 310-311—Discontent in Russia & Revolution."

GREGORY, THOMAS JEFFERSON. *History of Sonoma County, California, With Biographical Sketches of the Leading Men and Women of the County, Who Have Been Identified With Its Growth and Development from the Early Days to the Present Time.* Los Angeles, California: Historic Record Company, 1911. xv, 1112 pp., illus. HL 334820

Contents: History of Sonoma County.

Inscription: "Friend Jack[.]"

"I trust you will find of some interest this hist[.]—write-up of our grand rancho, our Imperial Sonoma. It hardly reaches the dignity of a history, this story I have told, or rather repeated; so we'll just 'blame the printer.' His scape-goat back can be another burden. In the matter of the biographies *I am inn-o-cent!* Who produced them I know not. T[h]om[as Jefferson Gregory.] To Jack London, Glen Ellen, Sonoma Co[.,] Cal."

Marginalia: Passages London marked deal with a historical account of Spanish California, the padres, Monterey, the Sonoma mission, the naming of San Francisco, and the beginnings of the 1905).

GRIEG, ALEXANDER. *Fate of the Blenden Hall, East Indiaman, . . . With an Account of Her Wreck, and the Sufferings and Privations Endured by the Survivors, For Six Months, On the Desolate Islands of Inaccessible and Tristan D'Acunha, . . . From a Journal Kept on the Islands, and Written with the Blood of the Penguin.* New York: William H. Colyer, 1847. 209 pp., illus. HL 336754

Contents: Historical account of a shipwrecked sailor.

Marginalia: "Novel[.] Present day[.] a similar wreck[.] only one or two shooting weapons[.] conduct of crew—of captain—of passengers. A love-story of course woven in. etc. etc." Borrowing the plot and theme of a factual account of a shipwreck, London planned to write a fictional story.

GRIERSON, FRANCIS. *The Invincible Alliance and Other Essays, Political, Social and Literary.* New York: John Lane Company, 1913. 235 pp., HL 336771
Contents: Political essays.
Bookseller: Paul Elder & Company, San Francisco, California.
Inscription: "To Jack with our love. Always faithfully yours, Georgia Loring Bamford. Fred I. Bamford[.] July, 1914."

GRIFFIS, WILLIAM ELLIOT. *Corea: The Hermit Nation.* New York: Charles Scribner's Sons, 1902. xxxi, 492 pp., illus. HL 332718
Contents: History of Korea.
Inscription: "Jack London."
Marginalia: London made a notation beside "A Body-Snatching Expedition," on page xxxi.
This was yet another of the volumes London took with him to Japan and Korea in 1904.

GROVER, MONTAGUE. *The Minus Quality and Other Plays.* Sydney: William Brooks & Company, Ltd., 1914. 89 pp., HL 337624
Contents: Dramas.
Inscription: "To Mr. Jack London from Montague Grover in memory of Southwell's Camp, Bondí, Australia[.] 1909[.]"

HAECKEL, ERNEST. *The Riddle of the Universe.* New York: Harper & Brothers, 1901. xii, 390 pp. HL 129923
Contents: Philosophical essay.
Marginalia: "Dualism and Monism—16—17—18—19—20. A plain statement of dualism & monism in relation to soul or mind—89–90–91—That some high plant lives or higher than some low animal lives, sponges & fly-catching plants, for instance—pp.160–161."
Unfortunately London's copy of *The Riddle of the Universe* is lost. He recorded the above findings in "Books I Have Read" in August 1901. Soon after, he used the book again for his notes on Christ: "Goth does not like Christian contempt of the body, and this comes out either through personal observation he makes in book, or

through discussion with Jewess, or with Pilate—see chapter (Our Monistic Ethics) *Riddle of the Universe*, pp. 354–5. See *Riddle of the Universe*, Chap. XVII for philosophy of Christ affair[.] *Riddle of the Universe*, pp. 327–328 etc." ("Christ Novel," HL).

Ernest Heinrich Haeckel's advocacy of organic evolution was quite popular at the turn of the century, and London mentions Haeckel's theories in his correspondence as early as 1898. Haeckel also turns up in many of London's books, including *The Kempton-Wace Letters, The Iron Heel, The Strength of the Strong*, and *The Star Rover* (pp. 161–62): "I think, had Oppenheimer had the opportunity for thorough education, he would have made a Marinetti or a Haeckel."

HALE, ANNIE RILEY. *Rooseveltian Fact and Fable*. New York: Published by the Author, 1910. 200 pp., illus. HL 332660

Contents: "The book is intended merely as a contribution to the truth of history, and is offered without malice, and without apology. Its author is neither Mr. Roosevelt's apologist nor his accuser—save as the Facts accuse him."—Author's Preface.

Marginalia: London underlined a quotation by Jacob Riis, and noted passages describing San Juan Hill, Roosevelt's book on the Rough Riders, and Roosevelt's fondness for William Howard Taft.

Enclosure: Postcard from Annie Riley Hale, dated 21 January 1911, expressing to London her delight at being able to send him a copy of her book.

HANKS, CHARLES STEDMAN. *Camp Kits and Camp Life*. New York: Charles Scribner's Son, 1906. xii, 259 pp., illus. HL 337122

Contents: Nature study.

Inscription: "For Jack London. With the compliments of The Author."

In a cover letter of 21 May 1906, Hanks claimed that London was in part to blame for the writing of *Camp Kits and Camp Life*, because of his "tremendous influence." He also begged London, as "a person . . . who really knows nature, looks at it," to write to him and let him know what he thought of the book.

HANNSSON, LAURA MOHR. *Studies in the Psychology of Women.* New York: Duffield & Company, 1906. 348 pp., HL 337292

Contents: Psychological study of the history of woman in society, traditional roles, and present social position.

Marginalia: London marked paragraphs dealing with the history of woman's illnesses and the history of man's conception of woman. On the rear endpapers, he made a few additional notes, including a few that later became part of *The Little Lady of the Big House:* "Aaron—the half-sex—quotes the Greeks that woman was nature's failure to make a man—.

"They appeal to Dick—or mayor Graham—who talks of the vagueness of souls, of personalities, male and female,—it's all fog & mist in the thick of the mystery.

"—Paula laughs, 'Maybe its mystification instead of mystery—man-made mystification[.]' Dick: 'There talks the true woman.' etc.

"49—chapter on types of women, cerebralés, etc.—Dandy stuff. 74—the cerebralés delusion of knowledge. Terry speaks it. 105—false exaltation of women—after man came back to earth, deterred from star-gazing by the stars[.] 112-13—Terrence develops the Madonna thesis[.] 120-21-22—[.] Testimony of painting that woman is as man has made her—Graham, perhaps[.]"

HAW, GEORGE. *No Room to Live: The Plaint of Overcrowded London.* London: Wells Gardner, Darton & Company, 1900. viii, 178 pp., illus. HL 336834

Contents: Sociological study of the London abyss.

Marginalia: In this source book for *The People of the Abyss,* London marked paragraphs dealing with the eviction of the poor from condemned tenements, the overcrowded living conditions (including many examples), piecework done at home, and examples of apartments covered with vermin and filth. He also noted the death rates among the London poor.

HAW, GEORGE. *Today's Work: Municipal Government, the Hope of Democracy.* London: The Clarion Newspaper Company, Limited, 1901. 240 pp., HL 336777

Contents: Appeal for municipal ownership.

Marginalia: The London tramways; examples of cities running their own municipal services, and providing cheaper rates and more benefits while doing it; conditions of the poor; the sale of human milk; and the establishment of municipal universities were all subjects London found stimulating in this book.

HAWKINS, SIR ANTHONY HOPE. *Second String.* Garden City, New York: Doubleday, Page & Company, 1910. v, 497 pp., HL 331741

Contents: Novel.

Bookseller: Derritt & Snelling. Old-Books-New. Oakland, Cal.

Marginalia: Paper aboard the *Snark* was scarce, and difficult to handle on deck in the wind, so books were often put into service as scratch pads. On pages 205, 280, and 355, London wrote "2:30," "3:30," and "4:30," then jotted down a few figures in order to plot the *Snark's* course.

HAWTHORNE, JULIAN. *The Subterranean Brotherhood.* New York: McBride, Nast & Company, 1914. xix, 329 pp., HL 336818

Contents: A description of life in prison and the effect of prison life on prisoners.

Marginalia: Descriptions of prison life, and "yeggs as best prisoners" were the subjects London noted in Hawthorne's prison study: "208—How yeggs stand together in prison."

Hawthorne and London first met in Los Angeles in January 1905. Hawthorne was on assignment for William Randolph Hearst's Los Angeles *Examiner,* and London was down for a visit. Although Hawthorne had written favorably of London's work, his harsh review of *A Daughter of the Snows* prompted London to criticize Hawthorne's "conventional mind" (London to Cloudesley Johns, 28 April 1905, HL).

HEADLEY, ALLANSON-WINN, ROWLAND GEORGE. *Boxing.* London: A. D. Innes & Company, 1897. x, 384 pp., illus. HL 336854

Contents: "In a former treatise the author of the following pages endeavoured to put beginners into the way of learning from first prin-

ciples; in the present work an attempt is made to go rather more
fully into the subject, and with this object in view, he has added
to certain chapters authentic accounts of important fights. . . ."
—Preface.
Marginalia: Leg work and straight hitting were the two subjects
London wished to study further in this book.
A great boxing fan, London wrote two novels on the subject: *The
Abysmal Brute* and *The Game,* and covered a number of important
bouts for the Hearst newspapers. Nor was he averse to putting on
the gloves himself—boxing bouts were common sport both at the
Beauty Ranch and aboard the *Snark.*

HEARN, LAFCADIO. *Shadowings.* Boston: Little, Brown & Company, 1910. 268 pp., HL 331752
Contents: Poems.
Marginalia: London made a mark beside a passage on page 181 mentioning favors of fathers and a mother's love.

HEART OF THE EMPIRE. *Discussions of Problems of Modern City Life
in England With an Essay on Imperialism.* London: T. Fisher
Unwin, 1902. xxiv, 417 pp., HL 336801
Contents: Socilogical study of London.
Marginalia: Before writing *The People of the Abyss,* London read a
great deal about the London poor. In this book, he found interesting descriptions of overcrowding and the number of poor in England's capital city.

HEINE, HEINRICH. *Heinrich Heine's Memoirs.* New York: John
Lane Company, 1910. 2 volumes, v, 299, vi, 303 pp. HL
334776
Contents: Memoirs.
Marginalia: In this book of memoirs, London marked a passage de-
scribing George W. F. Hegel, marked a few of Heine's letters, and
noted paragraphs that characterized people.
London drew the character Mulligan Jacobs, in *The Mutiny of the
Elsinore,* as a well-read, intellectual man, and for that reason put
Heine's books in Jacobs's library (pp. 95–96): "I talked on with him
about books and bookmen. He was most universal and particular.

He liked O. Henry. George Moore was a cad and a four-flusher. . . .
Ibsen's *Ghost's* was the stuff, through Ibsen was a bourgeois lickspittler. Heine was the real goods."

HEINEMAN, THEODORE WILLIAM. *The Physical Basis of Civilization: A Revised Version of 'Psychic and Economic Results of Man's
Physical Uprightness.'* Chicago: Forbes & Company, 1908. 241
pp., illus. HL 336770
Contents: "A demonstration that two small anatomical modifica-
tions determined physical, mental, moral, economic, social, and
political conditions."—Subtitle.
Bookseller: Smith Brothers, Oakland, California.
Marginalia: London marked paragraphs detailing primitive man's
causes of death and helplessness, his lack of defense abilities, and
the separation of the sexes.

HENDERSON, WILLIAM JAMES. *The Elements of Navigation: A Short
and Complete Explanation of the Standard Methods of Finding the
Position of a Ship at Sea and the Course to be Steered.* New York:
Harper & Brothers, Publishers, 1903. viii, 203 pp., illus. HL
336785
Contents: A beginner's handbook on navigation.
Marginalia: London and Captain Roscoe Eames both used this
book. London marked passages explaining the azimuth tables, longitude and latitude, altitude, Greenwich noon, the chronometer,
apparent mean time, Sumner's method of finding a ship's position
at sea, and finding latitude by means of meridian altitude of a star,
the polestar, or the exmeridian altitude of the sun.

This small blue book was the singlemost important volume in the
five-hundred strong *Snark* library. From its text London was able
to understand the more complicated and sophisticated passages in
his other books of navigation and, more important, to find the
ship's position at sea. In another copy of the book, picked up while
in the South Seas, London wrote an inscription for one of the later
captains of the *Snark:* "To Captain Warren:—Who introduced me
to 'Thorn.' Faithfully yours, Jack London. On Board The *Snark,*
Nov. 13, 1907."

HENLEY, WILLIAM ERNEST. *Poems.* New York: Charles Scribner's Sons, 1898. xiii, 255 pp., illus. HL 337658

Contents: Poems.

Bookseller: D. P. Elder & Morgan Shepard, San Francisco, California.

Inscription: "Jack London[.] From A. S. Jan. 6, 1903. N.Y."

"Anna Strunsky. From Jane A. Roulston[,] Christmas 1900[.]"

"I love this book and the woman who gave it to me. I recall every hour, at night in my room, in the day on the San Rafael hill-tops, when my soul read in it. I recall and I honor yet other times when others who were close read with me. Let it therefore carry my birthday greetings to you, dear Jack. Anna."

This book of poems is heavily marked both by London and Anna Strunsky Walling. It is likely that the two of them spent many evenings discussing Henley's poetry; for London was sending copies of his poems forth to Cloudesley Johns quite regularly just before the turn of the century. But London did not quote Henley in his own books quite as frequently. From Henley's *Poems,* London did find one or two lines, however, which fit into his story "Good-Bye Jack": "Life was a futile thing at best. A short two years and this magnificent creature, at the summit of her magnificent success, was one of the leper squad awaiting deportation to Molokai. Henley's lines came into mind:—'The poor old tramp explains his poor old ulcers; Life is, I think, a blunder and a shame.'"[39]

Jane Roulston was one of Anna Strunsky Walling's socialist friends.

HEWITT, JAMES FRANCIS KATHERINUS. *The Ruling Races of Prehistoric Times.* Westminster: Archibald Constable and Company, 1894. 2 volumes, lxv, 627, xxv, 382 pp., illus. HL 334747

Contents: Anthropological essays.

Marginalia: London marked paragraphs dealing with the beginnings of speech, the drinking of mead, akkadian astronomy, fire worship, Oedipus, the Satyrs, Troy, how myths evolved, Hindu historical mythology, and wolf legends. He noted his findings on the rear leaves of the two volumes: "Out of multitudinous memories I can trace the blending of the Southern astronomical myths with the hero myths of the north—thus—see p. 522—& earlier pp.

of this same essay. Also 556–57[.] 500—order of succession of races
& myths[.] 562—idem[.] 564—idem[.] 537–38–39—the over-
throw of moon goddess by sun god—good stuff[.] 539–40–41—
aryan myth."

"p. 214—dandy stuff for medium[.]"

London used Hewitt's book as a source for several planned fictional
episodes, and incorporated some of the material into *The Star Rover.*

HEWLETT, MAURICE HENRY. *Halfway House: A Comedy of Degrees.* New York: Charles Scribner's Sons, 1908. vi, 424 pp.,
HL 331750

Contents: Novel.

Marginalia: London marked a passage dealing with curates.

Maurice Hewlett was one of London's favored authors. Among the
books written by Hewlett that he owned were *Little Novels of Italy*
and *Mrs. Lancelot* and *Forest Lovers.* "Have just finished reading *Forest Lovers* by Maurice Hewlett[,]" London wrote in a letter of 10
March 1900 to Cloudesley Johns, "Read it by all means if you ever
get a chance" (*Letters,* p. 100). And to George Brett, who had sent
Jack a copy of *Little Novels of Italy,* London wrote: "My hearty
thanks for *Little Novels of Italy*—a favorite book of mine which I
did not possess. I think 'A Madonna of the Peach Trees' one of the
world's short story masterpieces" (*Letters,* p. 129).

HISTORICAL SKETCH BOOK AND GUIDE TO NEW ORLEANS AND
ENVIRNS. New York: Will H. Coleman, 1885. 324 pp., illus.
HL 331755

Contents: Guidebook to New Orleans and the Creole quarter.

Inscription: "To dear Jack London, from Fannie K. Hamilton. August 30, 1910. New Orleans' message to the visitor is something
like this: 'I offer you a rose, a palm-leaf fan, and an omlette soufflé. "

Enclosure: Newspaper clipping: "Jack London, in a recent sermon
by a San Jose minister, is characterized as 'an atheist, a scientist, a
philosopher, and thinker, questing the universe in a mad search for
God.' The clergyman also extols Mr. London's sincerity, and believes him to be 'essentially spiritual.'"

HODGE, JOHN W. *Corean Words and Phrases. Being a Handbook and*

To dear Jack London,
from Fannie K. Hamilton.
August 30, 1910.

New Orleans message to the
visitor is something like this:
"I offer you a rose, a palm-
leaf fan, and an omelette
soufflé."

Pocket Dictionary for Visitors to Corea and New Arrivals in the Country. Seoul: The Seoul Press—Hodge & Co., 1902. 369 pp., HL 332779

Contents: Phrasebook.

Inscription: "Jack London."

London purchased this dictionary in Seoul in 1904 while on assignment by William Randolph Hearst to cover the Russo-Japanese War.

HOLDER, CHARLES FREDERICK. *The Log of a Sea Angler: Sport and Adventures in Many Seas with Spear and Rod.* Boston: Houghton, Mifflin and Company, 1906. x, 385 pp., HL 336940

Contents: Incidents recounted from the author's continuous residence of five or six years "on the extreme southwestern portion of the Florida reef."—Preface.

Marginalia: A description of a Portuguese man-of-war and account of a shark being harpooned were used by London: "p. 32—Get a hermit crab out of shell by heating back of shell. p. 40—350[.] Portuguese man-of-war—virulent sting[.] 154—men killed by sharks."

HOLLAND, HENRY E. *The Tragic Story of the Waihi Strike.* Wellington: The 'Worker' Printery, 1913. 202 pp., illus. HL 336799

Contents: History of a worker's strike in New Zealand.

Inscription: "To Jack London in esteem and fraternity from Bob Ross[.] July, 1913."

HOLMES, THOMAS. *Pictures and Problems from London Police Courts.* London: Edward Arnold, 1902. viii, 224 pp., HL 334431

Contents: Sociological study of the justice system in London.

Marginalia: London marked many passages dealing with the conditions under which the poor of London lived, the hard work they endured, poor living conditions, poor pay, matchbox makers, and housekeeping in a London tenement. He used the descriptive material in *The People of the Abyss.*

HOLT, EDWIN BISSELL. *The Freudian Wish and Its Place in Ethics.* New York: Henry Holt and Company, 1916. vii, 212 pp., HL 336720

Contents: A review of the ethical aspects of Freud's work as applied to contemporary theory.

Marginalia: London marked many paragraphs in this heavily annotated book, including passages about dreams, suppressed wishes, the source of dreams, the doctrine of the wish, Freud on wit and humor, the physiology of wishes and their integration, a quotation from Darwin, the wish in ethics, the will and its relation to ethics, response, and cognition. His extensive notes include: "17—wit and humor merely 'letting the cat out of the bag.' 28—'Tell me what a man laughs at and dreams about and I will tell you what that man is.' 32—dandy illustration[.] 48—Freud's psychology the first psychology *with a soul*. 51-56—development of intelligence by integration of reflexes. 83–87—the 'secret' believed observed actions, to explain which is the source of myth-making. 89—also 96[—] William James'[s] denial of 'consciousness.' 93—also 96—denial of the 'subjective,' and affirmation of materialistic monism[.] 199—'Only the sane man is good, & only the sane man is free.' The man with suppressions is not sane, is not good, is not free."

HOLT, HENRY. *On the Cosmic Relations*. Boston: Houghton Mifflin Company, 1915. 2 volumes. HL 334750 PF

Contents: "an outline of the evolution of the relations between the soul and the external universe, and a summary of the recognized relations that are still so immaturely evolved as to be little understood."—Preface.

Marginalia: Among the passages London marked were a few defining consciousness, the origins of life, transferred senses, the soul, force, matter, and stream of consciousness. He also marked paragraphs dealing with the difference between thought and things, thought based on likeness and difference, the beginnings of fear, realism versus idealism, mediums, and Platonists versus Aristotlians. His notes include: "8—15—26—case of seeing with nose & earlobe[.] 52—proof of existence of a universe external to man. 390—spirits speaking telepathically to impress the medium." In the second volume, London marked paragraphs dealing with telepathy and William James's thoughts on the logic of presumption: "709—Wm[.] James on logic of presumption holding good against spirits conclusion. 708–9–10–11–12–13—James summing up of spiritism. 773—Podmare—on the slight scientific hope that some slight traces of spiritism have been discovered[.] 885–891—continuity of dreams like my farm dreams, etc. 896—Time & space annihilated in dreams."

Enclosure: "What is there in the Occult?" by Bailey Millard. Clipping from *Illustrated World*, pp. 631–36.

London's mother was an ardent spiritualist. His probable father, William Chaney, was a renowned astrologer. Although London rejected the dogma attached to these two pseudosciences, his interest in how they operated was strong, as evidenced by the marginalia in this book. London was also reading Holt's book about the same time he started studying Freud in depth—hence the strong emphasis on dreams.

HOOKER, BRIAN. *Poems.* New Haven: Yale University Press, 1915. vii, 146 pp., illus. HL 337617

Contents: Poems.

Inscription: Card inscribed: "With best wishes for a Merry Christmas & Happy New Year. Malcom Douglas."

HOOLEY, ARTHUR. *John Ward, M.D.* (*Pseudonym* Charles Vale). New York: Mitchell Kennerley, 1913. 320 pp. HL 331935

Contents: Novel.

Contents: Novel.

Marginalia: The disintegration of marriage and vanity were the two subjects of interest to London in this novel.

HOPPER, JAMES MARIE. *Caybigan.* New York: McClure, Phillips & Company, 1906. 340 pp., illus. HL 334332

Contents: Novel. *Inscription:* "Dear Jack:—Wish I'd known you about thirty years ago[.] James Hopper[.]"

A member of the "Crowd," James Hopper was a frequent visitor to the London's Piedmont bungalow. He later joined George Sterling in Carmel, and, finding the bohemian colony to his liking, wrote this and the following novel while living there.

HOPPER, JAMES MARIE. *The Trimming of Goosie.* New York: Moffat, Yard and Company, 1909. 216 pp., HL 83158

Contents: Novel.

Inscription: "To Jack London and Charmian London[.] From James Hopper[.] New York, November 10, 1909[.]"

HORNBLOW, ARTHUR. *The Lion and the Mouse: . . . A Story of American Life Novelized from the Play.* New York: G. W. Dillingham Company, 1906. 399 pp., illus. HL 331725

Contents: Novel about the Ruskin Club.

Bookseller: Smith Brothers, Oakland, California.

Inscription: "This, (in which we Ruskin men are,) for you, dear Jack & Charmian, with my love. Always faithfully yours, Frederick I. Bamford. Oct. 6, [']06."

Bamford's gift came at a time when he was trying to convince London to give a speech at the next Ruskin Club dinner. London, deep in the writing of his new novel *The Iron Heel,* replied that he did not have a paper to give, but offered a substitute:

   "The trouble is, I haven't got any paper to read at the Ruskin dinner; but I'll tell you what I'll do. Suppose I read a couple of chapters from my new novel. These are new in content and are devoted to the perishing middle class, and I think would go splendidly. Incidentally, I handle surplus value in them, and the inevitable breakdown of capitalism under the structure of profits it has reared. If this is satisfactory, suppose we set the date for the first Friday in November. And please let me know at earliest possible moment, if the first Friday in November is agreeable, because I put off from month to month all business engagements, etc., until such time as I am compelled to go to Oakland. Then I arrange all these business engagements to occur around the same date. In this instance, the date will be the Ruskin dinner. So you will see how important it is that I should know as soon as possible the date decided upon for the dinner.

"Heartiest thanks for *The Lion and the Mouse*. Charmian says that I must read it at once, in relation to my new novel [*The Iron Heel*] . . ." (Georgia Bamford, *Mystery*, p. 214).

HOUGH, EMERSON. *Getting a Wrong Start: A Truthful Autobiography*. New York: The Macmillan Company, 1915. 234 pp., HL 337227

Contents: Autobiography.

Marginalia: "Wittingly told, hard-headed, practical, thorough knowledge, no illusions—A man's adventure in life[.]"

London was often called upon to write advertisements or recommendations for new books. His notes at the back of this volume were probably printed in one of the Macmillan Company's many brochures.

HUGHS, ELIZABETH. *The California of the Padres, or Footprints of Ancient Communism*. San Francisco: I. N. Choynsky, 1875. 41 pp., HL 334762

Contents: History of California missions, drawing parallels between the system of government then in effect and modern socialism.

Marginalia: London marked paragraphs about the Jesuits.

Enclosure: Four-page autograph letter from Elizabeth Hughs to Mr. Spear, dated San Francisco, 19 October 1875, tipped in.

HULBERT, HOMER BEZALEEL. *The Passing of Korea*. New York:

Doubleday, Page and Company, 1909. xii, 473 pp., illus. HL
332717

Contents: "In the present volume I have attempted to handle the
theme from a more intimate standpoint than that of the casual tourist. Much that is contained in this present volume is matter that has
come under the writer's personal observation or has been derived
directly from Korean or from Korean works."—Preface.

Marginalia: London was mostly interested in gaining a general
background knowledge of Korea and Korean customs. He marked
paragraphs pertaining to agriculture, food products, ginseng, the
Korean disposition and character, Korean morality, the system of
judicial fines and the penal code, the social and political history of
the country, social activities and games engaged in by Koreans, and
Korean medicine.

HUNTER, ROBERT. *Poverty.* New York: The Macmillan Company, 1904. xi, 382 pp., illus. HL 336800

Contents: Sociological study of poverty in America.

Marginalia: In this source book for *The Iron Heel,* London found
information about the Boston poor, the number of poor people in
New York, the account of the death of a railroad worker, the poverty of the American farmer, Hunter's definition of poverty, a quotation about poverty by Maurice Hewlett, conditions of poverty,
the plight of poor children, sickness and the poor, child labor,
going to school hungry, and conditions in a Glasgow slum. He also
took extensive notes on the book, recording them on the flyleaf:
"24—poverty as bad in New York & Boston as in London. 27—
25% of N.Y. in constant poverty[.] 37—The thing happens—precariousness[.] 52–3–4–5—yearly earnings of labor in U.S. 57— of
the three dips of average workman into poverty in course of life.
71—struggle of worker, sinking down, before seeks poor-relief.
144—Ratio of deaths among rich, workers, poorer workers, etc.
148—Italian, dying of consumption, 'No, no. We gotta bring da
grub to ma chil.' 150–151–152—death of children. 178—a death-
scene in crowded room in tenement[:] 'Breath! Give me breath!'
216—60,000 to 70,000 children in New York City who go hungry
to school. 228—23,760,000 mechanical movements one worker per
year. 231—80,000 children at work in textile mills. Conditions of

Southern cotton-mill labor[.] 241—numbers of children at work[.]
320—Charity a failure—Hunter's experience.'

"Remember 'Appeal to the Young,' and make an appeal to the
soft & tender people, & at same time, another appeal to the
workers.

"Begin with poverty statements, etc.—work up concrete first,
then generalize—and then launch into appeal—clear, simple *lofty*
English. Ask what becomes of the strong young men, motormen,
etc. Bring in suicide among ways of accounting. In appeal portion—what world we should live in—all happy, healthy, etc. See
this book pp before 27 for Ruskin, Morris, Carlyle, etc. First half—
develop in concrete the thing happening. precipitating poverty.
Then give figures."

London's notes pertain to a sociological study of the New York
abyss he planned to write, as a companion to *The People of the Abyss*
which examined the plight of London's poor. Unfortunately, he
never got around to writing the book, perhaps letting his obvious
distaste for the city sway him from his task. London did use Hunter's
book, however, in a series first titled "Disappearing Class": "See
Hunter's *Poverty* page 61, for farmers' small earnings," ("Disappearing Class," HL) then evolved into *The Iron Heel* (p. 85): "One
would conclude from this that under a capable management of society modern civilized man would be a great deal better off than the
cave-man. But is he? Let us see. In the United States to-day, there
are fifteen million people living in poverty; and by poverty is meant
that condition in life in which, through lack of food and adequate
shelter, the mere standard of working efficiency cannot be maintained. . . . Robert Hunter, in 1906, in a book entitled *Poverty,*
pointed out that at that time there were ten millions in the United
States living in poverty."

HUNTER, ROBERT. *Socialists At Work.* New York: The Macmillan
Company, 1908. xiii, 374 pp., illus. HL 336774

Contents: Sociological account of modern socialism put to practical
application.
Marginalia: The right to work, a history of the French Revolution,
and violence as a sign of weakness are subjects London found interesting in this book: "23—Bismarck's state socialism[.] 240 241

242—expropriation with or without compensation. 255—peaceful methods[.] 256—good[.] 258—paradox of state socialism[.] 259— *quotations.* 262—quotations—excellent! 267—purchase by union of a statue[.] 276—*Gissing*[.]"

HYDE, WILLIAM DE Witt. *From Epicurus to Christ: A Study in the Principles of Personality.* New York: The Macmillan Company, 1905. viii, 285 pp., HL 337291

Contents: "The five centuries from the birth of Socrates to the death of Jesus produced five such principles: The Epicurean pursuit of pleasure, genial but ungenerous; the Stoic law of self-control, strenuous but forbidding; the Platonic plan of subordination, sublime but ascetic; the Aristotelian sense of proportion, practical but uninspiring; and the Christian spirit of love, broadest and deepest of them all.

"The purpose of this book is to let the masters of these same and wholesome principles of personality talk to us in their own words; with just enough comment and interpretation to bring us to their points of view, and make us welcome their friendly assistance in the philosophical guidance of life."—Preface.

Inscription: "To Jack & Charmian, with my love & happy memories of their tenderness & goodness to me. Always faithfully yours, Frederick I. Bamford. March 10—[']06.

By the first of July 1906, London had read this lengthy book and used it in a discussion of the Ruskin Club he was having with Bamford: "I quote the following from *Epicurus to Christ:* 'The reviling (shame) does not become a determining factor in my own mental state unless I choose to let it. If I feel humiliated and stung by it, it is because I am weak and foolish to stake my estimate of myself, and my consequent happiness upon what somebody who does not know me says about me, rather than on what I, who know myself better than anybody else, actually think.'

"Whatever is true of the individual and of yourself, should also be true of the Ruskin Club. With this big ethical principle to your mast, why should you deny it to the mast of the Ruskin Club?

"You were certainly false to the ethical principle you had nailed so high. To state that you had nailed this ethical principle to your mast, over thirty years ago, is no vindication of your having been false to it. There you are! Hip and thigh!" (Georgia Bamford, *Mystery*, p. 211).

London used the book again in *The Assassination Bureau, Ltd.*, placing a copy of the volume in the library of Ivan Dragomiloff (Sergius Constantine), chief of the bureau: "The front door closed behind them, and Winter Hall, stupefied, looked about him at the modern room in which he stood. He was more pervaded than ever by the impression of unrealness. Yet that was a grand piano over there, and those were the current magazines on the reading table. . . . He glanced at the titles of a table-rack of books—evidently Dragomiloff's. There incongruously cheek by jowl, were Mahan's *Problem of Asia*, Buckner's *Force and Matter*, Wells's *Mr. Polly*, Nietzsche's *Beyond Good and Evil*, Jacobs's *Many Cargoes*, Veblen's *Theory of the Leisure Class*, Hyde's *From Epicurus to Christ*, and Henry James's latest novel—all forsaken by this strange mind which had closed the page of its life on books and fared forth into an impossible madness of adventure." [40]

HYNDMAN, HENRY MAYERS. *The Record of An Adventurous Life.* New York: The Macmillan Company, 1911. xi, 422 pp., illus. HL 334422

Contents: Autobiography.
Marginalia: "122—shark episode" written on the rear endpaper.

IBSEN, HENRIK. *Lady Inger of Östrat. The Vikings At Helgeland. The Pretenders.* London: The Walter Scott Publishing Company, Limited, 1905. xvii, 379 pp., HL 337651 v. 3 1905

Contents: Three plays.
Inscription: "Dear Jack: I send you this book containing three works of varying degrees of greatness. *The Pretenders* to my mind is supreme as a whole tho' there are parts of *Lady Inger* that surpass it. They were written when Ibsen yet had the power (which is still yours) of seeing the whole world in one wide look, with the inner unerring sight of the poet. They are *his* 'Li Wan the Fair,' *his* 'Odyssey of the North,' *his* 'When God Laughs.' Then his eyes were towards the hills. He had not yet left the greater vision to sink sight in the man-made graves he etches for us in *Hedda Gabler* and *Little Eyolf.* Behold how infinitely greater is Hedda's prototype 'Hiordis' in *The Vikings* since she is conceived in the poet's sympathy and born of his genius—not drawn to scale as Hedda is. Look at such women as Lady Inger & see how pitiable a figure is even Mrs. Alving in *Ghosts* beside her. And for woman's love see Elina Gyldenlöve in *Lady Inger* and Ingeborg in *The Pretenders.* And wonder how a mere man could so comprehend The Allness of woman's love—and, having comprehended, could bend himself to the designing of Nora Helmers and Rebeccas. April 6th [']07. Constance Skinner."

Although London would later call Ibsen a "bourgeois lickspittler" in *The Mutiny of the Elsinore* (p. 96), in his earlier years he read quite a bit of the Scandinavian playwright. On 6 January 1901 London wrote to Anna Strunsky that he would "be glad to go in for the Ibsen circle. I need more of that in my life" (*Letters,* p. 21). And still in 1906, Charmian remembered London reading "numberless books of all sizes and titles, and we still found opportunity to share, aloud, H. G. Wells, de Maupassant, Gertrude Atherton, Sudermann, Phillpotts, Saleeby, Herbert Spencer, and countless others, including plays—among them Bernard Shaw's, Clyde Fitch's, Ibsen's;

and, above all, endless poetry. It is a curious jumble, I know; but Jack read rapaciously—both of the meatiest and the trashiest. He must know 'what the other fellow is doing'"(*Book of Jack London*, 1:123).

London also incorporates Ibsen's drama into *A Daughter of the Snows* (where Frona plays "Nora" in *A Doll's House*) and *The Mutiny of the Elsinore*.

IBSEN, HENRIK. *Letters of Henrik Ibsen*. New York: Fox, Duffield and Company, 1905. 456 pp., illus. HL 332469
Contents: Letters.
Bookseller: Paul Elder & Company, San Francisco.
Inscription: "Dear Jack—may this inspire you to 'attempt other attempts.' If not, you'll like it anyway. Blanche. Christmas, 1910."
A member of the "Crowd," Blanche Partington and London had a brief love affair in 1905.

IMRAY, JAMES FREDERICK. *Indian Ocean Pilot: The Seaman's Guide to the Navigation of the Indian Ocean*. London: James Imray & Son, 1886. 3 volumes, xcii, 1296 pp., illus. HL 337034
Contents: Sailing directions.
Marginalia: London was interested in the winds off the Cape of Good Hope, the winds in the Indian Ocean, and the Sey Chelle and Andaman islands.

IRVINE, ALEXANDER FITZGERALD. *From the Bottom Up: The Life Story of Alexander Irvine*. New York: Doubleday, Page & Company, 1910. x, 304 pp., illus. HL 334802
Contents: Autobiography.
Inscription: "To Jack London[.] My Dear Jack[.] You told me to write and I 'writ.' Here is installment number 1[.] Alexander Irvine[.] 1910[.]"
Alexander Irvine was an Irish-born socialist author and clergyman. When London met him in 1905, he was secretary of the Socialist Party of Connecticut and had, in that capacity, invited London to speak at Yale University. After the 1905 meeting, Irvine corresponded infrequently with London, occasionally sending him copies of books. *From the Bottom Up* contains a chapter recounting London's 1905 "Revolution" speech delivered at Yale. Irvine went on to become rector of St. Jude's Church in New York City.

IRVING, EDWARD. *How to Know the Starry Heavens: An Invitation to the Study of Suns and Worlds*. New York: Frederick A. Stokes Company, 1904. xvi, 307 pp., illus. HL 337219
Contents: "a careful selection of the most typical, interesting, and

instructive facts and theories concerning the Universe around us. The author has endeavored to describe and illustrate these in such a way as to attract, interest, and inform the general reader."— Preface.

Inscription: "To Jack London. With the Best wishes of the author, Edward Irving. Dec. 10. 1906. 1530 Shattuck Ave., Berkeley."

Marginalia: Passages that London marked include a description of the moon, the cluster of Hercules, an analysis of the laws of gravitation, and discussions of meteors and comets. His notes were taken in anticipation of a projected novel to be called *Farthest Distant:* "113—Farthest Distant[.] 169—power of attraction. 176[.] 219–20 etc.—for behavior of comet in space[.]"

JACOBSON, PAULINE. *A Fire-Defying Landmark.* San Francisco: Reprint from the *San Francisco Bulletin,* May 4, 1912. 15 pp., illus. HL

Contents: Short story.

Marginalia: "Fiction—San Francisco" written on front cover.

London categorized his voluminous pamphlet and clipping files by subject. "Fiction" was by far the largest category, containing hundreds of ideas for future stories and novels. This pamphlet deals with an episode that occurred after the 1906 San Francisco earthquake and fire.

JAMES, GEORGE WHARTON. *Heroes of California: The Story of the Founders of the Golden State as Narrated by Themselves or Gleaned from Other Sources.* Boston: Little, Brown and Company, 1910. 515 pp., illus. HL 981

Contents: Biographical sketches of California pioneers.

Marginalia: London put check marks beside the following books listed in the bibliography: *On the Trail of a Spanish Pioneer, The Personal Narrative of James O. Pattie, John Bidwell, History of the Donner Party, Death Valley in '49, Kit Carson's Life and Adventures, Seventy Years on the Frontier, Adventures of James Capen Adams, Mountaineering in the Sierra Nevada,* and Hittell's *History of California.* He also checked Leland's *The Life and Adventures of James P. Beckwourth,* and wrote beside it: "Ask about it. Is it the same one."

JAMES, GEORGE WHARTON. *Indian Basketry, and How to Make Indian and Other Baskets.* Pasadena, California: George Wharton James, 1903. 136 pp., illus. HL 338664

Contents: A history of and text for the making of baskets.
Inscription: "Dear Charmian: I send you this story of the work of struggling, striving, loving, thoughtful woman in her child days."
"My love & good wishes come with it, for I have sweet memories of your's and Jack's kindness & affection to me at Glen Elen. Ever your Comrade and Jack's, George Wharton James[.]"
An English-born explorer and interpreter of the southwestern United States, George Wharton James met Jack London in 1903. They soon became friends, and visited occasionally from 1905 to 1916. James later became editor of *Out West,* and published numerous books about the Southwest at his Pasadena-based press.

JAMES, GEORGE WHARTON. *The Rattlesnake Bite and How to Cure it.* Pasadena, California: George Wharton James, [1905?] 12 pp., illus. HL

Contents: Pamphlet describing the treatment of rattlesnake bites and poisoning.
Marginalia: London wanted to make sure that this pamphlet went with him on his four-horse driving trip: "World: Medicine Chest[.]"

JAMES, GEORGE WHARTON. *The Story of Scraggles.* Boston: Little, Brown and Company, 1906. vii, 88 pp., illus. HL 22908

Contents: Novel.
Inscription: "My Dear Jack. You whose heart goes out to all nature, from the highest to the lowest & who thoroughly & *really* lives the belief that we are akin to trees, rocks, birds & beasts, will gladly read this true story of my sweet little Scraggles. Your loving comrade[,] George[.]"

JAMES, WILLIAM. *The Varieties of Religious Experience: A Study in Human Nature Being the Gifford Lectures on Natural Religion Delivered at Edinburgh in 1901–1902.* New York: Longmans, Green & Company, 1911. xii, 534 pp., HL 336707

My Dear Jack,
You whose heart goes
out to all nature, from

The Story of Scraggles

the highest to the lowest,
& who thoroughly & really
lives the belief that we
are akin to trees, rocks,
birds & beasts will gladly
read this true story of my
sweet little Scraggles.
Your loving Comrade
George

Contents: "Religion and Neurology," "Circumscription of the Topic," "The Reality of the Unseen," "The Religion of Healthy-Mindedness," "The Sick Soul," "The Divided Self and the Process of Its Unification," "Conversion," "Saintliness," "The Value of Saintliness," "Mysticism," "Philosophy," "Other Characteristics," "Conclusion."

Marginalia: London marked many passages in this book, including paragraphs explaining James's theory on the meaning of religion, the controversy between religion and science, the history of early Greek morality, quotations from Tolstoy on religious melancholy, the sham of religious intellectualism, and James's belief that religion is caused by human egotism. He made cross references to Violet Pagét's *Gospels of Anarchy* on pages 118: "See Vernon Lee 198," and 122: "See Vernon Lee 198," and made brief mention of his "white logic" on page 141: "The white logic that enables us to see through all the vital lies whereby we live," made in reference to James's remarks on dying. On the rear pastedown London wrote: "491–2–3–95—Barleycorn. See Saltus'[s] *Philosophy of Disenchantment* for the whole list of the disenchanted thinkers[.]"

London made extensive use of this book for *John Barleycorn*. "How We Die: Sea captain, a la Chapman, lonely on ship of which he is lord and master, tries to read William James's *Varieties of Religious Experience* etc,"[41] and *The Mutiny of the Elsinore* (p. 75): "Sometimes I wonder what resides behind those clear blue eyes. Certainly I have failed to find any intellectual backing. I tried him out with William James's *Varieties of Religious Experience*. He glanced at a few pages, then returned it to me with the frank statement that it did not interest him. He has no books of his own. Evidently he is not a reader."

JAMES, WILLIAM. *The Will to Believe and Other Essays In Popular Philosophy.* New York: Longmans, Green, & Company, 1911. xvii, 332 pp., HL 336744

Contents: "The Will to Believe," "Is Life Worth Living?" "The Sentiment of Nationality," "Reflex Action and Theism," "The Dilemma of Determinism," "The Moral Philosopher and the Moral Life," "Great Men and Their Environment," "The Importance of Individuals," "On Some Hegelisms," "What Psychical Research Has Accomplished."

Marginalia: London wrote "The Why of Life" next to passages dealing with the risk of losing the truth. He also marked paragraphs discussing the impossibility of scientifically determined value, the definition of religion, and the concept of God. London made lengthy notations on the rear endpapers: "bondages of the will[.] marionettes of the belly & the loins.

"The cosmic ether[.] The gaseous invertibrates, etc. The flitting ghosts of gods, the dim-remembered duties in the day-dream of the world, the worships of the night, etc. etc. the brutal universe. p. 126—'Ignoramus, ignorabimus,' says agnosticism. All the weird gnosticisms, veils & tissues of words, ontological fantasies, from psychic hallucinations gibbering subjectivisms, groping & wanderings, the pulse of being[.] The beat of life. man wailing among shadows.

"The vital lies: That the strong is not vain[.] That there seems a special concern of the universe toward man. That man's destiny is somehow different from that of the other animals, and that the Noseless One, instead of waiting to drag him to the darkness of the grave, is in truth the way to life illumined, and more abundant."

The Will to Believe also appears in the *Mutiny of the Elsinore* (p. 55): "At four I lighted up and went to reading, forgetting my irritated skin in Vernon Lee's delightful screed against William James and his *Will to Believe.*"

JENSEN, JOHANNES VILHELM. *Braeen.* Copenhagen: Norsdisk Forlag, 1908. 294 pp., HL 338220

Contents: Novel.

Marginalia: London wrote: "Supposed to be a straight plagiarism of *Before Adam*" on the front cover.

JESSE, EDWARD. *Anecdotes of Dogs.* London: Henry G. Bohn, 1858. xvi, 491 pp., illus. HL 337234

Contents: Recollections of dogs and their behavior.

Marginalia: London made only one mark in this well-read book: a pencil marking on page 1. However, it seems quite evident that much of London's fictional characterizations of canine behavior came not only from his own pets but from the pages of this book.

Jack London and George Wharton James

JEVONS, WILLIAM STANLEY. *Studies in Deductive Logic: A Manual For Students.* London: Macmillan and Company, 1884. xxviii, 304 pp., illus. HL 336250

Contents: "In preparing these *'Studies'* I have tried to carry forward the chief purpose of my *Elementary Lessons in Logic,* which purpose was the promotion of practical training in Logic."—Preface.

Inscription: "Jack London[.] '1900' 1327—25th Ave[.] E. Oakland[.]"

Marginalia: London made many markings in this logic textbook. The format of the book is question-and-answer style, and London noted many of the discussions with his characteristic heavy pencil mark.

JOHNSON, EMILY PAULINE. *Legends of Vancouver.* Vancouver: David Spencer, Limited, 1911. xvi, 165 pp., illus. HL 332049 PF

Contents: "These legends (with two or three exceptions) were told to me personally by my honoured friend, the late Chief Joe Capilano, of Vancouver. . . ."—Author's Foreword.

Inscription: "Mr. and Mrs. London[.] With reminiscences of Waikiki Beach[.] T. S. H. Shearmen. Meteorological Office. Room 40, Post Office Building[,] Vancouver, B.C., Canada."

Enclosure: Newspaper clipping entitled: "Patriots of the Pacific," from the *Fielding Star,* 21 April 1915, page 2. At the top of the clipping is an inscription: "With the comps[.] of Tom L. Mills[,] Editor[.]" Clipping reads: "When the war is over! Many things are due when peace shall over all the earth again. One of the most interesting is that of which announcement is made in the issue just to hand of that splendid with-a-purpose publication the *Mid-Pacific Magazine,* which is printed in Honolulu. Editor Alex. Hume Ford announces a great big catch for the Hands-Around-the-Pacific Movement, of which Mr. Ford's magazine is the organ and booster. This catch is no less a personage than Jack London, who has once more been lured from his home in California to the South Sea Islands, which he voyaged with his bride on their honeymoon some few years ago, and out of which voyage the most forcible of America's novelists obtained much 'copy' which he has already converted into colourful stories. On his re-entry into the Pacific, Mr. London has acknowledged himself a keen convert to the Pacific Movement, with which he promises to closely identify all his personality and talents in the future. He has gone so far as to undertake, when the war is over, to participate in a Hands-Around-the-Pacific Movement tour. This delegation will touch at every land whose shores are washed by the Pacific Ocean, and Jack London will be the historian of the great cruise. Such a delegation may bank upon an enthusiastic reception when it reaches New Zealand."

JÓKAI, MÓR. *The Poor Plutocrats.* . . . New York: Doubleday & McClure Company, 1899. vii, 423 pp., HL 331775

Contents: "Essentially a tale of incident and adventure. . . ." —Preface.

Inscription: "Jack London." Also rubber stamp signature of Charmian Kittredge.

Marginalia: Jack and Charmian both marked passages in this book which illuminate Jókai's characterization and use of local color in description.

JORDAN, DAVID STARR. *To Barbara, with Other Verses.* Palo Alto, California: Printed for Private Use, 1897. 44 pp., HL 143858

Contents: Poems.

Inscription: "Mrs. Jack London, with the Kind regards of David Starr Jordan."

Jordan was the first president of Stanford University. Although London's early correspondence with Anna Strunsky and Cloudesley Johns indicated an affinity with Jordan's philosophy, he later rejected Jordan's writings as bourgeois.

JUNG, CARL GUSTAV. *Psychology of the Unconscious: A Study of the Transformations and Symbolisms of the Libido. A Contribution to the History of the Evolution of Thought.* Authorized Translation, with an Introduction by Beatrice M. Hinkle. New York: Moffat, Yard and Company, 1916. lv, 566 pp., illus. HL 336747

Contents: "Introduction," "Concerning the Two Kinds of Thinking," "The Miller Phantasies," "The Hymn of Creation," "The Song of the Moth," "Aspects of the Libido," "The Conception and the Genetic Theory of Libido," "The Transformation of the Libido: A Possible Source of Primitive Human Discoveries," "The Unconscious Origin of the Hero," "Symbolism of the Mother and of Rebirth," "The Battle for Deliverance from the Mother," "The Dual Mother Role," "The Sacrifice."

Marginalia: In reading this book shortly before his death, London made almost three hundred notations in it. Because of the influence Jung had on London, this is the most important book in his library. Surprisingly, he made relatively few notes at the back of the book: "P. xxvi—Libido defined—CKL." "15–16—sensuality of thought, of words, philosophy perfected animal sounds, the loneliness of the philosopher. 115–16—how, from libido of present man the genesis of Sun God still goes on. 165—good excerpts from the ancients of the symbolism of making fire by rubbing. 174—idem[.] 357–8–9—the hidden incest motif in the birth of Christ, the Light, the Sun God, reborn—the God reprocreating himself. 466—the sacrifice of the sacred horse symbolic of sacrifice of the world—a good illustration of symbolism for beginners."

During the last years of his life, London began to study psychology in depth, and, in turn, began to analyze himself in a similar context. He turned first to Freud, sometime after 1912, then to Jung in 1916 for the knowledge he had long needed and could now have. "I have quite a few books on psychoanalysis, which you could have access to any time you are visiting us," London wrote to Leo B. Mihan in a letter of 24 October 1916 (HL), "Also, I have just recently subscribed to the *Psychoanalytical Review*, which is a quarterly. Doctor Jung's book is a very remarkable book to me, and I do not hesitate to assert that you are no more excited about it than am I. It is big stuff. I used to rave to Hamilton about it when he was here." And to Charmian, London mentioned Jung in even stronger terms: "I tell you I am standing on the edge of a world so new, so wonderful, that I am almost afraid to look over into it" (Charmian London, *Book of Jack London*, 2:2).

The effects Jung and Freud had on London's literary output was very evident in his later work, and has been discussed at length in Earle Labor's *Jack London* and James McClintock's *White Logic*. Charmian, however, was cognizant of Jung's tremendous influence and, shortly after London died, invited Mary Wilshire, a student of psychology, to the ranch in order to analyze his markings in *Psychology of the Unconscious*. Together, Charmian and Wilshire made notes and copied those passages from Hinckle's introduction that characterized London's reading and grasp of Jung's book. Those notes were inserted in the back of *Psychology of the Unconscious*.

KALIDASA. *Translations of Shakuntala and Other Works by Arthur W. Ryder*. Evanston, Illinois: Thurland & Thurland, 1912. xxv, 216 pp., illus. HL 339170
Contents: Poems.
Marginalia: London marked two paragraphs describing the greatness of poetry.
Enclosure: Eight-page catalogue entitled: "Strange Books from the House of Gowrie."

KANNO, TAKESHI. *Creation-Dawn (A Vision Drama)*. Fruitvale, California: Takeshi Kanno, 1913. 63 pp., illus. HL 339613
Contents: Talks and meditations.

Inscription: "To the Seer of Glen Ellen and His Princess, With greet-ings, from Takeshi Kanno, The Hights[,] Oakland. August 11th[,] 1915."

KEELER, CHARLES AUGUSTUS. *A Light Through the Storm.* San Francisco: William Doxey, 1894. ix, 159 pp., illus. HL 1515

Contents: Poems.

Inscription: "Prof. John Fiske[.] With Compliments of the Author."

Keeler was a Berkeley poet, author, and naturalist whose acquaint-ances included a few of London's "Crowd": Herman Whitaker, James Hopper, and George Sterling. At the beginning of his career, Keeler made his name known through participation in the Harri-man expedition of 1899 to Alaska. After traveling around Cape Horn, and making a few other journeys to the South Seas, Keeler settled down in San Francisco, as director of the California Acad-emy of Sciences. London met him in Berkeley in 1899 or 1900.

KELLOGG, J. W. *Uses of Electricity on Shipboard.* New York: Ma-rine Engineering, 1904. 78 pp., illus. HL 337021

Contents: "The series of articles reprinted in the following pages were published to satisfy a demand for thoroughly practical infor-mation regarding the uses of electricity on shipboard, so that the man who has not had special electrical training, but who is called upon to care for an electric plant, can prepare himself for the work."—Preface.

London used this book to learn more about the *Snark's* generator.

KEYES, EDWARD LAWRENCE. *The Venereal Diseases, Including Stricture of the Male Urethra.* New York: William Wood & Company, 1880. xiii, 348 pp., illus. HL 336710

Contents: Medical book.

Marginalia: London marked paragraphs describing chancroid ul-cers, the symptoms of syphilis, vaccinal syphilis, the tertiary stage of syphilis, the treatment of syphilis with mercury, gonorrhea, and the treatment of gonnorhea.

London's large medical library included a number of sophisticated books about sex and sexual diseases, such as *The Treatment of Syphi-*

lis with Salvarsan or 606. Andrew Sinclair's *Jack: A Biography of Jack London* makes a strong case for London's belief that he suffered from the disease, and, more important, that he used the lethal remedies that the medical texts prescribed.

KILPATRICK, JAMES ALEXANDER. *Tommy Atkins at War, as Told in His Own Letters.* New York: McBride, Nast & Company, 1914. 127 pp., HL 334837

Contents: "This little book is the soldier's story of the war, with all his vivid and intimate impressions of life on the great battlefields of Europe."—Note.

Marginalia: London was quite interested in the personal emotions of man under conditions of war. He marked passages in this book dealing with that subject, including the sensation of freedom one has under fire, the humor in the trenches, and details of World War I trench warfare. London was specifically interested in passages on pages 1, 12, 28, 30, 33, 36, 40, 51, 55, 57, 62, 66, and 69, and recorded these page numbers on the rear endpaper.

KISH, ENOCH HEINRICH. *The Sexual Life of Woman in Its Physiological, Pathological, and Hygienic Aspects.* New York: Rebman Company, 1910. xi, 686 pp., illus. HL 336089

Contents: "In the following pages this sexual life of women will be considered both in relation to the female genital organs and in relation to the feminine organism as a whole."—Preface.

Marginalia: London marked a two-page passage dealing with feminine beauty.

KRAUSSE, ALEXIS SIDNEY. *The Far East: Its History and Its Question.* London: Grant Richards, 1903. xiv, 372 pp., illus. HL 333004

Contents: "The aim of the present volume is to afford in handy form a complete account of the history of the countries of the Far East, in so far as they have come into contact with Western Civilization." —Preface.

Inscription: "Jack London[.]"

Marginalia: In this background history of Korea, London noted passages about British imperialism in China, the contrast between China and Japan, an analysis of the Korean system of government, descriptions of the Chinese provinces, and Sino-Japanese friction. He also made a few notes on the endpapers: "Preface IX—Why China does not fear the Powers[.] Preface No. II-VI—Russian diplomacy superior to British. 4—Description of China's 18 provinces[.] 43—China & Japan quarreling over Corea in 1867[.] 47—China-Japanese War 1894[.] 48—Articles of treaty at conclusion of Chino-Jap War. 49—Protest of Powers and Japan recedes[.] 49—Secret Treaty between China & Russia. 137—The ulterior aim of Japan—what is it? 143—Corea—political & social constructive of[.] 199—Views of various authorities on the Far Eastern Question[.]"

"I[.] Just sum up the far Eastern Question. II[.] Japan as one of the Powers[.] III[.] Dalny[.] IV[.] Port Arthur[.] V[.] Wei Hai Wei[.] VI[.] Fusan Chung[.]"

KROPOTKIN, PETR ALEKSEEVICH, KNIAZ. *Fields, Factories and Workshops: Or, Industry Combined with Agriculture and Brain Work with Manual Work.* New York: G. P. Putnam's Sons, 1902. ix 259 pp., illus. HL 332045

Contents: "The following pages . . . contain a discussion of the advantages which civilized societies could derive from a combination of industrial pursuits with intensive agriculture, and of brain work with manual work."—Preface.

Marginalia: London's annotations concerned British agricultural statistics.

KROPOTKIN, PETR ALEKSEEVICH, KNIAS. *Memoirs of a Revolutionist.* London: Smith, Elder & Company, 1899. 2 volumes, xv, 258, 340 pp., illus. HL 332795

Contents: This "record of [Kropotkin's] . . . life contains the history of Russia during his lifetime, as well as that of the labour movement in Europe during the last half-century."—Preface.

Marginalia: London's interest centered on page 12 in the first volume, where he marked the paragraphs telling the story of Kropotkin's father, who received the cross for gallantry as a result of acts of bravery committed by his servant.

LADOFF, ISADOR. *American Pauperism and the Abolition of Poverty.* Chicago: Charles H. Kerr & Company, 1904. 230 pp. HL 336805

Contents: "An Appeal to the Reader: Pauperism and Poverty in the United States," "The Children of Poverty in the United States," "Pennsylvania Child Labor," "The Cause of Poverty in the United States," "The Industrial Evolution of the United States," "The Abolition of Poverty," "Supplement."

Marginalia: The conditions under which poor children live, child labor, the factory system, an account of a six-year-old boy working twelve hours a day, the case study of a fourteen-year-old candy dipper, and the base ignorance of factory workers are subjects that London noted in this book, marking them down for future reference on the endpapers: "64—Carmen—a child sufferer[.] 64—boys of the dumps[.] 75—child laborers in New Jersey[.] 78—child laborers in Southern cotton factories[.] 80—average age of starting to work—9 yrs—report of N.Y. Factory Inspector[.] 85—an instance (striking) of a child laborer[.] 94—instances of child laborers in Pa[.]"

London's opposition to child labor was vocal and persuasive, especially in his most notable short story on the subject: "The Apostate."

LAFARGUE, PAUL. *Social and Philosophical Studies.* Chicago: Charles H. Kerr & Company, 1906. 165 pp., HL 336742

Contents: "Causes of Belief in God," "The Origin of Abstract Ideas," "The Origin of the Idea of Justice," "The Origin of the Idea of Good."

Marginalia: London marked paragraphs that discussed the origin of abstract ideas, instinct, education, and the lack of interest in religion among the masses. On page 88 he noted a paragraph listing "great mathematicians" and on the previous page noted " Germany[.]"

LAMSZUS, WILHELM. *The Human Slaughter-House.* Evanston, Illinois: Thurland & Thurland, 1913. vii, 116 pp., HL 331724

Contents: "This book deals chiefly with the physical and mental horrors of war."—Introduction.

Marginalia: London marked a quotation from Emperor Frederick the Noble on the business of war, and the influence of technology and science on the battlefield.

LARKIN, EDGAR LUCIEN. *Radiant Energy and Its Analysis: Its Relation to Modern Astrophysics.* Los Angeles: Baumgardt Publishing Company, 1903. 335 pp., HL 275720

Contents: Scientific treatise on radiant energy.
Inscription: "To Jack London, With highest regards of the Author, Edgar L. Larkin. Lowe Observatory[,] May 21—[']06[.]"
Marginalia: London marked a passage dealing with the positions of the stars in the Southern Hemisphere.

Larkin was director of Lowe Observatories atop Echo Mountain, a few miles from Pasadena. As one of the most respected astronomers on the West Coast, he was the obvious expert to turn to with a controversy on stellar navigation, and London did just that in 1906. The book came as a "thank-you note" for Larkin's stay at the London ranch in April.

LAURIAT, CHARLES EMELIUS, JR. *The* Lusitania's *Last Voyage, Being a Narrative of the Torpedoing and Sinking of the* R.M.S. Lusitania . . . Boston: Houghton, Mifflin Company, 1915. vii, 158 pp., illus. HL 336860

Contents: Factual account of the sinking of the *Lusitania.*
Bookseller: Charles E. Lauriat Company, Importers & Booksellers, Boston.
Marginalia: London made several pencil marks on pages of this book, mostly concerning the sinking of the ship.

LECKY, SQUIRE THORNTON STRATFORD. *The Danger Angle, and Off-Shore Distance Tables.* London: George Philip & Son, Limited, 1905. xxvi, 138 pp., illus. HL 336143

Contents: Tables and handbook on navigation.
Bookseller: Louis Weule Company, Chronometers and Nautical Instruments, San Francisco, California.
Marginalia: The passage London marked in this book deals with the measurement of distance by using a mountain top visible on the horizon.

LECKY, SQUIRE THORNTON STRATFORD. *Wrinkles in Practical Navigation*. London: George Philip & Son, Limited, 1904. xxvii, 812 pp., illus. HL 336794 PF

Contents: "The particular aim of this treatise is to furnish seamen with thoroughly *practical* hints, such as are not found in the ordinary works on Navigation . . . ."—Preface.

Marginalia: In this heavily marked and annotated book on navigation, London noted passages explaining the irregular shape of the earth, a guide for the taking of azimuths and bearings, an explanation of the steering compass, chronometer, and sextant, how to use Mercator's chart, taking a bearing, using a horn protractor and string, the azimuth tables, the station pointer, dragging a lead, dead reckoning, compass errors, the Mariner's creed, the Azimuth mirror, barometer readings, equinoctial gales and Cape nor'westers, the constellations and observations of stars, including latitude by a star on the meridian, and "373–4—meridian altitude before hand for star[.]"

Enclosure: "Hurricanes" by R. L. Holmes. 20 November 1901. London wrote on this pamphlet: "run 24[.] southing 3.5[.] Westing 23.5 — 25 longitude[.]"

LEE, GERALD STANLEY. *Inspired Millionares: A Forecaste*. Northampton, Massachusetts: Mount Tom Press, 1908. 308 pp., HL 336811

Contents: "Part One (Which Says They Are Coming)," "Part Two (Which Considers Ways and Means)," "Part Three (Which Is Concerned with Signs and Tokens)."

Inscription: "With Love & Greetings to Jack London. Gerald Stanley Lee[.] Dec[.] 12[,] 1909[.]"

An ordained minister, Lee was a popular author of novels during London's day. He also lectured on literature and modern art at Smith College, and was editor of the Mount Tom Press in Massachusetts.

LEE, GERALD STANLEY. *The Voice of the Machines: An Introduction to the Twentieth Century*. Northampton, Massachusetts: The Mount Tom Press, 1906. iv, 190 pp., HL 331728

Contents: Novel.

Inscription: "To Jack London. Today, but especially Day After To-
morrow. Sincerely yours, Gerald Stanley Lee. Northampton[,]
Mass."

LE GALLIENNE, RICHARD. *Omar Repentant.* New York: Mitchell
Kennerley, 1903. 22 leaves. HL 339690
Contents: Poem.
Inscription: "For the Wolf[,] in memory of a Manhattan Night, from
the littlest of the Pack. M[ichael] M[onahan.] Jan[.] 17—1912."

LE GALLIENNE, RICHARD. *The Quest of the Golden Girl: A Ro-
mance.* New York: John Lane Company, 1910. x, 308 pp., HL
332122
Contents: Romance.
Inscription: "To Jack London and his golden girl from Richard and
Irma Le Gallienne, with love. January 12, 1912.
    "So Jack was born today! & we're
    d——d glad of it!
    All glory & joy of life, Jack & no
    sad of it—
    It's a good world, Jack take the
    lass-&-lad of it!"
English-born author Richard Le Gallienne was acquainted with
Jack London only through their mutual profession. Le Gallienne
was the author of numerous books, a few of which found their way
into London's library.

LEWIS, ALFRED HENRY. *Wolfville.* New York: Frederick A. Stokes
Company, 1887. 337 pp., illus. HL 332387
Contents: Tales of the Old Cattlemen.
Inscription: "153 Collins—S.F. Send Hoffman 500 Places Ms."
London refers here to James Knapp Reeve's *Five Hundred Places to
Sell Manuscripts,* which he did send to fledgling author Elwyn Hoff-
man. (*See* REEVE, JAMES KNAPP for a transcription of the letter Lon-
don wrote to Hoffman.)

LEWIS, ARTHUR MORROW. *The Struggle Between Science and Su-*

perstition. Chicago: Charles H. Kerr & Company, 1916. 188 pp., HL 337225

Contents: "The Antagonists," "Struggles in Greece," "Science in Alexandria," "Christians and Emperors," "The Alexandria Tragedy," "Bruno the Wanderer," "Bruno, the Martyr," "Galileo to 1616," "Trial and Sentence," "Recantation and After," "The Future."

Inscription: "Dear Jack London: My one regret in sending you this book of lectures is that you did not get to hear them as originally delivered by our good friend Comrade Lewis. And I hope you will get as much enjoyment out of reading them as I did in listening to them, which I cannot begin to describe. Your sincere Ralph Kasper[.] Nov. 7, 1915."

Socialist Ralph Kasper, who sold cigarettes by mail order for awhile, was one of London's many friends.

LEWIS, AUSTIN. *The Rise of the American Proletarian.* Chicago: Charles H. Kerr & Company, 1907. 213 pp., HL 336807

Contents: "The object of the following pages is to show briefly the causes of the origin of this proletarian class in the United States and to describe the mode in which it has made its existence manifest up to the present time."—Preface.

Inscription: "With my undying love, dear Jack. Fred."

Marginalia: London underlined only one sentence in this book. It appears on page 47: "the iron of the machine has eaten into the soul of the artisan."

Austin Lewis (whom London characterized as the best expert on historical socialism) was London's friend, mentor, and critic, especially during the days of the Oakland "Crowd." Lewis knew much about socialism, and it is likely that he (along with Frank Strawn-Hamilton) was an influential source of London's knowledge of the subject.

London finished reading *The Rise of the American Proletarian* 17 February 1908, and immediately wrote to Cloudesley Johns to praise it: "just finished Austin Lewis's *American Proletariat [sic]*. It's good stuff" (*Letters*, p. 257).

LEWIS, AUSTIN. *The Rise of the American Proletarian.* Chicago: Charles H. Kerr & Company, 1907. 213 pp., HL 336808

Contents: Origin and activities of the American proletarian class in America.

Inscription: "Jack London[.] With love & fraternal greetings[,] Austin Lewis[.] April, 1907[.] From the top of the list down to the bottom. With all that has happened between, of Marty & me & Jim Hopper[.] You'll be keeping the memory going."

Xavier "Marty" Martinez, James Hopper, and Austin Lewis were all (along with London) members of the original "Crowd" of East Bay artists, writers, and socialists.

LIEBKNECHT, WILHELM PHILIP CHRISTIAN MARTIN LUDWIG. *Karl Marx: Biographical Memoirs.* Chicago: Charles H. Kerr & Company, 1901. 181 pp., HL 336048

Contents: Memoirs.

Marginalia: London marked a paragraph describing some of the lies that were told about Marx's life.

LILIUOKALANI, QUEEN OF THE Hawaiian ISLANDS. *Hawaii's Story.* Boston: Lee and Shepard Publishers, 1899. viii, 409 pp., illus. HL 332600

Contents: Autobiographical reminiscences and accounts of Hawaiian history.

Marginalia: Charmian London made most of the markings in this book, except for a brief excerpt on page 213 describing Kalakaua's funeral.

LLOYD'S CALENDAR, 1908. London: Lloyd's, 1908. iv, 532 pp., illus. HL 336857

Contents: "Lloyd's Calendar is intended to furnish information of value to Officers of the Mercantile Marine, to Yachtsmen, and others."—Preface.

Inscription: "From C[.] Wooley[,] Mr. Jack London[.] Suva[,] 1908[.]"

Marginalia: London was interested in the length of degree in latitude and longitude, an explanation of the charts, and finding latitude and longitude at sea.

LOEB, JACQUES. *The Mechanistic Conception of Life: Biological Essays*. Chicago: The University of Chicago Press, 1912. 232 pp., illus. HL 336729

Contents: Philosophical essays.

Bookseller: Smith Brothers, Oakland, California.

Marginalia: London was interested in the first two essays in this book: "The Mechanistic Conception of Life" and "The Significance of Tropisms for Psychology." He marked paragraphs explaining the beginnings of scientific biology, the definition of life and death, chromosomes and heredity, a definition of ethics, and the physico-chemical explanation of psychic phenomena.

LONDON, JACK. *Adventure*. New York: The Macmillan Company, 1911. viii, 405 pp., HL 12697

Contents: Novel.

Enclosure: Letter from George Darlishire to Jack and Charmian London, dated 30 April 1911. Darlishire pointed out the following errors in *Adventure:* "page 7. No man suffering from dysentery would be carried on a Sol[oman] I[s]l[and] Native's back. It would be infinitely easier to walk with an arm round the boy's neck. (The case you are thinking of was Bernays, at Langa, who had a poisoned foot & could not bear to place same on the ground. I was laid up at the same time with dysentery & when I got really bad, just getting out of bed & back again gave me such pain that I could not move at all for about 2 minutes until after swallowing chloradyne which Bernays used to have ready for me on every such occasion. I could not have hung on to a boy's neck to save my life.

"p 8. 4th line from Bottom. 'shrieks & screams' should be 'wails & moans'

"p 10. 6—B. No man weak with dysentery would strike with his hand.

"15. 8—T. Lavo is not visible from P[en]d[u]f[ry]n verandah. (Immaterial anyway though)[.]

"17. 12—T Never been a case yet where runaways returned on their own account.

"18. 3—B. full moon rises over the village of Tasimloko on Guadalcanal not Malaita, & *at 6-0* P.M. punctually."

"22. The Chief of Tasimloko village would probably catch Malaita runaways as they would make for Marah. Balesuna is to the West.

"25. 12—B. Woman & picanninies were never assembled at floggings.

"27. 12—B. "'to fella whip three times' should read '3 ten,' but excessive 15 was limit at P[en]d[u]f[ry]n & in 50% cases such natives were in a fainting condition & *also* in 90% were not shrieking natives, taking punishment in dead silence.

"27. I never heard of a native doing the flogging, I don't think you could get a malaita boy to flog another even under the threat of a rifle.

"28. Any sign of amusement most improbable under the circumstances.

"37[.] 6—T[.] 'Cane press' should read 'leave of Ivory nut–palm' (sago palm). A N. W. swell would have been better indication of approaching N. W. than barometer.

"40[.] 2—B. There was no prayer book at P[en]d[u]f[ry]n."

"43. 2—T. The Jessie would have been waiting for wind to come & the moment it struck her, the anchor would have been weighed. 2 anchors down in a N[.] W[.] would mean that she was unable to get out & meant to ride it through.

"p. 43[.] 4 from Bt. Berande shoal, not Balesurua, anyway the shoal only exists on the chart & not in nature.

"p. 44. dysentery as a rule disappears after heavy rain, not after wind. dysentery epidemics occur usually during the dry portions of S[.] E[.] Season.

"Most improbable for a vessel to go ashore when running before in N[.] W[.] to Neal Bland.

"p. 47. 13 from T. A whale boat caught in N[.] W[.] off Florida would very probably turn up at P[en]d[u]f[ry]n. It has happened."

"p[.] 91[.] 1 from Bt. Breakfast at P[en]d[u]f[ry]n at 11–0 A[.]M[.]

"p[.] 283[.] 1 & 2 from Btm. In any such case the gang would be separated into different gangs.

"These are a few of the mistakes I noticed on reading it through the first time . . ."

LONDON, JACK. *Before Adam*. New York: The Macmillan Company, 1907. vii, 242 pp., illus. HL 5714

Contents: Short novel.

Enclosure: Postcard from Ernst Haekel, 8 July 1907, thanking London for a copy of *Before Adam.* Also, original pencil sketch by Charles Livingston Bull, illustrator of *Before Adam.*

LONDON, JACK. *Burning Daylight.* New York: The Macmillan Company, 1910. v, 361 pp., illus. HL 12760

Contents: Novel.

Enclosures: Magazine clipping: "Rhymed Reviews. Burning Daylight by Arthur Guiterman." Also a letter from George Sterling to Charmian London which mentions that Sterling saw "Uncle Frank this morning and talked *Burning Daylight* with him. He begs me 'for Christ's sake' to tell Jack that the portrayal gave him nothing but pleasure and interest."

LONDON, JACK. *The Call of the Wild.* New York: The Macmillan Company, 1903. 231 pp., illus. HL 337700

Contents: Novella.

Enclosures: Photograph of the Bond brothers, and Buck tipped onto verso of frontispiece. London wrote "Buck." "Atavism" (poem) by John Myers O'Hara has been tipped onto page 14. The poem was originally published in *The Bookman,* November 1902.

LONDON, JACK. *The Cruise of the Snark.* New York: The Macmillan Company, 1911. xiv, 340 pp., illus. HL 337699

Contents: Essays.

Enclosures: Clipping from *The Evening News* [Sydney], 21 December 1912: "Dying Out. New Hebrides Natives. . . ." Letter from George Darlishire, 7 July 1910, concerning the *Snark.* Poem by Elwyn Hoffman: "A Chant of the Wanderers." Clipping: "The Robber Crab of the South Sea Islands." "Description of Yacht *Snark.*" Chronometer Method. "The Story of Captain Weaver's Gold." "A Brief Explanation [of the abandonment of the *Snark* voyage]."

LONDON, JACK. *A Daughter of the Snows.* Philadelphia: J. B. Lippincott Company, 1902. 334 pp., illus. HL 337691 PF

Contents: Klondike Novel.

Marginalia: London marked paragraphs on pages 7, 8, 16, 17, 32, 33, 39, 40, 66, 67, and 69.

Enclosures: Two letters from Del Bishop, a Klondike miner, relating to his experiences in the Klondike in 1904. Also typewritten copy of the song lyric: "The Moon Shone Bright on the Wabash. . . ." (written by Paul Dresser).

LONDON, JACK. *The Faith of Men and Other Stories.* New York: The Macmillan Company, 1904. v, 286 pp., illus. HL 12701

Contents: Short stories.

Enclosure: Newspaper clipping: "Hangs Himself at Rampart. John Snell, Formerly of Sausalito, Commits Suicide. Seattle (Wash.), March 18.—H. J. Mignery of Great Barrington, Mass., who arrived from Skagway last night direct from the Minook district, reports the suicide by hanging at Rampart City of John Snell, a resident of Sausalito, Cal. Samuel Fertig, a partner in mining ventures, returned to the cabin after an absence of several days and saw on a card pinned to the door the words "Gone Out." Forcing an entrance, Fertig saw Snell suspended by a wire rope from a rafter of the cabin cold in death. It was his second attempt at self-destruction. Snell left San Francisco last July with 1,500 dozen eggs with which he hoped to reach Dawson. Low water prevented his getting beyond Rampart, and there he found that a majority of the eggs had spoiled. Brooding over this misfortune drove him to suicide. He has a son and a daughter residing at Sausalito."

LONDON, JACK. *The Game.* New York: The Macmillan Company, 1905. 182 pp., illus. HL 337698

Contents: Novel.

Enclosures: Clipping from San Francisco *Sunday Call:* "The Conquering Hero As He Sees Himself" by Helen Dare. Clipping from San Francisco *Examiner,* 10 September 1905, page 41: "Britt Knocked Out by Nelson." Clipping from San Francisco *Examiner,* August 1905: "Jimmy Britt Reviews *The Game.*" Letter from London to the Editor of the New York *Saturday Times,* 18 August 1905 complaining about their attack on the realism of *The Game* and defending it.

LONDON, JACK. *The God of His Fathers, & Other Stories.* New

York: The Macmillan Company, 1901. 299 pp., illus. HL
337697

Contents: Short stories.

Marginalia: London marked the contents pages beside "The God of
His Fathers," "Which Make Men Remember," and "The Grit of
Women." He also marked paragraphs on pages 223, 258, 259, 262,
288, 289, 293, 294, 295, 296, and 297.

Enclosures: Two letters from Freada Maloof (a Klondike Dance-hall
girl) to London dated San Francisco, 10 July 1903, and Seattle, 2
August 1903, conveying greetings to London and admiration for
his book.

London's annotations were made for a dramatic version of *Scorn of
Women*.

LONDON, JACK. *The House of Pride and Other Tales of Hawaii.*
New York: The Macmillan Company, 1912. v, 232 pp., illus.
HL 12753

Contents: Short stories.

Enclosures: Clipping from San Francisco *Chronicle,* 26 August 1916.
London wrote at top of clipping: "Stick into *House of Pride* my shelf
copy, at beginning or end of story entitled 'Chun Ah Chun.'":
"Death of Judge Humphreys Removes Island Legal Light. It Also
Marks Passing Within Month of Second Son-in-Law of Chun
Afong, Wealthy Chinese. Honolulu (H.T.), August 25.—The death
here of Judge A. S. Humphreys, one of the most prominent members of the Hawaiian bar, marks the passing of the second within a
month of the sons-in-law of the late Chun Afong, wealthy Chinese, twelve of whose thirteen daughters were married to prominent white men.

"Judge Humphreys died last Sunday, after an illness of several
weeks, and after improvement in his condition had led to hope of
his recovery.

"Humphreys was appointed Judge of the Circuit Court in Honolulu just after the annexation of the islands to the United States. His
attempt to revise the rules and practices of the Hawaiian bar caused
a bitter attack upon him by some of the lawyers, who carried the
matter to Washington. The prominence given the affair made Judge
Humphreys at the time a national figure. He went to Washington in

his own behalf and was upheld by Attorney-General Knox."

LONDON, JACK. *The Iron Heel.* New York: The Macmillan Company, 1908. xiv, 354 pp., illus. HL 337696 PF
Contents: Novel.
Enclosures: Clippings from the Oakland *Tribune,* 17 July 1909: "The Deadly Parallel drawn on Jack London" and "I am a Sucker, But Not Thief." (Charmian London wrote at top: "Book Room. *The Iron Heel.* Plagiarism.") Clipping from *Colliers,* 26 June 1909: front page (London wrote at top: "Refer to the Quarryman—Chapter VIII)." Clipping from the New York *World,* 11 March 1911: *"The Iron Heel."* Letter from W. G. Henry to London, dated Oakland, 10 March 1911, enclosed, in which Henry states that he has "taken the liberty to dramatize . . . [*The*] *Iron Heel* into three acts for the Socialists of Oakland." Also, a letter from London to Comrade Harris, 26 October 1914, stating: "There's no use in suggesting my writing another book of that sort [*The Iron Heel*]. It was a labor of love, and a dead failure as a book. The book-buying public would have nothing to do with it, and I got nothing but knocks from the socialists."

LONDON, JACK. *The Kempton-Wace Letters.* New York: The Macmillan Company, 1903. 256 pp., illus. HL 337693
Contents: Fictional collection of letters.
Enclosure: Poem entitled "The Passionate Author to His Love" by Puck.

LONDON, JACK. *Love of Life and Other Stories.* New York: The Macmillan Company, 1907. v, 265 pp. HL 12705
Contents: Short stories.
Marginalia: "By the way, 'Keesh the Son of Keesh' & 'Story of Keesh' are different. I think you have pinned on page of latter data that belongs to former."
London's note was probably intended for his secretary, Jack Byrne.

LONDON, JACK. *Love of Life and Other Stories.* New York: The Macmillan Company, 1906. v, 265 pp. HL 406409

Contents: Short stories.
Bookseller: John F. Hendsey.
Inscription: "Jack London. Glen Ellen, Sonoma Co., Cal. Sep[.] 10, 1906[.] Joan London. Hartford—February 17—1930[.] Dear Uncle Charley: When did you say you were going to vote the socialist ticket? Jack London[.]"

LONDON, JACK. *Martin Eden.* New York: The Macmillan Company, 1909. 411 pp., illus. HL 337692
Contents: Semiautobiographical novel.
Enclosures: Open letter from London to the Reverend Charles Brown, 17 June 1910, defending *Martin Eden* as an attack on individualism. Also letter from William T. Holmes to Jack London, 4 January 1911, stating that "unless I am greatly mistaken some of the characters in *Martin Eden* are real living persons, and have been also my most intimate friends and comrades." Article written by London, "My Faith," published in *The Workingman's Paper,* 18 June 1910, and letter from London to *The Workingman's Paper* dated 5 June 1910.

LONDON, JACK. *The People of the Abyss.* New York: The Macmillan Company, 1903. xiii, 319 pp., illus. HL 337689
Contents: Sociological study.
Marginalia: London marked paragraphs on pages 142, 148, 157, 192, 196, 202, 210, 215, 216, 218, 219, 220, 221–27, 230, 231, 250, 251, 256, 260, 267–69, 292–96, 302, and wrote on page 310: "I want to say right here, that I do not think there is one of you who is not riding—blood of sweatshops on your clothing."
Enclosures: Poem entitled "At London's Edge" by George H. Maitland. Also clipping from January 1905 San Francisco *Call:* "Poor of London Are Ready to Battle for Bread."

LONDON, JACK. *Revolution and Other Essays.* New York: The Macmillan Company, 1910. ix, 309 pp., illus. HL 12709 PF
Contents: Essays.
Enclosure: Four-page pamphlet: "What They Think of Crime and Criminals." Los Angeles: Prison Reform League.

LONDON, JACK. *The Road.* New York: The Macmillan Company, 1907. xii, 224 pp., illus. HL 12708 PF
Contents: Short stories.
Enclosures: Letter from ex-member of the United Brew Workers Union to London. Letter from Eugene J. McCarthy to London, 19 October 1894.

LONDON, JACK. *The Sea-Wolf.* New York: The Macmillan Company, 1904. vii, 366 pp., illus. HL 12696
Contents: Novel.
Enclosures: "Wolf Larsen." Poem by Thomas E. Winecoff dated 27 June 1910. Also newspaper clipping: "Romance of Seal Riding. Men Who Have Made Literature in The North Pacific. Real Exploits of the Men Who Are the Heroes of Tales and Poems by Kipling, Jack London and Others—Their Places Taken Now by the Japanese."
". . . Clustered in the upper harbor of Victoria, their mooring chains rusting, their hulls cracking, lies a fleet of some sixty sealing schooners, few of which have been sent out for some years now. If these schooners had voices they could tell tales of many adventures of daring raids on faraway seal rookeries of smuggling—for some of them were once smuggling craft carrying opium and contraband Chinese—of many romantic cruises.
"Some are famous craft. The *Casco* was the schooner which Robert Louis Stevenson made his notable South Sea cruise; the *Vera* was the mysterious smuggler *Halcyon,* the *Thomas F. Bayard* was a New York pilot boat. Alex McLean, the 'Sea Wolf' of Jack London, the hero of the late Frank Norris stories of the 'Three Black Crows,' now master of a prosaic harbor tugboat was one of the best known of the sealers who achieved notoriety. A Nova Scotian, like most of the more noted sealers, Sandy McLean, with his tremendous mustache, burst upon the waterfront of San Francisco about a quarter century ago and engaged in many seafaring adventures.
"He was first of the sealers to penetrate into Bering Sea with his schooner *City of San Diego.* He went treasure hunting in the *Sophie* [*sic*]*Sutherland,* following a will of the wisp to the Solomon Islands. . . . The treasure hunting expedition was a failure, for the Dane had given *The Sea-Wolf* a gold brick. . . .

"Then the adventurer turned to Bering Sea and the Russian seal islands, defying the revenue cutters of the Czar and Uncle Sam. . . . He succeeded in disabling the Czar's patrol boat by throwing a chain over her screw. . . ."

LONDON, JACK. *The Son of the Wolf.* Boston: Houghton Mifflin and Company, 1900. 251 pp., illus. HL 21717

Contents: Short stories.

Inscription: "Dear Jim [Whitaker]—A true Son of the Wolf, receive this in seal of blood brotherhood from one of the pack. London."

Enclosures: Two pictures of Jack London. Poem by George Sterling read at London's funeral. Letter from London to Herman Whitaker, New York City, 23 July 1902:"I was most grieviously disappointed in my S. A. trip. But shall cross over to England & the Continent for a couple of months.

"Mr. O. J. Smith, American Press Association. 45 Park Place, New York City.

"I recommend you to him today, in reply to his desire for humorous stories—which I imagine are similar to those accepted by *Harpers.*

"He is starting a magazine, & wants good stuff for it. Don't think of sending him anything but good stuff. You see, it was for this magazine that I was to be sent to S. A.—& so you can see that connection with him may be valuable, especially if the thing arrives, & anyway as President of the Am. Press Ass."

LONDON, JACK. *The Star-Rover.* New York: The Macmillan Company, 1915. 329 pp., illus. HL 12704

Contents: Novel.

Enclosures: Clipping bearing the following notes: "Paste into *Star Rover*—my shelf copy." "20 years after Jack's death I found this note home, and now, in 1936, I do his request. Charmian London." Also, "The Star Rover Dedicated to the Hero of Jack London's *Star Rover'* by Sing Sing no. 65368. Also newspaper clipping with the following notes: "'The Star Rover' Am. title. 'The Jacket.' Eng." and London's notes for *The Star Rover:*

"BIG NOVEL—Some day write great prison story of Ed Morrell. BEGINNING with how he came up from Mexico and met Joe

King and Diamond Nell, on to love affair with Evans's daughter. Meets King in Folsom. LATER meets him in San Quentin—coaching him, and warning him what to avoid when he got out. Follow Morrell's history closely, to his own emergence, and regaining of health, and going after scalps of men and women who injured him in prison. Morrell—landing at Ferry—alone, lonely, stunned by speed of people. Had never seen automobiles nor motor cycles—all the world whirling. Goes into a saloon. Sits at table. Orders whiskey and beer; turns his stomach. On street again, frightened—carrying suit case. Another saloon—sits and cries. Goes to ferry and catches boat to Oakland—then Davy Crockett Saloon. In bed six weeks. Then mountains. 22 weeks alone. Well, starts back—typhoid tent, etc., etc.

"Christ Novel. Barrabas—Marie Corelli. Page 17. Description of Christ's trial before Pilate. Emphasize the passion-distorted faces of the straining mob; the stern disreagrd [sic] of Pilate; the imperturbable Roman soldiers; the passivity of Christ—paint a picture, trenchant, clear-cut, short, striking. Don't capitalize adjectives, pronouns, etc. of Christ's. Just the same as with any ordinary mortal. On the night he was captured he was briefly tried by the Sanhedrim at the house of Caiaphas the high-priest; also before the tetrarch, Herod. The next day he was taken before Pilate, evidently in the morning. Look up Roman soldiers' accouterments. Get Josephus from Whittaker. See Bessie about some books she has on it."

"*Star Rover* Episode—he condensed in it the novel he had planned. I asked him about it. Charmian."

"CHRIST NOVEL. Keynote and words, apart at beginning of 'Christ Novel;' 'There is only one thing more wonderful than the reality of Christ, and that is, Christ never existing, that the imagination of man should have created him.' Copy[.]"

Clipping: "How to Handle Men, A Practical Application of the New Penology." "Put in front of my— *Star Rover.*"

LONDON, JACK. *Tales of the Fish Patrol*. New York: The Macmillan Company, 1905. 243 pp., illus. HL 12763 PF
Contents: Short stories.
Enclosures: "List of Books By Jack London." Note at top written by

Charmian London: "Put in J. L.'s 1st Edition." Also a note on the "list" by London, with arrow pointing to *Tales of the Fish Patrol:* "Translated 3 stories from this book without my permission; and I am now going after the publisher." Also enclosed is a letter dated 9 March 1903 from London to the *Youth's Companion* explaining the actual conditions on which the *Fish Patrol* stories were built.

LONDON, JACK. *The Valley of the Moon.* New York: The Macmillan Company, 1913. 530 pp., illus. HL 12752
Contents: Novel.
Enclosure: Advertising pamphlet issued by the *Cosmopolitan Magazine.*

LONDON, JACK. *What Life Means to Me.* Chicago: Charles H. Kerr & Company, 1906. 21 pp., HL 426332
Contents: Essay.
Marginalia: Marginal scoring beside passage on page 8 recounting London's days as a work beast.

LONDON, JACK. *White Fang.* New York: The Macmillan Company, 1906. vii, 327 pp., illus. HL 11561 PF
Contents: Novel.
Enclosure: "White-Fang is conceived Feb. 1. White-Fang is born April 3. White-Fang is blind for 21 days. White-Fang finished suckling by June 5. Had begun to eat meat (disgorged by mother) by May 3. He quit his mother for good in December. Was grown in three years[.] Lived 15 years[.]"
"WOLF. Average length 4 ft. Average tail 17 to 20 inches[.] Average height at shoulder 27 to 29 inches[.] Timber-wolf, buffalo-wolf, etc.—are all different names for the gray wolf, as distinguished from the prairie wolf or coyote[.] The gray wolf commonly sports reddish and blackish individuals. Maybe the mother of White-Fang had a moderately red tinge; his father was the regular gray wolf. White Fang himself was gray, but with reddish tints and glints in his full coat."
"The Wolf. In spring and summer wolves are solitary or in pairs, in the autumn in families, and in winter in packs. The pairing season is in December and January, when the males fight savagely to-

gether; those who are fortunate enough to secure a mate remain with her till the young are well grown. The young are born in burrows usually excavated by the wolves themselves, and during her confinement the female is fed by the male. The period of gestation is 63 days, and from 3 to 9—(usually 4 to 6) cubs are found in a litter; these are blind for 21 days, and are suckled for 2 months, but at the end of one month are able to eat half-digested flesh disgorged by the mother. They quit the parents in November or December, but many remain together 6 or 8 months longer. They are fully grown in 3 years, and live from 12 to 15 years. *Encyclopedia Americana* Article: 'Wolf.'"

Frederick Irons Bamford wrote the above in response to a query London posed.

LUBBOCK, ALFRED BASIL. *Round the Horn Before the Mast.* New York: E. P. Dutton & Company, 1902. x, 375 pp., illus. HL 337223

Contents: "Frisco," "Oakland Creek and Porta Costa," "The North Pacific," "The South Seas," "Running Easting Down," "Off the Horn," "The South Atlantic," "In the Tropics," "The Western Ocean," "In British Waters."

Marginalia: London was interested in the chorus of Duckfoot Sue, Captain Slocum, a list of sea chanties, and a fresh-water allowance for sailors. He recorded these in notes on the endpaper: "slab-footed Swede. blue-nose[.] blending a squaresail—57[.] shanty—75[.] songs—101[.] song for pulling on a rope—11[.] song of the tradewind—116[.]   Chanty—206[.]   Chanty—227–228–229[.] Chanty—244–246[.] Reuben Ranzo—342[.] Sally Brown—370[.] Leave her Johnnie—371[.]"

LYDSTON, GEORGE FRANK. *The Blood of the Fathers: A Play in Four Acts.* Chicago: The Riverton Press, 1912. 241 pp., HL 337678

Contents: Four-act play dedicated to Jack London, describing the degeneration of man.

Inscription: "To Jack London, From G. Frank Lydston. With deep admiration and profound esteem. May 20th[,] 1912[.]"

LYDSTON, GEORGE FRANK. *Sex Hygiene for the Male and What to Say to the Boy.* Chicago: The Riverton Press, 1912. 304 pp., illus. HL 336085

Contents: Popular treatise on sex hygiene.

Inscription: "To Jack London. With regards of G. Frank Lydston[.]"

LYNCH, JEREMIAH. *Three Years in the Klondike.* London: E. Arnold, 1904. 280 pp., illus. HL 55678

Contents: Description of the author's adventures in the Klondike.

Ex-senator Jeremiah Lynch traveled to the Klondike to seek gold, and wound up writing about others who found it instead. His book was a popular, entirely readable account of the strike, and London used it, in part, for his short story "To Build a Fire": "*KLONDIKE.* (A Study) Of a strong man wetting his feet, freezing to death in struggling to make a fire. (*See* Lynch's *Three Years in Klondike,* pages 64, 65, 66" ("To Build a Fire: Notes," HL).

The passage which London marked in this book was a particularly powerful one, and it is not surprising that, after reading it, London decided to revise his juvenile story of the same name: "The day after (November 18) there came to us at Dawson the news of a dreadful death. . . . A miner was walking up the Klondike ten miles from here going to his claim. . . . It was only 6 inches of water that the miner stepped into, and in a moment he was out, and hastening to the brush hard by, started to light a fire: for the clothes freeze, the feet freeze, and in five minutes one may find that part of his body and garments which has been immersed in water, through only a few inches deep, as rigid as solid steel. Rapidly he cut a few fragments of wood with his heavy pocket-knife. But the unlighted match dropped from his already chilled fingers, for he had rashly removed his mitts in order to use the knife with more freedom. Then he lighted a second and a third, and finally several at one time; but either his haste, or perhaps a sigh of the air, caused them to fall on the ever-ready snow. And all this time the frost was seizing his limbs, his body, his heart, his mind. He turned to the fatal mitts, which he never should have taken off; but his already frozen fingers could only lift them from the ice where they had fallen, and after a vain attempt he hurled them from him, and strove once again to light a last match. But it was too late."

LYONS, NORBERT. *Lays of Sergeant Conn*. Manila: Times Press, 1914. vii, 117 pp., illus. HL 337669
Contents: Poems.
Inscription: "Honolulu, May 17, 1916[.] To Jack London, Writer of Man's Stories—who, I hope, will be imbued with a small hankering to visit the Pearl of the Orient after reading this little volume—with compliments of the author, Norbert Lyons[.]"

McCARTHY, JUSTIN HUNTLY. *A History of Our Own Times, From the Accession of Queen Victoria to the General Election of 1880*. Chicago: Thompson & Thomas, Publishers, 1887. 2 volumes, iv, 591 pp., illus. HL 334511(v.1)
Contents: General history of England.
Marginalia: London marked a paragraph about William the Conquerer. He also noted the book in his "Flight of Duchess" (HL): "See Justin McCarthy's *History of Our Own Times* for political & parliamentary data."

MACDONALD, ALEXANDER. *The Island of Traders: A Tale of the South Seas*. London: Blackie and Son Limited, 1909. 292 pp., illus. HL 332058
Contents: Novel.
Inscription: "To Mr. Jack London with kindest Regards from Alexander MacDonald[.] Sydney[.] Jan[.] 8 1908[.] [*sic*]Coo-ee!"

MACDONALD, ALEXANDER. *The Lost Explorers: A Story of the Trackless Desert*. London: Blackie & Son Limited, 1907. 380 pp., illus. HL 332057
Contents: Novel.
Inscription: "To Mr. Jack London[.] With the Author's Kindest Wishes. Alexander MacDonald[.] Sydney[,] Jan[.] 8 / 1900[.]"

MACGILLIVRAY, E. J. *A Treatise Upon the Law of Copyright in the United Kingdom and the Dominions of the Crown, and in the United States of America*. London: John Murray, Albemarle Street, 1902. 403 pp., illus. HL
Contents: Guide to international copyright law.

Marginalia: London marked passages dealing with the assignment of copyrights, infringement of dramatic copyright, prohibited acts, and copyright ownership.

MacKaye, James. *The Economy of Happiness.* Boston: Little, Brown and Company, 1906. xv, 533 pp., illus. HL 336727
Contents: "The present work aims to be a contribution to the English school of philosophy."—Preface.
Inscription: "To Jack London[.] greetings from his friend[,] Percy MacKaye[.] Feb[.] 1 / 11[.]"
Poet and dramatist Percy MacKaye was one of Cloudesley Johns's cousins.

MacKaye, Percy. *Fenris, the Wolf: A Tragedy.* New York: The Macmillan Company, 1905. 150 pp., HL 274452
Contents: Drama.
Inscription: "The Wolf, 'him who was brought forth a glorious miscarriage of the gods to be exalted to a man.' Dear Jack—To my friend[,] From your friend[,] Constance [Skinner]. July[,] 1906."
Marginalia: London marked the speech of Thordis on page 117.

McNamara, Robert Emmette. *Chiropractic: Other Drugless Healing Methods.* Davenport, Iowa: Universal Chiropractic College, 1913. 395 pp., illus. HL 336135
Contents: Text extolling the benefits of chiropractic.
Inscription: "Compliments of the author[,] R. E. McNamara to Jack London[.]"

Maeder, Alphonse E. *The Dream Problem.* New York: The Nervous and Mental Disease Publishing Company, 1916. 43 pp., HL
Contents: Psychology text discussing dream analysis.
Marginalia: London marked a paragraph on artists and a number of passages describing the function of dreams.

Maeterlinck, Maurice. *Wisdom and Destiny.* New York: Dodd, Mead and Company, 1903. xxi, 353 pp., HL 332009

Contents: "In this book morality, conduct, life are surveyed from every point of the compass, but from an eminence always."— Introduction.

Bookseller: Smith Brothers, Oakland, California.

Marginalia: Most of the marginalia were made by Charmian; however London marked paragraphs on wisdom, sacrifice, religion, and the illusion of God, and noted them on the rear endpaper: "177–188[.]"

London enjoyed Maeterlinck's works enough to have portions of them copied out for circulation among his friends. In a letter to Frederick Bamford, dated 2 August 1905, he mentions the philosopher: "Do you care much for Maeterlinck? I have some more beautiful excerpts from him, which I shall be sending you in a couple of days—as soon as they are typed out.

"Do you know the thing that startles and surprises and satisfies me these days? It is, that the big men of the world all agree as to how life should be lived, no matter how much they disagree about the meaning and essence of life. Take, for instance, three divergent thinkers such as Nietzsche, Maeterlinck, and Schopenhauer. I have been reading a good deal of them recently, and they agree—quite, quite agree" (Georgia Bamford, *Mystery*, pp. 193–94).

MAITLAND, EDWARD. *The Pilgrim and the Shrine, Or, Passages from the Life and Correspondence of Herbert Ainslie, B. A.* New York: G. P. Putnam & Sons, 1871. 471 pp., illus. HL 334501

Contents: Autobiography.

Marginalia: London's interest in this book was centered on page 416, where he marked a paragraph discussing the divinity of Christian worship.

MANN, ALEXANDER. *Yachting on the Pacific, Together with Notes on Travel in Peru, and an Account of the Peoples and Products of Ecuador.* London: Duckworth and Company, 1909. xi, 286 pp., illus. HL 336876

Contents: Travel log.

Inscription: "To 'Jack London,' with respectful regards, A. Mann[.] June 12[,] / 09[.]"

MANN, ARTHUR SITGREAVES. *Prince Ivo of Bohemia: A Romantic Tragedy in Five Acts.* New York: The Grafton Press, 1906. 84 pp., HL 337676

Contents: Play.

Inscription: "St. Johns College, Shanghai[,] China[.] To Jack London from a fellow traveller on the *Siberia,* Jan. 1904. Have you got any idealism in you yet? Arthur S. Mann."

The *Siberia* was the steamer that carried London and Mann from San Francisco to Yokohama in 1904.

MARBLE SAFETY AXE COMPANY. *Marble's Game Getter Gun and Other Specialties for Sportsmen.* New York: Marble Safety Axe Company, 1910. 60 pp., illus. HL

Contents: Catalog.

Marginalia: London marked advertisements for the "No. A-18 Game Getter Cleaning Rod, Long brass shell power, 22-long powder, 22 long rifle powder, 22 short powder," and ".44-40 round ball cartridges."

MARSHALL, HENRY. *Marshall's Navigation Made Easy, Or the Mariner's Daily Assistant and Self-Instructor.* Milwaukee, Wisconsin: Henry Marshall, 1877. 72 pp., illus. HL 336752 PF

Contents: Introduction to navigation.

Marginalia: London marked passages on parallel sailing, finding a course and distance by Mercator's sailing, the logline and glass, longitude by chronometer, and finding longitude by the sun at noon.

Enclosure: A typed worksheet, entitled "Chronometer Method," and signed and dated: "Jack London, Nov. 30, 1907."

MARSHALL, HENRY. *Marshall's Navigation Made Easy, Or the Mariner's Daily Assistant and Self-Instructor.* Milwaukee, Wisconsin: Henry Marshall, 1877. 72 pp., illus. HL 336753

Contents: Introduction to navigation.

Marginalia: In this, the first of two copies of the book carried aboard the *Snark,* London marked passages describing the use of the compass in parallel sailing, and finding longitude.

MARSTON, EDWARD. *Fishing for Pleasure and Catching It.* London: T. Werner Laurie, 1906. xiii, 152 pp., illus. HL 336750
Contents: Stories about fishing.
Marginalia: On the cover of this book London wrote: "Carpenter's *History of Our World About India*[.]"

MATHE, HELEN. *One Summer in Hawaii.* New York: Cassell Publishing Company, 1891. 298 pp., illus. HL
Contents: Hawaiian travel guidebook.
Bookseller: Thrum's, Honolulu.
Marginalia: London marked a passage about the people of Hawaii who "once went about 'barefooted to their eyes' and who smacked their lips over a cannibal feast."

MAXWELL, WILLIAM BABINGTON. *The Devil's Garden.* Indianapolis: The Bobbs-Merrill Company, 1914. 444 pp., HL 332976
Contents: Novel.
Marginalia: London's notes for this novel were taken in anticipation of a review of the book: "greatly human, even balanced with a deep & certain knowledge of life—of man's life, of woman's life. *The Devil's Garden* is masterly, and William Dale is a fresh figure in fiction not lightly to be forgotten. Mr. Maxwell's portrayal is . . . regret delay in sending this caused by absence[.]"

MAYBRICK, FLORENCE ELIZABETH (CHANDLER). *Mrs. Maybrick's Own Story: My Fifteen Lost Years.* New York: Funk & Wagnalls Company, 1905. vii, 394 pp., illus. HL 334790
Contents: Autobiographical account of the author's imprisonment in Woking and Aylesbury prisons.
Marginalia: London was interested in the sentencing of Mrs. Maybrick, the discussion of her conviction on little evidence, and the insanity of the judge who presided over her trial.

MELVILLE, HERMAN. *Typee: A Real Romance of the South Seas.* Boston: Dana Estes & Company, 1892. xxxvi, 389 pp., HL 334784
Contents: Novel.

Bookseller: Smith Brothers, Oakland, California.

Marginalia: London marked paragraphs about the French battle with the natives at Typee, a description of the valley at Typee, the bay of Nukuheva, remarks about natives' dental problems, and a passage about keeping a fire alive. The book was also annotated by George Sterling and Charmian London.

Enclosure: Unsigned article from *Current Opinion:* "The Mystery of Herman Melville."

MELVIN, FLOYD JAMES. *Socialism as the Sociological Ideal: A Broader Basis for Socialism.* New York: Sturgis & Walton Company, 1915. 216 pp., HL 336797

Contents: "This study has grown out of an attempt to formulate a generic definition of socialism."—Preface.

Enclosures: Cover letter from Lawton L. Walton to Jack London, 24 March 1915, telling him about the book and requesting to say "a word for the book . . . a few lines that can be used in a circular." Also a letter of 27 July 1915 from Jack Byrne to Walton explaining that London was away from the ranch.

MEYER, JOSEPH ERNEST. *Protection: The Sealed Book. A Treatise and Guide for the Protection of Players of Games of Chance, Such as Dice, Cards, Roulette, Slot Machines, Etc. . . .* Milwaukee, Wisconsin: Joseph E. Meyer, 1909. 121 pp., illus. HL 336962

Contents: Guide to winning at gambling games.

Marginalia: London underlined a hint on how to win at poker.

MIGHELS, PHILIP VERRILL. *The Inevitable.* Philadelphia: J. B. Lippincott Company, 1902. 361 pp., illus. HL 332973

Contents: Novel.

Inscription: "To Jack London with the sincere regards of the Perpetrator, Philip Verrill Mighels. Piedmont, Cal. Dec. 12th[,] 1902."

MIKKELSEN, EJNAR. *Conquering the Arctic Ice.* Philadelphia: George W. Jacobs and Company, 1910. 470 pp., illus. HL 332751

Contents: Narrative of the Anglo-American Polar Expedition.

Marginalia: London marked a passage describing in great detail the treatment, care, and equipment necessary for Arctic sled dogs, as well as marking: "399—Herschel island quite a metropolis[.]"
For a dog story he was contemplating, London referred to this book: "Novel[.] A Dog Story[.] Trip over the ice pack a la *Conquering the Arctic Ice* by Ejnar Mikkelsen[,] especially Chapter V for all details of dogs."[42]

MILLER, JOAQUIN. *As It Was in the Beginning: A Poem.* San Francisco: The Whitaker & Ray Company, 1903. 99 pp., HL 338609

Contents: Poem.
Inscription: "Dear Jack: I know you'll like this. George Sterling[.]"
Marginalia: London marked a number of the cantos in this book for Charmian to copy.

Although he belonged to an earlier generation, Joaquin Miller was a revered and honorary member of the "Crowd." George Sterling often paid homage to the aging poet at his cabin located at the "Hights" of the Piedmont Hills. He managed to interest London in Miller's poetry through this book. London thanked Sterling for the book in a letter of 8 July 1903 (HL) from Glen Ellen: "*As It Was in the Beginning* came last night. I began at once reading aloud from it. All were delighted, and I am delighted that you, and no one else, should have sent it to me."

MILLIS, HARRY ALVIN. *The Japanese Problem in the United States: An Investigation for the Commission of Relations with Japan Appointed by the Federal Council of the Churches of Christ in America.* New York: The Macmillan Company, 1915. xxi, 334 pp., illus. HL 336965

Contents: Discussion of the treatment and admission of Japanese immigrants into the United States.
Enclosure: A business card: "With the Compliments of Rev. Sidney L. Gulick, Associate Secretary of the Commission on Peace and Arbitration."

MILLS, WALTER THOMAS. *The Struggle for Existence.* Chicago: In-

ternational School of Social Economy, 1904. 640 pp., HL
336768

Contents: Sociological study of oppression.

Marginalia: London marked many paragraphs in this book, including passages discussing the struggle for existence, the history
of the divine rights of kings, competition, exploited fame, and the
power of the workers. On the endpaper, he wrote: "441—Farmer's
earnings."

MITCHELL, EDMUND. *Tales of Destiny.* London: Constable and
Company, Limited, 1913. 190 pp., HL 332566

Contents: Short stories.

Inscription: "To Jack London, with kindest regards from a brother
Bohemian, the Author, Edmund Mitchell[.] Grove of Bohemia,
Cal. 9th August 1913."

Mitchell gave this book to London during the annual "High Jinks"
of the Bohemian Club held at their forest retreat in a Russian River
redwood grove.

MITCHELL, JOHN. *Organized Labor: Its Problems, Purposes and
Ideals and the Present and Future of American Wage Earners.* Philadelphia: American Book and Bible House, 1903. 436 pp.,
illus. HL 323531

Contents: Discussion of trade unionism.

Marginalia: London put check marks beside the following chapter
headings: "The Problem of the Unskilled," "The Case Against the
Trade Union," "The Unionist and the Non-Unionist," "Labor
and Capital at War," and "Strikes in Their Moral and Economic
Aspects."

MODERN LOVE. *An Anthology.* New York: Mitchell Kennerley,
1906. 75 pp., HL 337665

Contents: Poems.

Marginalia: London made markings beside the following poems:
"Modern Beauty" by Arthur Symons, "Requiescat" by Oscar
Wilde, "Night (After All)" by T. W. Rolleston, "A Shropshire Lad"
by A. E. Housman, "The Rune of the Passion of Women" by Fiona

Macleod, and "True Love" and "A Song of Farewell" (author un-known).

MONAHAN, MICHAEL. *At the Sign of the Van, Being the Log of the Papyrus With Other Escapades in Life and Letters.* London: Mitchell Kennerley, 1914. 439 pp., HL 332914

Contents: Short stories.
Inscription: "Dear Wolf—Here's a place on the Van just for you—and send me your book of short stories with 'Samuel' Michaelis[.] Jul[.] 1914[.]"
Enclosure: Photograph of the author, inscribed "Yours sincerely, Michael Monahan."
Irish-born poet and editor Michael Monahan was the founder of *Papyrus* magazine and literary editor for the Chicago *Evening Post.*

MONAHAN, MICHAEL. *Palms of Papyrus, Being Forthright Studies of Men and Books, with Some Pages from a Man's Inner Life.* New York: The Papyrus Publishing Company, 1909. 240 pp., illus. HL 339876

Contents: Literary essays.
Inscription: "To Jack London with sincere gratitude and admiration for his brain genius. Michael Monahan[.] Anno domini 1910[.]"

MOORE, GEORGE. *Hail and Farewell Ave.* New York: D. Appleton and Company, 1911. 260 pp., HL 332974

Contents: Novel.
Bookseller: Brentano's, New York, New York.
Marginalia: London wrote "254—description of metaphysics" on the rear pastedown.

MOORE, GEORGE. *Mike Fletcher: A Novel.* New York: Press of The Minerva Publishing Company, 1889. 302 pp., HL 332979

Contents: Novel.
Marginalia: London marked a passage on page 258 describing Mike Fletcher's character.

MOORE, JOHN HOWARD. *The Universal Kinship*. Chicago: Charles H. Kerr and Company, 1906. x, 329 pp., illus. HL 336819

Contents: "*The Universal Kinship* means the kinship of all the inhabitants of the planet Earth. . . . the chief purpose of these pages is to prove and interpret the kinship of the human species with the other species of animals."—Preface.

Marginalia: London characterized this book as "splendid virile English[.] appreciation of the value of words[.] makes alive the dull[.] heavy prose of the big books. Up to date[.] Reads like a novel[.] uses always the right word[.] Interest never flags. Masterly knowledge of the subject. pragmatic[.] broad grasp."

London marked paragraphs describing a gibbon, man as a primate, the development of the brain, the evolution of Earth, the genealogy of animals, kinship, the story of Eden and evolution, the human soul, and the emotions of anthropoid races. On the rear endpapers, he made the following notes: "30–31–32–33–34–35[.] pp. 100–101. pp. 142–143–144[.] For future book—see pp. 32–33–34—Future book—in the midst of the decay of a colossal civilization—forgotten machines—vast canals etc[.]—and the cold, always the cold creeping in. maybe, creatures are highly developed mentally—but helpless against the invading cold of space 270°C below zero—or 400°F below zero[.]"

London's notes on this book, aside from those for a future story, were made for Charles Kerr (28 April 1906, HL): "At last, after being thrown out of gear by the earthquake, I am getting around to dropping a line about Mr. Moore's *The Universal Kinship*.

"I do not know of any book dealing with Evolution that I have read with such keen interest. Mr. Moore has a broad grasp and shows masterly knowledge of the subject. And withal the interest never flags. The book reads like a novel. One is constantly keyed up and expectant. Mr. Moore is to be congratulated upon the magnificent way in which he has made alive the dull, heavy processes of the big books.

"And then, there is his style. He uses splendid, virile English and shows a fine appreciation of the values of words. He uses always the right word."

MOORE, JOHN MURRAY. *New Zealand for the Emigrant, Invalid, and Tourist.* London: Sampson Low, Marston, Searle and Rivington, Limited, 1890. xiii, 253 pp., illus. HL 334368
Contents: Travel book on New Zealand.
Marginalia: London was interested in the globetrotter, the state of farmland in New Zealand, the climate in Wellington, the Maoris, the Panama Canal, natural wonders of New Zealand, and electricity on shipboard, probably in preparation for the *Snark* voyage.

MORGAN, LOUIS. *The Modern Tattooist.* Berkeley: The Courier Publishing Company, 1912. 80 pp., illus. HL
Contents: Complete history of the art of tattooing and its uses, and also a text on modern methods of tattooing.
Inscription: "With regards to Mr. London from Louis Morgan[.] Jan. 17,—1916."

MÖRNER, BIRGER. *Byllene Bin.* Stockholm: Bokforlag, 1911. 142 pp., HL 338606
Contents: Poems.
Inscription: "To Jack and Charmian London from their friend the Author."

MÖRNER, BIRGER. *KGL. Mayestaets Plaisir.* Copenhagen: Nordisk Forlag, 1907. 111 pp., illus. HL 332481
Contents: Novel.
Inscription: "To Mrs. Jack London from her and her Jack's sincere friend[,] Birger Mörner. Sydney[,] 10 / 3 1909."

MÖRNER, BIRGER. *Söderhafvets Sagor.* Stockholm: Bokförlag, 1910. 193 pp., illus. HL 337102
Contents: Novel.
Inscription: "To Jack London and Mrs. Jack from theirs very truly Birger Mörner."

MORRIS, GOUVERNEUR. *The Pagan's Progress.* New York: A. S. Barnes & Company, 1903. xix, 258 pp., illus. HL 332557
Contents: Story of primeval man similar in content to *Before Adam.*

Inscription: "To Jack the Fighter from a Brother in Arms[.] Austin Lewis. Sept. 1904[.]"

MORRISON, ARTHUR. *To London Town.* London: Methuen & Company, 1899. 312 pp., HL 332556

Contents: Novel.

Marginalia: London checked off a number of books in the publisher's advertisements to this book: *Pierre and His People, The Translation of a Savage, The Trail of the Sword, An Adventurer of the North, The Seats of the Mighty, The Pomp of the Lavilettes, The Battle of the Strong,* and *The Rural Exodus.* On the rear endpapers, he recorded some dialect: "ketchin (catching[.])] bin (been)[.] D'year (do you hear)[.] ole (old)[.] 'ere (here)[.] doucher (don't you) [.] trouseys (trousers)[.] cop it (get it, catch it)[.] Lawr (law)[.] Lud (would)[.] Git (get)[.] O' (of)[.] respeck (respect)[.] laugwidge (language)[.] nachural (natural)[.] cons'kently (consequently)[.] Jus-so (just so)[.] pint (point)[.] edication (education)[.] unforchuate (unfortunate)[.] ullo (hello)[.] pore (poor)[.] Mar (md)[.] be'ave (behave)[.] Yus (yes)[.] seleck (select)[.] 'Olludy (holiday)[.] arf (half)[.] 'Di em the enny, enny-seckle, yew aw ther bee. Di'd like ter sip the enny from those red lips, yew see!![']] 'Ere, I si, gev'ner, we cawn't.' 'garn (go on)[.] fr(for). 'a 'eard (have heard)[.]]"

MORTON, HENRY HOLDICH. *Genito-Urinary Disease and Syphilis.* Philadelphia: F A. Davis Company, 1908. xii, 521 pp., illus. HL 336177

Contents: Medical text.

Marginalia: London put a match in the book beside page 406 to mark his place, and on page 520 made a pencil mark beside "phlebitis."

MOSBY, THOMAS SPEED. *Causes and Cures of Crime.* St. Louis: C. V. Mosby Company, 1913. x, 354 pp., illus. HL 336114

Contents: Sociological text on crime.

Inscription: "To Jack London with the Compliments of The Publisher. 5 / 22—16[.]"

MUMFORD, JAMES GREGORY. *Surgical Memoirs and Other Essays.* New York: Moffat, Yard & Company, 1908. ix, 358 pp., illus. HL 336740

Contents: Medical essays, including essays on the history of medicine.
Marginalia: "9—Oath of Hippocrates[.] 19—Galen discovers circulation of the blood[.]"

MUNRO, HECTOR HUGH. *The Rise of the Russian Empire.* Boston: L. C. Page and Company, 1900. xii, 334 pp., illus. HL 334782

Contents: Detailed history of the Russian Empire.
Marginalia: London kept a diary only a few times in his life: during the Klondike, while on the road with Kelly's Army, and during his Japanese-Korean trip. He recorded a portion of his Japanese train schedule in this book: "1:50 P.M. Leave Kohara for Moji[.] 2:01 3:20 P.M. 3:33 P.M. 4:08 5:10 5:23 6:56 7:10 7:48 8:31 8:45 10:09 10:27 10:48 J Hashimoto[.] J Hashimoto in Nagasaki[.]"
Enclosure: Memo from the Sanyo Hotel, Shimonoseki.

London stayed at the Sanyo Hotel the night after his arrest in Moji. (He was arrested for taking photographs in the war zone.)

NAUGHTON, W. W. *Heavy-Weight Champions . . . Being an Account of Every Heavy-Weight Championship Contest from Sullivan and Corbett to Jeffries and Johnson, together with a Complete Record of Every Contestant, Extended Sketches of Jeffries and Johnson, and Story of the Making of the Big Match.* San Francisco: John Kitchen, Jr., Company, 1910. xxx, 208 pp., illus. HL 336976

Contents: History of boxing champions.
Marginalia: London marked the statistics of the records of Tommy Burns, James Corbett, Robert Fitzsimmons, and Jack Johnson.

An avid sports fan, particularly of boxing, London covered many of the fights as a sports writer for the Hearst newspapers. He is also generally credited with originating a minor literary genre: the boxing novel. Two of his books are primarily about boxing: *The Game* and *The Abysmal Brute.*

NAUGHTON, W. W. *Heavy-Weight Champions . . . Being an Account of Every Heavy-Weight Championship Contest from Sullivan and Corbett to Jeffries and Johnson, together with a Complete Record of Every Contestant, Extended Sketches of Jeffries and Johnson, and Story of the Making of the Big Match.* Milwaukee, Wisconsin: Riverside Printing Company, 1910. 223 pp., illus. HL 336977

Contents: History of boxing champions.
Inscription: "To Jack London compts. of W. W. Naughton[.]"

NEIDIG, WILLIAM JONATHAN. *The First Wardens: Poems.* New York: The Macmillan Company, 1905. viii, 99 pp., illus. HL 339907

Contents: Poems.
Inscription: "For Jack London, from his friend, W. J. N. Madison, Wis. May 14, 1906."

NELSON, BATTLING. *Life, Battles and Career of Battling Nelson, Lightweight Champion of the World.* Hegewisch, Illinois: Battling Nelson, 1908. iii, 265 pp., illus. HL 336978

Contents: Autobiography.
Inscription: "With kind remembrances of the Jeffries-Fight, Reno[,] July 4. To my old Pal—Jack London, who dubbed me the Abysmal Brute—Compliments of Author Battling Nelson[.] Hegewisch, Ill[.] July 14, 1910. If Jeffries or Johnson had only showed a—just a little of that stuff.—Abysmal Brute[.]"

Oscar "Battling" Nelson's nickname "Abysmal Brute" came as a result of his fight against Jimmy Britt in Colma, California, 10 September 1905. London covered the fight for the Hearst newspaper chain, and, in the article he wrote, came up with the nickname (*Jack London Reports,* pp. 253–54): "Nelson is a fighting animal. Britt is an intelligent animal with fighting proclivities. This is another way of telling the story.

"It was the abysmal brute against a more highly organized intelligent nature. Now, do not misunderstand me. I do not wish to call Nelson a brute; but what I wish to say is that Nelson possesses to an unusual degree the brute you and I and all of us possess in varying degrees.

"Let me explain. By abysmal brute I mean the basic life that resides deeper than the brain and the intellect in living things. It is itself the very stuff of life—movement; and it is saturated with a blind and illimitable desire to exist. This desire it expresses by movement.

"No matter what comes it will move. It came into the world first. It is lower down on the ladder of evolution than is intelligence. It comes first, before the intellect. The intellect rests upon it; and when the intellect goes it still remains—the abysmal brute."

NELSON, BATTLING. *Life, Battles, and Career of Battling Nelson, Lightweight Champion of the World.* Hegewisch, Illinois: Battling Nelson, 1909. iii, 265 pp., illus. HL 336975
Contents: Autobiography.
Inscription: "To Jack London, the man who called me an 'Abysmal Brute,' thereby paying me the biggest compliment ever accorded me by any writer. With the Compliments and best wishes of his friend, Battling Nelson[.] Hegewisch Ill. How would you like to be an 'Abysmal Brute?'"
Enclosure: Publisher's advertisement and order form.

NIETZSCHE, FRIEDRICH WILHELM. *The Case of Wagner, The Twilight of the Idols, Nietzsche Contra Wagner.* New York: Macmillan and Company, 1896. xx, 351 pp., HL 336791 PF
Contents: At one time the friend and follower of Wagner, Nietzsche wrote this book after reaching a position that strongly opposed Wagner in both art and philosophy.
Marginalia: Most of the annotations in this book were made by Charmian, although London did mark the paragraphs on pages 86 and 254 that criticize the Christian concept of God. London's specific interests were the essay "The Case of Wagner" and the epilogue to "Nietzsche Contra Wagner."
Enclosure: "New Revelations of Nietzsche," a clipping from *Current Literature,* pp. 644–46.

Nietzschean philosophy permeates much of London's work. *The Sea-Wolf,* for example, was written as an attack on Nietzsche. In a letter of 21 February 1912 to George Brett, London states emphatically his opposition to the German philosopher: "I, as you know, am in the opposite intellectual camp from that of Nietzsche. Yet no man in my own camp stirs me as does Nietzsche or as does De Casseres" (*Letters*, p. 361).

NIETZSCHE, FRIEDRICH WILHELM. *The Dawn of Day*. New York: The Macmillan Company, 1903. xxix, 387 pp., HL 336748
Contents: Philosophical essay.
Marginalia: London marked passages noting the beginnings of customs, the bearing of insanity on the history of morality, the value of the belief in superhuman passions, the problems of words, the apostate of the independent mind, Christianity, and the Christian revenge on Rome.

NIETZSCHE, FRIEDRICH WILHELM. *A Genealogy of Morals*. New York: The Macmillan Company, 1897. xix, 289 pp., HL 336791 PF
Contents: Philosophical essays.
Enclosure: "Nietzsche and the Will to Power" by Vernon Lee. [Violet Pagét]. Clipping from the *North American Review*, December 1904, pp. 842–59.
London's reading of Nietzsche was in full swing by September 1904. In a letter to Charmian dated 29 September, he remarked: "Have been getting hold of some Nietzsche. I'll turn you loose first on his *Genealogy of Morals*—and after that, something you'll like—*Thus Spake Zarathustra*" (*The Book of Jack London*, 2:31).
London recommended Nietzsche to his friends as well, as he did in a letter of 27 June 1905 to Ida Winship (Kingman Collection, Glen Ellen, California): "I am just going to begin *Iconoclast*. Get hold of Nietzsche's *The Case of Wagner*—or read his *Genealogy of Morals* or his *Thus Spake Zarathustra*."

NILES, BLAIR. *Our Search for a Wilderness: An Account of Two Ornithological Expeditions to Venezuela and to British Guiana*. New York: Henry Holt and Company, 1910. xix, 408 pp., illus. HL 332791

Contents: Travel in South America.

Inscription: "Compliments of Gaylord Wilshire[.]"

Gaylord Wilshire was a prominent socialist, a friend of Anna Strunsky Walling, and publisher of *Wilshire's Magazine*. London first contributed to *Wilshire's Magazine* in 1906. He wrote to Wilshire often, first only on business matters, then on the basis of a firmly based friendship.

NOEL, JOSEPH J. *Love's Bread Line*. New York: The Claridge Press, 1914. 99 pp., HL 337324

Contents: Poems.

Inscription: "To Jack of the golden heart. Noel."

Oakland journalist Joseph Noel involved London in a number of ill-advised business arrangements, most notably the Millergraph company. When the business deals fell through, Noel abandoned London to the mercy of the creditors. Noel also managed to acquire the dramatic rights to *The Sea-Wolf,* which, when the motion picture interests became hopelessly confused and intertwined, he sold back to London for a monstrously steep price. Noel's *Footloose in Arcadia* (New York: Carrick & Evans, Inc., 1940) presents a one-sided view of London and Sterling and Bierce. The book characterized London as hedonistic, with little self-control.

NORDAU, MAX. *The Interpretation of History*. New York: Moffatt, Yard and Company, 1911. 419 pp., HL 336759

Contents: "History and the Writing of History," "The Customary Philosophy of History," "The Anthropomorphic View of History," "Man and Nature," "Society and the Individual," "The Psychological Roots of Religion," "The Psychological Premises of History," "The Question of Progress," "Eschatology," "The Meaning of History."

Bookseller: Hochschild, Kohn & Company.

Marginalia: London marked passages discussing the use of history to justify meaningless institutions, the place of political history, the historical acceptance of God, the hiding of facts about one's life, and the definition of abstraction. He marked the following pages on the rear pastedown: "50, 53, 89, 120, 123, 132, 162, 168, 174. 'The awful privilege of reason[.]' bog-lights[.] will-o-wisps[.]"

London's introduction to Nordau came in 1900 when he read "The Natural History of Love." The essay had a positive effect on him, and he wrote to Johns about it: "If you ever get a chance, read Max Nordau's essay, 'The Natural History of Love.' Its thought is similar to yours, and it also goes down to the physical basis of the physiological basis. God! he does and the average man or woman in society on account of their love-making ways, etc." (*Letters*, p. 96).

NORIE, JOHN WILLIAM. *A Complete Epitome of Practical Navigation, Containing all Necessary Instructions for Keeping a Ship's Reckoning at Sea, With the Most Approved Methods of Ascertaining the Latitutde and Longitude and Every Requisite to Form the Complete Navigator: The Whole Being Rendered Perfectly Easy, and Illustrated by Numerous Examples, Diagrams and Charts, Together with a Correct and Extensive Set of Tables, Preceded by a Copious Explanation of Each Table*. London: Imray, Laurie, Norie and Wilson, 1904. 2 volumes bound together, xi, 424, xl, 573 pp., illus. HL 337036
Contents: Sailing instructions.
Marginalia: London marked ten pages dealing with plane and traverse sailing.

NORMAN, GERTRUDE. *A Brief History of Bavaria*. Munich: Heinrich Jaffe, 1910. x, 211 pp., HL 337311
Contents: Popularized history of Germany.
Inscription: "Dearest Charmian[,] I hope this little history of the land where I live and study will interest you. I happen to have rooms on the top floor of the little palace Ludwig the first built for Lola Montez. Always[,] Pauline[.] München Barer str. Sept[.] 1912[.]"
Pauline French was one of Charmian London's close personal friends.

NORRIS, FRANK. *The Octopus*. New York: Doubleday, Page & Company, 1901. 651 pp., HL 153007
Contents: Historical novel.
Marginalia: London marked a passage on page 549 dealing with the

"great voice of the centuries: let my people go" and the "cry of the nations."

NOTABLE SHIPWRECKS. *Being Tales of Disaster and Heroism at Sea.* London: Cassell and Company, Limited, 1899. viii, 310 pp., illus. HL 336831

Contents: Historical accounts of famous shipwrecks.
Marginalia: "Sharks[.] Bryan 345—shark head, Japanese man's hand."

NUMBER 1500. *Life in Sing Sing.* Indianapolis: The Bobbs-Merrill Company, 1904. 276 pp., HL 339669

Contents: Journal of time spent in prison, with general remarks about prison conditions.
Marginalia: *Life in Sing Sing* provided London with a rich description of prison life, which he exploited for use in *The Star Rover.* In this copy of the book (he had two), he marked paragraphs describing a cell, relating the case of Duncan Young, a prisoner who was framed, and: "15—description of cell house. 142 to 145—story idea or part of a prison setting for a novel."

NUMBER 1500. *Life in Sing Sing.* Indianapolis: The Bobbs-Merrill Company, 1904. 276 pp., HL 336751

Contents: See preceding entry.
Marginalia: In this copy of the book, London found descriptions of Sundays in prison and prisoners isolated on the brink of madness.

O'HARA, JOHN MYERS. *Pagan Sonnets.* Portland, Maine: Smith and Sale, 1910. ix, 42 pp., illus. HL 339874

Contents: Poems.
Inscription: "To Jack from John With best regards. March 25, 1911."
"Ave, Victor!
   I mark you from a rabble-circled space
Emerge as some great gladiator would,
   Triumphant from the combat, with the blood
And dust of the arena in his face;

Behind, the roar of thousands that abase
Themselves before such prowess as withstood,
  Herculean to meet a multitude,
Onslaught of rabid beast and savage race."
"Dear Genius of 'Wake-Robin Lodge!'
  Dear Friend!
A sonnett-call across the continent;
  An answer to the cordial one you sent
in *Martin Eden!* May you, to the end,
  In single-handed battle never err,
And die beside your sword, a conqueror!
—John Myers O'Hara[.]"

"I am sending you with this mail" O'Hara wrote to London, "a copy of *Pagan Sonnets.* On the fly page you will find a sonnet that is a tribute to yourself. I think you will like the book—anyway let me know what you think about it whenever you have the leisure . . ." (27 March 1911, HL).

O'HARA, JOHN MYERS. *The Poems of Sappho. An Interpretative Rendition into English.* Chicago: Privately printed, 1907. 97 pp. HL 336659

Contents: Poems.

"I trust that you will enjoy my translation of the fragments of Sappho" O'Hara wrote. "The reviews which I have so far received have been laudatory beyond my wildest expectations. Let me know whether the copy reaches you safely" (11 August 1907, HL).

O'HARA, JOHN MYERS. *Songs of the Open.* Portland, Maine: Smith & Sale, 1909. ix, 41 pp., HL 339675

Contents: Nature poems.

Inscription: "My dear London; This book owes, in a large measure, its inspiration to yourself and your immortal classic of the open, *The Call of the Wild.* Therefore, I have taken the honor to myself of dedicating these poems to you not only as a tribute of admiration for your genius, but [as] a token of sincere friendship. Faithfully yours, John Myers O'Hara. July 22, 1909."

O'HARA, JOHN MYERS. *Songs of the Open*. Portland, Maine: Smith & Sale, 1909. ix, 41 pp., HL 339674

Contents: Nature poems.

Inscription: "My dear London, Here is another copy of *Songs of the Open* in the added garb of a box. Ever yours, John Myers O'Hara[.] July 15, 1910[.]"

OLDFIELD, L. C. F. *The Law of Copyright*. London: Butterworth Company, 1912. 266 pp., HL 336419

Contents: Explanation of the new (1909) British and U.S. copyright acts.

Marginalia: London marked a paragraph on page 170 dealing with the deposit of copyrighted works.

OMAR KHAYYAM. *The Quatrains of Omar Khayyam*. London: Kegan Paul, Trench, Trübner & Company, Ltd., 1893. 124 pp., HL 339657

Contents: Poems.

Inscription: "Jack London seems not to have cut into this volume farther than the preparatory pages—torn rather. As to the *Rubáyát* of Omar, he preferred the arrangement made by Richard Le Gallienne to that of Fitzgerald. Charmian Kittredge London. 'House of Happy Walls' which contains Jack's library, never before assembled. 1944[.]"

OMAR KHAYYAM. *Rubáiyát of Omar Khayyam. A Paraphrase From Several Literal Translations by Richard Le Gallienne. A New Edition With Fifty Added Quatrains*. New York: John Lane Company, 1909. 102 pp., HL 339668

Contents: Poems.

Inscription: "To Jack London & Jack's wife, with the love of Richard & Irma Le Gallienne—in memory of the night of the Festival at St. Michael & All Angels! January 10, 1912.

This book seems worthwhile, Jack. I'm glad I wrote it—
Hearing you tell how, in the Klondike snow,
    You read & cared about it long ago—
And I have lived to hear your sweetheart quote it!"

London wrote an extensive discussion of Omar Khayyam's *Rubái-yát* in *The Sea-Wolf.*[43] He also discussed the book with Johns in a letter dated 30 March 1899 (*Letters,* pp. 24–26):"Thanks for the criticism of poem—merely an experiment, you know. . . . It was not till after I had completed it that I noticed the debt owing to Omar Kayam [*sic*]. And by the way, what do you think of Le Gallienne: As a writer, I like him. As a man, I have no respect for him, dislike him; yet I know nothing about him as a man. Perhaps it's the ideas I got of the man, Le Gallienne, from reading his work. In his version of the *Rubáiyat,* I was especially struck by the following, describing his search for the secret of life:
'Up, up where Parrius' hoofs stamp heaven's floor,
  My soul went knocking at each starry door,
Till on the stilly top of heaven's stair,
  Clear-eyed I looked—and laughed—and climbed no more.'
But I prefer Fitzgerald's."

OSBON, BRADLEY SILLICH. *A Sailor of Fortune: Personal Memoirs of Captain B. S. Osbon.* New York: McClure, Phillips & Company, 1906. ix, 332 pp., illus. HL 332440
Contents: Recollections of a life at sea, edited by Albert Bigelow Paine.
Marginalia: London marked a description of a cyclone and a squall, and the practice of burying a man alive up to his neck in order to rid him of a fever. On the endpapers he wrote: "16—idea for South Sea yarn—wood-rats a yard long where he's buried. 14[.] 60[.]"

OSBOURNE, LLOYD. *The Queen Versus Billy and Other Stories.* London: William Heinemann, 1900. 308 pp., HL 332200
Contents: Short stories.
Inscription: "To Jack from Lloyd in friendship and esteem. 1916."

OSTRANDER, W. M. *How Money Grows.* Philadelphia: W. M. Ostrander, 1904. 19 pp., illus. HL
Contents: Financial "self-help" pamphlet.
Marginalia: London marked a paragraph on page 5 explaining how to succeed in the world.

OTT, EDWARD AMHERST. *How to Use the Voice in Reading and Speaking: A Text Book of Elocution for Colleges, High Schools, and for Self-Instruction.* New York: Hinds & Noble, 1901. vi, 275 pp., illus. HL 336756

Contents: Speech textbook.

Marginalia: London was interested in breathing exercises, pausing, and general speech techniques. Unfortunately, he was never regarded as a dynamic speaker.

PAGÉT, VIOLET (*pseudonym* Vernon Lee). *Gospels of Anarchy, and Other Contemporary Studies.* New York: Brentano's, 1909. 372 pp., HL 336056

Contents: "Gospels of Anarchy," "Emerson as a Teacher of Latter-Day Tendencies," "Deterioration of Soul," "Tolstoi as a Prophet," "Tolstoi on Art," "Nietzsche and the 'Will to Power,'" "Professor James and the 'Will to Believe,'" "Rosny and the French Analytical Novel," "The Economic Parasitism of Women," "Ruskin as a Reformer," "On Modern Utopias: An Open Letter to Mr. H. G. Wells," "A Postscript on Mr. Wells and Utopias."

Marginalia: London wrote: "See James 118" on pages 197 and 198, referring to William James's *The Varieties of Religious Experience.*

PAGÉT, VIOLET (*pseudonym* Vernon Lee). *Vital Lies: Studies of Some Varieties of Recent Obscurantism.* New York: John Lane Company, 1912. Two volumes, xi, 262, 217 pp. HL 334788

Contents: "First Part: Theoretical Obscurantism," "The Two Pragmatisms" "What Is Truth?" "The Truths of Mysticism," "Fruits for Life." "Second Part: Applied Obscurantism," "Father Tyrrell and Modernism," "Mr. Crawley and Anthropological Apologetics," "Monsieur Sorel and the Syndicalist Myth," "Third Part: True In So Far As Misunderstood," "The Rehabilitation of Obscurity," "Humanism."

Marginalia: The two pragmatisms, a definition of truth, and Father Tyrrell's modernism and the will to continue believing are the subjects that London found interesting in Vernon Lee's book.

PALACIO VALDES, ANTANASIO. *The Fourth Estate.* New York: Brentano's, 1901. vi, 461 pp., HL 332389
Contents: Novel.
Bookseller: The Burrows Brothers Company, Cleveland, Ohio.
Marginalia: London used this novel as a source for Spanish names for his characters, including "sapristi!"

PALMER, AGNES LIZZIE (PAGE). *The Salvage of Men: Stories of Humanity Touched by Divinity.* New York: Fleming H. Revell Company, 1913. 214 pp., HL 332495
Contents: History of the Salvation Army.
Inscription: "Compliments of the author[,] Agnes L. Palmer[.] New York, January 1914."

PANCRAZIO, G. *Opere.* Florence: Casa Editrice Nerbini, 1915. 283 pp., HL
Contents: Novella.
Inscription: "To Mr. J. London[.] G[.] Pancrazio[.]"

THE PAPYRUS: *A Magazine of Individuality.* Edited by Michael Monohan. New Series, Volume 5 (July–December, 1909). HL 149826 (v.5 2nd copy)
Contents: Literary essays and articles.
Inscription: "With Papyrian Greetings from Michael Monahan[.] June 1910[.]"
Born in County Cork, Ireland, in 1865, Michael Monahan was best known as a poet and editor. Shortly before the publication of this issue, London wrote to Ninetta Eames asking her to "please write to the editor of *Papyrus* merely mentioning that I am away off on the other side of the world on the *Snark,* and that it would be better, under the circumstances, to let the subscription expire" (*Letters,* p. 266).

PARKMAN, FRANCIS. *The California and Oregon Trail: Being Sketches of Prairie and Rocky Mountain Life.* New York: A. L. Burt, Publisher, [19—]. 320 pp., HL 332667
Contents: History of the West.

Marginalia: The western movement, local color of the West, and Indians are the subjects that London noted in this book.

PARKMAN, FRANCIS. *The Oregon Trail: Sketches of Prairie and Rocky-Mountain Life*. Boston: Little, Brown and Company, 1872. xii, 381 pp., HL 337235
Contents: Account of a western expedition.
Marginalia: London marked passages about ants, Fort Laramie, George Catlin and Daniel Boone, the Rocky Mountain trappers, and buffalo robes.

PASKE, CHARLES THOMAS. *The Sea and the Rod*. London: Chapman and Hall, Limited, 1892. xvi, 224 pp., illus. HL 336749
Contents: Fishing as a hobby and sport.
Bookseller: The Burrows Brothers Company, Cleveland, Ohio.
Marginalia: Game fish (bass and grey mullet) and the Ceylon and Bombay harbors are the subjects that London noted here, evidently in anticipation of visits to those places aboard the *Snark*.

PATON, JOHN GIBSON. *John G. Paton, D. D.: Missionary to the New Hebrides*. London: Hodder and Stoughton, 1894. viii, 493 pp., illus. HL 332641
Contents: Autobiography.
Marginalia: London used this book as a source for his South Sea fiction, and marked paragraphs describing the sandalwood traders, the intentional killing of natives with a measles epidemic, and the narrow escape of a missionary from a native uprising.

PATTEN, WILLIAM. *Short Story Classics*. Volume Four. New York: P. F. Collier & Son, 1905. 351 pp., illus. HL 338679
Contents: Short stories.
Marginalia: London marked his short chapter (from *The Call of the Wild*) "For the Love of a Man."

PATTERSON, JOSEPH MEDILL. *A Little Brother of the Rich: A Novel*. Chicago: The Reilly & Britton Company, 1908. 361 pp., illus. HL 333321

Contents: Novel.

Enclosure: Calling card inscribed: "Miss Catherine Mather. 494 East Colorado Street. Just to prove that all the mental incompetants [*sic*] don't stay with 'the Bourgeoisie."

PENNOLL, JOSEPH. *San Francisco: The City of the Golden Gate, Being Twenty-five Reproductions in Photogravure from Etchings and Drawings.* New York: [1915?]. 25 leaves, illus. HL 20847

Contents: Photographs of San Francisco.

Inscription: "Dear Jack—You may have my number, but I have yours—this is a belated birthday present. Affec—Carrie Feb. 1915."

Carrie, or Carolyn Rand Sterling, was George Sterling's wife.

PERRY, MATTHEW GALBRAITH. *Narrative of the Expedition of an American Squadron to the China Seas and Japan, Performed in the Years 1852, 1853, and 1854 . . .* New York: D. Appleton & Company, 1857. vii, 624 pp., illus. HL 334818

Contents: "among the expressed motives which induced the Commander of the Expedition to desire the execution of the work by other hands than his own, none seemed more prominent than this consideration; that, as the facts here embodied were to be gathered not merely from the pages of his own journal, but from those also of several of his officers as well as from their official reports to him, he thought it better to confide the compilation to a disinterested third party . . ."—Preface.

Inscription: "Presented to Jack London by Wm. S. Porter[,] Dec[.] 27 / 13[.]"

Marginalia: "113" written on front flyleaf.

William S. Porter operated on London for an attack of appendicitis in 1913, and, thereafter, took him on as one of his patients.

PHELPS, GUY FITCH. *Ethel Vale, The White Slave.* Chicago: The Christian Witness Company, 1910. 217 pp., illus. HL 333345

Contents: "In the sad story of Ethel Vale is to be found the full fruit of those *twin monstrosities,* Poverty and Drink. . . . It has been the desire of the author to outline . . . some of the tragic features of the White Slave Traffic."—Preface.

Inscription: "Presented to Jack London by one of his admirers, the Author. March 14, 1911. Dallas Oregon[.] Box 71."

PHILLIPS, ARTHUR EDWARD. *Effective Speaking. An Exposition of the Laws of Effectiveness in the Choice of Material in Speech, With Examples and Exercises.* Chicago: The Newton Company, 1913. 314 pp., illus. HL 336935

Contents: This "book presents in a practicable way the essentials of effectiveness in all departments of speaking, whether it be impressiveness, entertainment, convincingness, persuasion. . . . Also it offers a logical way to effective Extemporaneous Speaking."—Preface.

Inscription: "Sincerely[,] Arthur Phillips[.]"

PHILLPOTTS, EDEN. *The Good Red Earth.* New York: Doubleday, Page & Company, 1901. 328 pp., HL 332493

Contents: Novel.

Marginalia: London marked a paragraph on page 193 illustrating characteristics of human nature.

PHILLPOTTS, EDEN. *The Whirlwind.* New York: McClure, Phillips & Company, 1907. 407 pp., HL 332488

Contents: Novel.

London recommended the *Whirlwind* to Frederick Bamford shortly after reading it in 1907. He made no inner markings in the novel, however.

THE PHOENIX. Volume 1 (June 1914–November 1914). 192 pp., illus. HL 181457 (v.1 2nd copy)

Contents: Literary essays and articles.

Inscription: "Dear Jack—Speak not of the Dead but put me in your book-rack—the one you reach to o'nights. *The Phoenix.* M. M. August 4—1915[.]"

Michael Monahan, editor of *The Phoenix,* frequently corresponded with London.

THE PIRATES OWN BOOK, *Or Authentic Narratives of the Lives,*

Exploits, and Executions of the Most Celebrated Sea Robbers.
Portland: Francis Blake, 1855. 432 pp., illus. HL 336788
Contents: Sea sagas and tall tales of pirating.
Bookseller: Raymer's Old Book Store, Seattle, Washington.
Inscription: "To Jack London from the Book Pirate[,] Chas[.] D.
Raymer[.] Seattle, Wa. July 30th[,] 1912[.]"

THE PITIFUL STORY OF THE PERFORMING ANIMAL. London: Animals' Friend Society, 1914. 31 pp., illus. HL 379916
Contents: Examples of human cruelty to animals.
Marginalia: The descriptions of animal acts and trainers found in
this pamphlet were heavily incorporated into London's exposé on
the subject: *Michael, Brother of Jerry.*

POE EDGAR ALLAN. *Letters of Poe and His Friends.* New York:
The University Society, 1902. viii, 452 pp., illus. HL 338984
(v. 17)
Contents: Volume XVII of *The Complete Works of Edgar Allan Poe,*
edited by James A. Harrison.
Marginalia: London marked paragraphs on pages "47[,] 48[,] 101[,]
111[,] 227[,] 229[,] 263[,] 264" which concerned Poe's "The Fall of
the House of Usher," Washington Irving, and the business affairs
and dealings Poe had with his publishers.

POE, EDGAR ALLAN. *Prose Tales, Poems.* New York: The University Society, 1902. vi, 288 pp., illus. HL 338984 (v. 6–7)
Contents: Volumes V and VII of *The Complete Works of Edgar Allan
Poe,* edited by James A. Harrison.
Inscription: "Edgar Allan Poe," a holograph poem written by George
Sterling, tipped onto page xlvi.

POLLARD, PERCIVAL. *Their Day in Court.* New York: The Neale
Publishing Company, 1909. 486 pp., HL 221160
Contents: Literary criticism and essays on women, men, and
manners.
Inscription: "To Jack and Charmian London—To Mate-Man and

Mate-Woman! Christmas Greetings! And love! From Edith De Long Jarmuth. Dec. 25—1910.''

POND, JAMES BURTON. *Eccentricities of Genius: Memories of Famous Men and Women of the Platform and Stage.* New York: G. W. Dillingham Company, 1900. xxvi, 564 pp., illus. HL 332824

Contents: Sketches of famous orators, pulpit orators, women lecturers and singers, humorists, explorers, travelers and war correspondents, actors and dramatic critics, literary lecturers, authors, readers, etc.

Marginalia: London marked passages and paragraphs containing anecdotes by Wendell Phillips, William Lloyd Garrison, Charles Sumner, Chauncey M. Depew, and Horace Porter.

POWELL, Edward Alexander. *Fighting in Flanders.* New York: Charles Scribner's Sons, 1914. xvi, 231 pp., illus. HL 334496

Contents: First-person narrative of the fall of Belgium during World War I.

Marginalia: On page 176, London characterized a description of being under mortar fire as "a good fiction episode[.]"

POWELL, EDWARD PAYSON. *The Country Home Library.* New York: McClure, Phillips & Company, 1905. 382 pp., illus. HL 337098

Contents: Interior design ideas.

Marginalia: London used this book while planning the Wolf House: "p. 42—good storage cellar for milk, meat, etc. p. 43—permanent seats & lockers in kitchen[.] 44—kitchen vestibule & locker for slop buckets[.]"

POWERS, STEPHEN. *Tribes of California.* Washington, D.C.: Government Printing Office, 1877. 635 pp., illus. HL 338626

Contents: A survey of the Rocky Mountain region "containing information in regard to the habits and customs, legends, religious beliefs, and geographical distribution of the California Indians. Information collected during three years' residence and travel among

At Robert Louis Stevenson's Grave

these tribes."—Second Letter of Transmittal.

Marginalia: Tribes of California was used as a source for *The Acorn-Planter* (and was also used incidentally in *The Little Lady of the Big House*): "23[.] 39—Origin of fire—good[.] 60—snaring the sun. 94—Fighting with miners because muddy water destroyed salmon[.] 277—Ishi's tribe—Deer River & Mill River Indians[.] 278—Indians of west side of the Sacramento[.] 308—Acorn Song. 338—clothes of Calif[.] Indians[.] 339—Nishinam Adam & Eve[.]"

THE PSYCHOANALYTIC REVIEW. Volume III, Number 3 (July 1916). HL

Contents: Articles on psychoanalysis.

Marginalia: London marked paragraphs discussing the significance of psychoanalysis, a Freudian review of *Sons and Lovers,* and Freud and sociology.

PUFFER, JOSEPH ADAMS. *The Boy and His Gang.* Boston: Houghton Mifflin Company, 1912. xi, 187 pp., illus. HL 332487

Contents: A sociological study of children's gangs.

Marginalia: This book reminded London of his road kids and gay cats days, and he marked paragraphs listing the names of gangs, the life span of a gang, and the sentiment of ownership: "I can write my *Gang Autobiography,* from beginning, to my gang of thinkers from the books, when I retired from all gangs, the last including the socialists. p. 14[,] 29—develop that the tougher gangs were more permanent, the nicer were ephemeral. 32—property in territory."

RAMBLES IN POLYNESIA. London: European Mail, Limited, 1897. ix, 207 pp., HL 332474

Contents: Personal history of Polynesia.

Marginalia: London marked passages describing New Caledonia, the Kanaka rebellion, the red shirt of a sailor, government graft, and Kai-oui-oui.

RAMÉE, LOUISE DE LA *(pseudonym* Ouida). *Puck: His Vicissitudes, Adventures, Observations, Conclusions, Friendships, and Philosophies.* Philadelphia: J. B. Lippincott & Company, 1870. 607 pp., HL 332551

Contents: Novel about a dog.

Marginalia: A description of spring, summer bees, the effects of priest-ridden times, celebrities, and the hooting and howling of a crowd are subjects that caught London's eye in this book.

RAMÉE, LOUISE DE LA *(pseudonym* Ouida). *Signa. Folle-Farine. Sir Galahad's Raid.* New York: P. F. Collier, 1889. 815 pp., illus. HL 334843

Contents: Three novels.

Marginalia: The people's loss of hope and power was the subject of the one marking London made in *Signa*. His markings in *Folle-Farine* included passages describing an attempt to find the right way (London wrote "Aug '91" by this entry), "The Law of all creation is cruelty," and a statement that love casts out fear.

In her *Book of Jack London,* (1:42–43) Charmian remembered the day London bought this book: "In the spring of 1912, Jack London, one day browsing in a dingy second-hand shop in Harlem for books to add to our traveling library on a voyage around Cape Horn, came across a cheap reprint of *Signa.* Home to our Morningside apartment he carried the small-typed story which, he had all his life declared, had had more influence in the shaping of his career than any other, not even excepting Herbert Spencer's *Philosophy of Style.* Upon the lurching poop-deck of the big four-master *Dirigo,* off the unseen coast of Brazil, I listened, not always with dry eyes, to the rhythmic, caressing voice, as Jack reread the loved romance which had opened to his groping intelligence the gates to unsurmised beauty."

The story of *Signa* and its effect on him was told many times by London during his lifetime. With less than two years to live, London told it one last time, to an instructor of children's literature at the University of Wisconsin, Marion Humble, on 11 December 1914: "Two wonderful things happened to me when I was a small boy that practically deducted the entire course of my life, and I doubt if neither of these two wonderful things had happened to me that I should ever have become a writer."

"The first wonderful thing was, when I was a little boy on a poor California ranch, finding a tattered copy of Ouida's novel entitled *Signa*. The end of this book was missing but I read and reread and reread countless times the story of *Signa* and it put in me an ambition to get beyond the skylines of my narrow California valley and opened up to me the possibilities of the world of art. In fact it became my star to which I hitched my child's wagon" (*Letters,* p. 438).

RANK, OTTO. *The Myth of the Birth of the Hero: A Psychological Interpretation of Mythology.* New York: The Journal of Nerv-

ous and Mental Disease Publishing Company, 1914. iii, 100
pp., HL

Contents: Psychoanalytic essay.
Marginalia: On page 25, London marked the first paragraph, which
discusses the myth of Kyros.

RAPPAPORT, PHILIP. *Looking Forward: A Treatise on the Status of
Women and the Origin and Growth of the Family and the State.*
Chicago: Charles H. Kerr & Company, 1906. 234 pp., HL
336714

Contents: Psychoanalytic treatment of women.
Marginalia: A discussion of the first scientific attempt to write a history on the theory of materialism was marked by London.

RAUSCHENBUSCH, WALTER. *Christianity and the Social Crisis.* New
York: The Macmillan Company, 1907. 429 pp., HL 336699

Contents: Historical analysis of Christianity and the involvement of
the church in social action.
Inscription: "Bamford to London. To Charmian with my love.
Fred. Jan 31, 08."
Marginalia: London marked passages discussing the failure of the
church to undertake its fundamental purpose, Jesus' mistake in calling earth "The Kingdom of God," Old Testament hostility to rit-
ual, and Jesus' agreement with Mary of Bethany.

READE, WINWOOD. *The Martyrdom of Man.* New York: Peter
Eckler, 1900. 543 pp., HL 336718

Contents: Quasi-Darwinian history of man.
Inscription: "Leon Bly, Red Bluff, Cal." London wrote *"Before
Adam"* beside the inscription.

London put a copy of *The Martyrdom of Man* in Mulligan Jacobs's
library, one of the sailors aboard the *Elsinore* in *The Mutiny of the
Elsinore.*

REEVE, JAMES KNAPP. *Five Hundred Places to Sell Manuscripts: A
Manual Designed for the Guidance of Writers in Disposing of Their
Work.* Franklin, Ohio: The Editor Publishing Company, 1899.
v, 74 pp., HL

Contents: Directory of serial and book publishers.

Marginalia: London added quite a few names and addresses to the ones already listed in the book: "*The Bookman:* 372 Fifth Avenue, N.Y.C. (Arthur B. Maurice). *The Critic:* 27 West 23rd St., N.Y.C. *The Reader:* 10 West 23rd St., N.Y.C. *The Red Book:* Trunbull White (editor): 158 State St., Chicago. Lecture Agent:-Heber Mac-Donald: 209 West 43rd St., New York City. Associated Sunday Magazines: 52 East 19th St., N.Y.C. Wm. A. Taylor (Editor). The Blanchard-Venturer Co. Lecture crowd. Los Angeles, Calif. James B. Pinker, Effingham Place, Ariendel Street, Strand, London. W.C. Sir Isaac Pitman & Sons, 11. Armen Corner, London, E.C. England. Charles Dryer, *The Delineator,* 17 West 13th St., N.Y.C. Mrs. Fannie K. Hamilton, 703 Stockton St., S.F. Also, care the *Reader,* N.Y.C. I. M. Hazzard, American Press Association. 45 Park Place, N.Y.C. Katharine N. Birdsall, (Newspaper Syndicate) 34 Union Square, New York City. Herbert P. Williams, Macmillan Co. R. W. Johnson (Ass. Ed.[)] *Century Magazine,* Union Square, N.Y.C. Arthur I. Street, Associated Sunday Magazines, 52 East 19th St., N.Y.C. *Century Magazine.* R. W. Gilder—editor. R. W. Johnson—assoc. [editor.] C. C. Buel—asst[.] [editor.] Chester—Treasurer[.] Witter Bynner, *McClure's Mag.* Heber MacDonald, 209 West 43rd St. N.Y.C. Edward Stratton Holloway, J. B. Lippincott Company, Washington Square, Philadelphia Pa. *The Outlook,* 287 Fourth Avenue N.Y.C. Orlando J. Smith, Pres.—Am. Press Association, 45 Park Place, N.Y.C. C. A. Moody, *Out West,* Los Angeles, Calif. C. S. Aiken, *Sunset,* 4 Montgomery St., S.F. C. F. Bourlse, Managing Editor, *Collier's Weekly.* 416 West 13th. St., N.Y.C. [On business card]: Paul R. Reynolds, No. 70 Fifth Avenue. Representatives of Wm. Heinemann, Sampson Low, Marston & Co., Limited, Archibald Constable & Co., of London. *N.Y. Independent,* 130 Fulton St., N.Y.C. Mr. George P. Brett, The Macmillan Co., 66 Fifth Avenue, New York City. H. Perry Robinson, Isbister & Co., 15 Tavistock Street, Convent Garden, London, W.C. *Woman's Home Companion,* 35 West—21st St. N.Y.C. Mr. Frank Chapin Bray, *Chautauquan,* Cleveland, Ohio. Hjmar H. Boyesen, Jeanette L. Gilder, *The Critic,* G. P. Putnam's Sons, 27 West 23rd St. N.Y.C. Caspar Whitney, *Outing,* 239 Fifth Avenue, N.Y.C. Mr. D. E. Wheeler, *Collier's Weekly,* 416—West 13th. St., N.Y.C. *Pearson's Magazine* 43–45 East Nineteenth St., N.Y.C.

Marvin Dana *Smart Set,* 1135 Broadway N.Y.C. *The Critic,* 27 West 23rd St., N.Y.C. Ellery Sedgwick *Frank Leslie's Popular Monthly,* 143 Fifth Avenue, N.Y.C. Will M. Clemens (Lit. agent)—70 Fifth Avenue, N.Y.C. J. O'H Cosgrave. *Everybody's Magazine,* Doubleday, Page & Co., 34 Union Square, N.Y.C.
Enclosures: Listing of Publishers, "The New Competiton" (a contest launched by *Collier's Magazine*), and "Registration in the Rural Free Delivery Service."

An early *Writer's Market,* Reeve's book was a popular guide to the magazine market. London's first mention of the book comes in a letter of 6 September 1899 to Cloudesley Johns. In 1903, he gave a copy to author Elwyn Hoffman: "Dear Elwyn—May this do as well for you as an earlier edition has done for me. With best wishes and the grip of good luck, Jack London. The Bungalow, June 26, 1903."

REEVE, JAMES KNAPP. *Practical Authorship. . . . A Work Designed to Afford Writers an Insight Into Certain Technical, Commercial and Financial Aspects of the Profession of Letters as Followed by the General Writer for Current Publications.* Cincinnati: The Editor Publishing Co., 1900. v, 287 pp., HL 336123

Contents: Guide for writers.

Inscription: "Sincerely Yours[,] James Knapp Reeve. Franklin, O. 2/26/1903."

REEVE, SIDNEY ARMOR. *The Cost of Competition: An Effort at the Understanding of Familiar Facts.* New York: McClure, Phillips & Company, 1906. xix, 617 pp., illus. HL 335830 PF

Contents: Sociological text.

Marginalia: Public corruption is the subject of a paragraph marked by London in this book.

Enclosure: Letter of 28 February 1906 from McClure Phillips & Company to London, requesting that he review Reeve's book.

RENAN, ERNEST. *Anti-Christ, Including the Period from the Arrival of Paul in Rome to the End of the Jewish Revolution.* Boston: Roberts Brothers, 1897. vi, 442 pp., HL 336826

Contents: "Paul in Prison," "Peter at Rome," "The Churches in Judea," "Latest Acts of Paul," "Nearing the Crisis," "Conflagration of Rome," "The Christian Martyrs," "Death of Peter and Paul," "After the Crisis," "The Revolt in Judea," "Massacres in Syria and Egypt," "Vespasian in Galilea," "Terror at Jerusalem," "The Death of Nero," "Disasters and Signs," "The Apostles in Asia," "The Apocalypse," "Later Fortunes of the Book Accession of the Flavii," "The Fall of Jerusalem," "Results of the Fall of Jerusalem."

Marginalia: London was interested in the churches in Judea A.D. 62, the revolt in Judea, and the massacres in Syria and Egypt. His notes include: "Apocalyptic nightmares—[.] 63–67—Class struggle in Jerusalem. 192–3–4—Christ novel. 206–7."

RENAN, ERNEST. *The Apostles.* New York: Carleton, Publisher, 1866. vi, 353 pp., HL 336702

Contents: History of the beginnings of Christianity, including the life of Jesus.

Marginalia: London marked passages about Saint Paul's legendary love, and his life, and the story of women in Judea.

RENAN, ERNEST. *Life of Jesus.* Boston: Little, Brown and Company, 1903. x, 481 pp. HL 336723

Contents: "Widely recognized as the one great literary monument of a century of New Testament criticism."—Editor's Note.

Marginalia: London drew heavily on this and the two preceeding books for material to use in his Christ novel. On the endpapers of this book, London's novel begins to take shape: "Girl is from the west of Antipas. At first not converted. But at the End of story is. Hero meets her after crucifixion. She is weeping. She does not speak. Hero marks strange charm of Jesus—even over himself. Pilate tells Priests Jesus is not political. They threaten by saying they will make it political. 335—They instance woman taken in adultery. Pilate applauds. The man is no fool. He is a philosopher. The Pharisees will never forgive him that. 337—Again Pilate applauds— 'a wise man of the Christ!' 342—He is stoned. 347—Council called against him. 360—Council called against him. 362—Judas did not betray for money. Pilate laughs it to scorn.

"175–253–54—Girl denies Jesus is son of David—She tells of his people in Galilee. Galilee—names relations. 192—Pilate says he was a fisherman—Girl says he was a carpenter before that. Chaps. X & XI—The king of the beggars. 214–15—company he kept—publicans, sinful women, etc. 216—his progress over country. 224— When claim is made that John is Elijah raised from the dead, Pilate—'shows insanity.' 'What is political there?' One replies that the Jews can make anything political, even dead men's bones. 229–30— Jerusalem priests. 297—Charlatanism of Jesus & apostles. 307— prosperity is sin—Pilate retorts that they had a treasurer that malfeased. 313—Jesus insane, possessed. 322—Some Roman sneers at the religiosity of the Jews.

"Herod contends that Jesus is a harmless fanatic—simple-minded, lunatic[.] Jewish girl contends he is sane[.] 135—reign of God on earth—over-throw of Roman rule, therefore—this the girl denies. But somebody else affirms it. 140—Pilate argues, priests are wrong because Christ is putting out of a job. 146–48–9–etc.—Hero asks about John the Baptist—Pilate & girl give different accounts of John. 156–7—Pilate tells of reports of John & Jesus working to-

gether—putting priests out of commission—also, of row raised by
priests & execution of John by Antipas. 162-63—'End is at hand—
etc.'—revolutionist. 165—When peasants tried to make Christ
a king—Pilate's agents reports of the matter. Pilate instances the
episode[.]

"'Hero says: I prefer the Greek attitude of practicing virtue without hope of recompense. Be good because it is good to be good,
rather than to be good in order to escape hell or win to some future
heaven.'—p. 116–17[.] Foregoing in some discussion at Pilate's
court. Pilate's attitude on miracles—Missouri ["show me"]. Bring
in Pilates wife[.] I tell, at Pilate's, that I saw lepers healed—if they
were lepers.

"110—Religious tensions of Jews. 118-19—Herod & Herod's 3
sons. 119—The Roman procurators including Pilate. 146—Hero
asks about John the Baptist—Pilate & Jewish girl both give different accounts of John. 179—Landscape description[.] 193—Great
road from Aere to Damascus. 231—The phrase 'foolish Galileans.'
239—Nicodemus, the rich Pharisee[.] 240—Jesus destroys the
Law[.] 369—Arrest & trial[.] 373, also 384—Jesus was guilty of a
capital crime under the law—Pilate recognizes this[.] 377—Pilate
states that he hates the Jewish law; but—379—Pilate: 'It has been
our policy to remain neutral in these quarrels of sectaries.' 381—
riot threatened. Pilate has me and all men, in readiness. 382—Still
Pilate tries to save Jesus. 382—Jews had caused 'trouble with Rome
over votive shields.'

"106—Christ[.] 122—Hero argues that Jesus is not a political
revolutionist[.] 132—The Divine is within Christ—a personal
awareness of the indwelling of God. 387—passed back on Romans
to execute Jesus[.] 389—the bitter cup—prophesied[.] 390—Shape
of cross: T[.] 391—Pilate's sneer—'King of the Jews[.]' 398—theories that he did not die but Lodbrog says it is gossip. 399—Pilate is
surprised at quick death and summons Centurion to corroborate.
Practically all Pilate's troop were anxious[.]"

This book was one of the primary sources for London's Christ
novel—a book that found publication as a chapter in *The Star Rover*.

RICKLIN, FRANZ. *Wish Fulfillment and Symbolism in Fairy-Tales.*

New York: Nervous and Mental Disease Publishing Company, 1915. iii, 90 pp., HL

Contents: Psychological analysis of children's literature.

Marginalia: London marked several pages of text dealing with the symbolism of the fairy tale.

RIIS, JACOB. *The Battle with the Slum.* New York: The Macmillan Company, 1902. xi, 465 pp., illus. HL 337289

Contents: "*The Battle with the Slum* is properly the sequel to *How the Other Half Lives,* and tells how far we have come and how." —Preface.

Marginalia: London made only one mark in this book, on page 27, which he indexed on the rear flyleaf: "English Slum (dead) compared with American slum (yeast) 27[.]"

Author and journalist Jacob Riis devoted most of his life to the improvement of conditions in New York schools and tenements, including the establishment of parks and playgrounds, and the Jacob A. Riis Neighborhood House. Riis's books often appeared on the same advertising bill with London's.

RILEY, JAMES WHITCOMB. *Good-Bye, Jim.* Indianapolis: The Bobbs Merrill Company, 1913. 27 leaves, illus. HL 337661

Contents: Juvenile picture book.

Inscription: "To Jack London with all kinds of good wishes from Howard Chandler Christy[.] Oct. 15th. 1913."

Christy was most famous as an illustrator for *Scribner's, Harper's, Collier's Weekly,* and *Cosmopolitan.* He also illustrated many of James Whitcomb Riley's books. On 13 July 1913, London wrote to Christy (HL) from Oakland's Merritt Hospital: "As you will see from the heading of this letter, I am on my back. It was my appendix, and I had it out last Tuesday. Everything's going beautifully; and now, my very first letter since the operation is to be dictated to you, to tell you the delight I have taken in your illustrations of *The Valley of the Moon.* I have to confess that I had had my misgivings about your being able to handle successfully my sort of types; I didn't think you could do it, but by golly! you did—you did! And I have keenly enjoyed your depicting of Billy and Saxon and the rest."

George Sterling, Edwin Markham, and Jack London at Bohemian Grove

ROBERTSON, H. A. *Erromanga: The Martyr Isle*. London: Hodder and Stoughton, 1902. ix, 467 pp., illus. HL 332615

Contents: A history of Erromanga written by a missionary who lived on the island for nearly thirty years.

Bookseller: "Throp's Subscription Library, Reading, Pennsylvania."

Marginalia: London marked paragraphs discussing Erromanga, Dillon Bay, Hawaii, and wives.

ROBINSON, VICTOR. *Comrade Kropotkin*. New York: The Altrurians, 1908. 127 pp., illus. HL 332654

Contents: Biography of Kropotkin.

Inscription: "To Jack London with the high regards of Victor Robinson."

ROESLER, FRANK EMILE. *The World's Greatest Migration: The Origin of the "White Man."* Kansas City: F. E. Roesler, 1913. 15 pp., HL

Contents: Theory of the origins of the Anglo-Saxon.

Marginalia: On the cover, London wrote: "I have memories of vast run migrations through many lives—snow & ice—I take it that we came south. Ethnology."

London's annotations concern the origins of the white man. He wrote "game" on page 7.

ROESLER, FRANK EMILE. *The World's Greatest Migration: The Origin of the "White Man."* Kansas City: F. E. Roesler, 1913. 15 pp., illus. HL

Contents: See previous entry.

Marginalia: "Ethnology[.] Gather all the Sun sickness, etc. under 'Ethnology.'"

London was forced to cancel his *Snark* voyage around the world because of a mysterious ailment that caused his extremities to swell to tremendous size, and generally left him completely incapacitated. As a result, he began to amass a large library of medical and ethnological books which explained what he felt were the racial causes of his illness.

ROSSE, FLORENCE JAMES. *Philosophy & Froth.* New York: Broadway Publishing Company, 1905. 27 pp., illus. HL 337619

Contents: Philosophical quips and sayings.

Inscription: "For J. London. Compliments of the Author[.]"

ROSSER, WILLIAM HENRY. *The Yachtman's Handy-Book, For Sea Use, and Adapted to the Board of Trade Yachting Certificate.* London: Norie and Wilson, 1896. viii, 144 pp., illus. HL 336827

Contents: "this work . . . has been written to give, in as plain terms as possible, a complete knowledge of the intent and purpose of Practical Navigation."—Preface.

Marginalia: London marked paragraphs explaining how to correct a compass course, departure, the conversion of departure into difference of longitude, tides and times of high water, the chronometer, and the rules of navigation.

RUSSELL, ADDISON PEALE. *Library Notes.* Boston: Houghton, Mifflin and Company, [19—]. 402 pp., HL 336758

Contents: "Insufficiency," "Extremes," "Disguises," "Standards," "Rewards," "Limits," "Incongruity," "Mutations," "Paradoxes," "Contrasts," "Types," "Conduct," "Religion."

Enclosures: Clippings from *Western Christian Advocate*; 21 August 1912, page 17: "Addison P. Russell: Moral Knight of English Letters," and 15 May 1912, pages 11-12: "William Henry Venable, Cincinnati's Arnold of Rugby." Also clipping dated 8 September 1906: "To A. P. Russell, (on His Eightieth Birthday)."

SALEEBY, CALEB WILLIAMS. *The Cycle of Life According to Modern Science, Being a Series of Essays Designed to Bring Home to Men's Business and Bosoms.* New York: Harper & Brothers, 1904. iii, 342 pp., illus. HL 337230

Contents: Popular essays on a variety of subjects.

Marginalia: London marked paragraphs which dealt with a number of subjects including external evidence of the existence of the mind, atomic power, a comparison of human versus geologic history, speculation of the future progress of civilization, the evolutionary process, and Herbert Spencer. London recorded the distance run aboard the *Snark* on the endpaper: "117 miles, S.S.W. run from yesterday noon to my sight."

Read aboard the *Snark, The Cycle of Life* was incorporated into *Martin Eden* (pp. 318-19), the novel London was writing at the time: "Down town he stopped off long enough to run into the library and search for Saleeby's books. He drew out *The Cycle of Life,* and in the car turned to the essay Norton had mentioned on Spencer. As Martin read, he grew angry."

SALEEBY, CALEB WILLIAMS. *Worry: The Disease of the Age.* New York: Frederick A. Stokes Company, 1907. xi, 311 pp., HL 336163

Contents: Essays commenting on the effects, types, and cures of anxiety, and the relation between worry and religion.

Marginalia: London marked a quotation from Spencer, a quotation from Huxley ("Public opinion called that chaos of prejudices"), and paragraphs discussing the emotion of love and the irrationality of the worry of growing old.

SALT, HENRY STEPHENS. *Cruelties of Civilization: A Program of Human Reform.* London: William Reeves, 1896. Two volumes, various paginations. HL 336200

Contents: "Humanitarianism: Its General Principles and Progress," "I Was in Prison," "Plea for Mercy to Offenders," "Women's Wages: And the Conditions under Which They Are Earned," "Dangerous Trades for Women," "The Humanizing of the Poor Law," "Vivisection," "Sport," "The Extermination of Birds," "The Horse," "Cattle Ships and Our Meat Supply," "Behind the Scenes in Slaughter Houses."

Marginalia: London was interested in the description of Ceylon divers, making matches, and the list of dangerous trades for women, such as fur and cape making, glass blowing, and the use of white lead.

SCHEFFAUER, HERMAN GEORGE. *Of Both Worlds: Poems.* San Francisco: A. M. Robertson, 1903. 144 pp., illus. HL 83234

Contents: Poems.

Inscription: "For Jack London, this little book with the hope of a closer intimacy with me whose incomparable work has ever found its greatest admirer in Herman Scheffauer."

Marginalia: London marked the following poems: "The Song of the Slaughtered Disarmament," "Shangalon of the Pole," "The Night Bells of Noel," "Lines on a Dead Dog," "Poe," "The Sea of Serenity."

Herman George Scheffauer was a San Francisco-born poet and member of the Crowd. He was a protégé of Ambrose Bierce, and wrote poetry in a style similar to that of Bierce's star pupil, George Sterling. Scheffauer left the Bay Area in 1910 for Germany, where, like Sterling, he committed suicide.

SCHNACK, FERDINAND J. H. *The Aloha Guide: The Standard Handbook of Honolulu and the Hawaiian Islands for Travelers and Residents with a Historical Resumé, Illustrations and Maps.* Ho-

nolulu, Hawaii: Honolulu *Star-Bulletin,* 1915. 202 pp., illus.
HL 332737

Contents: Travel guide to Honolulu and the Hawaiian Islands.
Marginalia: London marked passages on pages 20, 29, 33, and 114
dealing with Hawaiian vocabulary, Walter F. Frear (governor of the
Territory of Hawaii in 1907), Hawaiian climate and weather, and
Mauna Loa and the Polo Grounds.

SCHOPENHAUER, ARTHUR. *The Art of Controversy and Other Post-
humous Papers.* London: Swan Sonnenschein & Company,
Limited, 1896. vi, 120 pp., HL 336725

Contents: "The Art of Controversy," "On the Comparative Place of
Interest and Beauty in Works of Art," "Psychological Observa-
tions," "On the Wisdom of Life: Aphorisms," "Genius and Virtue."
Bookseller: Smith Brothers, Oakland, California.
Marginalia: The passage London marked in this book concerned
possible strategies to follow in the course of an argument.

"I have read Schopenhauer and Weininger," London wrote in a
copy of *Before Adam* which he gave to Charmian, "and all the German misogynists, and still I love you. Such is my chemism—our
chemism, rather" (Charmian London, *The Book of Jack London,* 2:
121).

London criticized Schopenhauer publicly in *Smoke Bellew:* "For
the first time in his life he was really learning woman, and so clear
was Labiskwee's soul, so appalling in its innocence and ignorance,
that he could not misread a line of it. All the pristine goodness of
her sex was in her, uncultured by the conventionality of knowledge
or the deceit of self-protection. In memory he reread his Schopenhauer and knew beyond all cavil that the sad philosopher was
wrong. To know woman, as Smoke came to know Labiskwee, was
to know that all woman-haters were sick men."[44]

SCHULTZ, ALFRED PAUL KARL EDWARD. *Race or Mongrel: A Brief
History of the Rise and Fall of the Ancient Races of Earth: A The-
ory that the Fall of Nations Is Due to Intermarriage with Alien
Stocks; A Demonstration that a Nation's Strength Is Due to Racial
Purity; a Prophecy that America Will Sink to Early Decay Unless*

Immigration Is Rigorously Restricted. Boston: L. C. Page & Company, 1914. 369 pp., illus. HL 334748

Contents: Racial history.

Marginalia: This book is heavily marked by London. Some of the paragraphs he marked concern the Chaldeans and history of the Phoenicians, a conclusion that the future lies with the pure race, an account of the destruction of the Carthaginians by intermarriage, discussions of Jesus, an Aryan and not a Jew by race (thus Christianity is an Aryan religion), the Hindus, history of the Greeks, the degeneration of the Romans into a mongrel race, the rise of the Anglo-Saxon, a nonmongrelized race, Anglo-Saxons in America, and the doom of the Anglo-Saxon through interbreeding with other races. On the rear pastedown, he wrote: "Big Essay: 'Ragnarok' Perishing Anglo-Saxon in U.S.—War is a divine beneficence compared with mixed breeding.

"A book for Socialist autobiography[.] 59—Golden Rule—Indian poetry[.] 182-183—Why not write a 'Ragnarok' when men fight side by side with the geniuses of the race—a la key motif of *Mutiny of the Elsinore.* 212—Bit of Edda[.]"

Enclosure: Notepaper with "Edward. List of Jack's books" written on it by Charmian London. Also, arithmetic scribbled on verso by Jack London.

SCHWOB, MARCEL. *Mimes.* Portland, Maine: Thomas B. Mosher, 1901. xxviii, 96 pp., illus. HL 332395

Contents: Twenty-one prose songs which are "reiterations of a dead and vanished time, reincarnations of the Greek soul."—Foreword.

Inscription: "To Jack London, about to start on a trip around the world.

A reveller he gives, of the
serious kind, farsighted with
    fire, not wine, beneath the
region of his heart.
"He's drunk sheer madness!
    not with wine
But old fantastic tales he'll arm
    His heart in heedlessness divine.

And dare the road nor dream
of harm.
Fannie K. Hamilton. September, 1906."

Newspaper writer Fannie K. Hamilton first met London in 1903.
(*See* Joseph Conrad, *Tales of Unrest.*)

SCOTT, LEROY. *The Shears of Destiny.* New York: Doubleday,
Page & Company, 1910. 333 pp., illus. HL 332220
Contents: Novel.
Inscription: "To Comrade Jack London: With the hearty regards of
Leroy Scott[.] Caritas Island, Stamford, Conn[.] July 15, 1910[.]"

SCOTT, LEROY. *The Walking Delegate.* New York: Doubleday,
Page & Company, 1905. 372 pp., illus. HL 334760
Contents: Novel.
Marginalia: London disagreed with Leroy Scott's description of the
St. Ettienne Hotel: "It was a push button" he wrote on page 8. And
on page 18, Charmian noted, "If all floors are 30 ft., the building is
660 feet high already!" London also marked paragraphs dealing
with a union fight, the dialect of a workman, and graft and corruption. On the rear endpapers, he made notes for a book review:
"Author Shares familiarity with his subject—with the lives of the
people with whom he speaks. Graphic, interest maintains from first
page to last—the book once begun cannot be laid down; it is to be
feared that the average reader, held by the story, will race through
the pages and miss—not the lesson, but the vital facts of the story—.
It is a transcript from life, from 20th Century life, from 20th Century life in New York City where the steel fabrics (skyscrapers) are
reared into the sky to constitute themselves mountain ranges, as
upstanding peaks, outjutting spurs, in the Jungle of Commercial
empire—Then, next, the deeds of the Jungle.
  "Begin with graft & rottenness everywhere in business life.
Then—production for profit instead of service—a sample. Then—
the old sinning and the new. The old primitive struggle for existence, & the new struggle for existence[.] Did the author know
what he was doing.
  "How Baxter sold out Foley when discovered, by informing the
district attorney—& the contractors are called for it, 'Public Bene-

factors.' 363—and then, the one honest man, Tom, the hero of the book & the battler for the Truth & the right, sells out the right & the truth, not that he may benefit, but that the union may benefit— he blackmailed the horses.

"Rottenness of walking delegate[,] of Employers—See Baxter, p. 57[.] The ethics of industry—86—of the battle of the strong—of society based upon elusiveness that is for profit rather than service of baseness that is of betrayal & chicane rather than the positive struggles & efforts of primitive times—otherwise it is primitive."

"67—care more for dollars than self-respect[.] 82—86—Employers traitors to each other[.] Rottenness of the union—betrayal[.] 207—What Foe said when his union rottenness failed, of the business rottenness of Baxter[.] 263—The futile rebellion of Mr. Driscoll & the rottenness & betrayal[.] The double cross of thieves' parlance[.] 276—336[.]"

London's opinions of *The Walking Delegate* were published in the San Francisco *Examiner,* 28 May 1905.

SEELEY, SIR JOHN ROBERT. *The Expansion of England.* Evanston, Illinois: Thurland & Thurland, [19—]. viii, 309 pp., HL 338649

Contents: Lecture courses.
Marginalia: London was interested in a passage on page 244 asserting that modern civilization is great because it has more demonstrated truths. He noted this on the rear pastedown: "244—The text of truth[.]"

SELIGMAN, EDWIN ROBERT ANDERSON. *The Economic Interpretation of History for Its Marxist Theory.*
New York: The Columbia University Press, 1902. ix, 166 pp., HL 336772

Contents: "We may state the thesis succinctly as follows: The existence of man depends upon his ability to sustain himself; the economic life is therefore the fundamental condition of all life."— Introduction.
Marginalia: London was interested in Marx's manifesto, property, and the fundamentals of Marxist theory.

SERVICE, ROBERT WILLIAM. *The Spell of the Yukon and Other Verses*. Philadelphia: Edward Stern & Co., Inc., 1907. 99 pp., illus. HL 338570

Contents: Poems.
Bookseller: Smith Brothers, Oakland, California.
Inscription: "For 'Cuz' and Uncle Jack. 1910."

SERVICE, ROBERT WILLIAM. *The Trail of '98. A Northland Romance*. New York: Grosset & Dunlap, Publishers, 1910. xi, 514 pp., illus. HL 332506

Contents: Poems.
Inscription: "I have had two ambitions—one *was* to meet Jack London (I just met him) [—] the hell with the other ambition. This is for 'Jack' from Ed Wynn. 10 / 29 / 1913[.]"

SERVISS, GARRETT PUTNAM. *Other Worlds: Their Nature, Possibilities and Habit-ability in the Light of the Latest Discoveries*. New York: D. Appleton and Company, 1901. xv, 282 pp., illus. HL 337044

Contents: This book "presents the latest discoveries among the planets of the solar system, and shows their bearing upon the question of life in those planets"—Preface.
Marginalia: Check mark at top of page 18, beside "Mercury, A World of Two Faces and Many Contrasts."

SEVERANCE, CAROLINE MARIA (SEYMOUR). *The Mother of Clubs*. Los Angeles: Baumbart Publishing Co., 1906. 191 pp., illus. HL 334806

Contents: "The Genesis and Purpose of the Club Idea," "From Boston to Los Angeles," "Woman's Club and Friday Morning Club of Los Angeles," "A Bit of Personal Evolution," "Letters and Addresses," "Contributions to Current Thought," "Reminiscences," "Extracts from Letters Written to Madame Severance."
Inscription: "To Jack London—as a slight token of my keen sympathy in his heroic efforts by tongue & pen for social betterment—& in the hope that if he have time, and wish to go over the little volume, he may find sympathetic interest in many of its topics, and

share its hopes of a peaceful solution of our appalling problems. From C. N. Severance. 'El Nido.' 806 W. Adams[.] Los Angeles, June 1906[.]"

Enclosure: Letter from London to Severance: "Thank you heartily for your kindness in sending me the book. It just arrived this mail, and when I tell you I have already delved into it to the extent of finding N. O. Nelson's correspondence with you, you will see that I am going to enjoy it."

"Mr. Nelson, by the way, has been up to see us. He just left this morning. Yesterday afternoon we were out riding over the hills and through the canyons, and in the evening we had a swim in Sonoma Creek. Mr. Nelson is one of the youngest men I ever met. He's a perfect joy."

"Facing page 143 in your book, is the photograph of you, Rebecca Spring, and Susan B. Anthony. Can you tell me how I can go about it to get this photograph? You see, I know Mrs. Rebecca Spring very well, and I have not forgotten the evening I spent at El Nido."

SINCLAIR, MAY. *The Helpmate.* New York: Henry Holt and Company, 1907. 438 pp., HL 332518

Contents: Novel.

Inscription: "Jack and Charmian, my dear friends, this tender, this exquisite, this delicate, this masterful revelation of a spiritual battle, to you, with my love & happy memories of radiant, happy vital days. Fred I. Bamford. Sept. 12, [']07[.]"

In a letter to Frederick Bamford (19 August 1907, HL), Charmian London sent her thanks for May Sinclair's book: "No, we haven't read May Sinclair's latest book. I wish you would send it to us. I love to get books from you, and if *The Helpmate* is half as wonderful as *The Divine Fire,* I'll be doubly grateful. If you are so kind, brother, send to us at Papeete, Tahiti, which is our next address."

SINCLAIR, UPTON BEALL. *The Cry for Justice. An Anthology of the Literature of Social Protest. The Writings of Philosophers, Poets, Novelists, Social Reformers, and Others Who Have Voiced the Struggle Against Social Injustice.* Philadelphia: The John C. Winston Company, Publishers, 1915. 891 pp., illus. HL 12771

Contents: Essays on social topics.
Inscription: "My Dear Jack London: This is the second time you have done me a great favor—The other time with *The Jungle*—and I must not fail to send you my very sincere appreciation. Upton Sinclair[.] Gulfport, Miss. June 29th, 1915[.]"
Enclosures: Letter from Upton Sinclair to Mr. Armond Carroll. Flyer entitled: "A Collection of the Literature of Socialism."

The favor Sinclair refers to is the introduction London wrote for *The Cry for Justice*. In it, London compared the book to the Bible, Koran, and Talmud.

SINCLAIR, UPTON BEALL. *The Industrial Republic. A Study of the America of Ten Years Hence.* New York: Doubleday, Page & Company, 1907. xiv, 284 pp., illus. HL 317406
Contents: Novel.
Inscription: "To Jack & Charmian & the *Snark* with the greetings of Upton Sinclair[.] 'Caelum non animum mutant qui trans mare currunt.'"

SINCLAIR, UPTON BEALL. *The Jungle.* New York: The Jungle Publishing Co., 1906. 413 pp., HL 332436
Contents: Novel.
Inscription: "To Jack London, with all my heart. Upton Sinclair."
"'Where savage beasts through forest midnight roam, Seeking in Sorrow for each other's joy!'"
Enclosure: "Sustainers' Edition: An appeal was published in the Socialist press for advance orders to make possible the publication of this book. About five thousand copies were ordered, of which this is one. The Author."

SINCLAIR, UPTON BEALL. *The Jungle.* New York: The Jungle Publishing Co., 1906. 413 pp., HL 332437
Contents: Novel.
Inscription: "To Jack London with all my heart. The Author. Princeton, N.J. Feb. 17[, ']06."
Enclosure: Newspaper review of *The Jungle:* "Upton Sinclair's Great Work."

"To Jack London,
with all my heart.

Upton Sinclair

'Where savage beasts through
forest midnight roam,
Seeking in sorrow for each-
other's joy!'"

SINCLAIR, UPTON BEALL. *The Metropolis*. New York: Moffat,
Yard & Company, 1908. 376 pp., HL 332438
Contents: Novel.
Inscription: "To Jack London with the greetings of Upton Sinclair[.]
March 10th[,] '08."

SINCLAIR, UPTON BEALL. *The Overman*. New York: Doubleday,
Page & Company, 1907. 90 pp., illus. HL 332523
Contents: Fiction.
Inscription: "To Jack London with the greetings of Upton Sinclair."

SINCLAIR, UPTON BEALL. *Samuel the Seeker*. New York: B. W.
Dodge & Company, 1910. 315 pp., HL 294335
Contents: Novel.
Inscription: "To Jack London with the greetings of Upton Sinclair[.]
A little squib for the Cause & don't expect too much of it!"

173   Treaty of Paris
after the Crimea

267   Slavophils

219   Origin of Nihilism

235
236 }   Russophobes & Russophiles.
237

268 — Tsar agrees to delegate his
authority to the people through a
fear of Nihilists

300 — Russo-French Understanding

307 — Strain caused by nihilism
To Alexander III

311   Nicholas II asserts he will
maintain unflinching autocracy

312 — Declaration of friendship for
France — Treaty

314 — Trans-Siberian Railway.

339 — Japan Chinese War

344 — Resemblance of situation
of China to Turkey.

SINCLAIR, UPTON BEALL. *Springtime and Harvest. A Romance.* New York: The Sinclair Press, 1901. viii, 281 pp., illus. HL 332524

Contents: Novel.
Inscription: "To Jack London[.] If there were any telepathy about the Mystery, or any power of vicarious achievement, I would bid these lost dreams of mine to visit you. U.S. Written in the summer of 1900[.]"

SKOTTSBERG, CARL JOHAN FREDERICK. *The Wilds of Patagonia: A Narrative of the Swedish Expedition to Patagonia, Tierra Del Fuego, and the Falkland Islands in 1907-1909.* New York: The Macmillan Company, 1911. xix, 336 pp., illus. HL 332500

Contents: Account of an expedition to South America.
Marginalia: "Main-yard—sail was being furled. Gooseneck of the Truss broke[.] Yard swinging back & forth. Chain-sling broke[.] Then banging on the lifts & lower-topsail sheets over lee side[.]"

SKRINE, FRANCIS HENRY BENNETT. *The Expansion of Russia: 1815–1900.* Cambridge: At the University Press, 1903. vii, 386 pp., illus. HL 334779

Contents: Political history of Russia.
Marginalia: London marked paragraphs describing Russian tsarist society, the Treaty of Paris of 1856, the death of the tsar, and the Russian involvement in Korea. His notes include: "173—Treaty of Paris after the Crimea[.] 207—Slavophils[.] 219—Origin of Nihilism[.] 235-236-237—Russophobes & Russophiles. 268—Tsar agrees to delegate his authority to the people through fear of nihilists[.] 300—Russo-French understanding[] 307—Strain caused by nihilism to Alexander III[.] 311—Nicholas II asserts he will maintain his unflinching autocracy[.] 312—Declaration of friendship for France—Treaty[.] 314—Trans-Siberian Railway. 339—Japan Chinese War. 344—Resemblance of situation of China to Turkey."

SMALL, ALVION WOODBURY. *Between Eras from Capitalism to Democracy. . . . A Cycle of Conversations and Discourses with Occa-*

sional Side-Lights upon the Speakers. Kansas City, Missouri: Inter-Collegiate Press, 1913. 431 pp., HL 336793

Contents: Socialist essays.

Inscription: "Dear Jack London: Sincerely yours, Ralph Kasper[.] November 21, 1915[.]"

SMITH, ARTHUR HENDERSON. *China in Convulsion.* New York: Fleming H. Revell Company, 1901. 2 volumes, xiv, 770 pp., illus. HL 332758

Contents: Account of the Boxer Rebellion.

Marginalia: London marked passages discussing the paying of tribute in China at the turn of the century and German aggression in 1897.

SMITH, MILES STANIFORTH CARTER. *Handbook of the Territory of Papua.* Melbourne: J. Kemp, Acting Government Printer, [1907?] 108 pp., illus. HL 332736

Contents: Description of the geography, history, and sociology of Papua.

Marginalia: London marked a paragraph describing the treatment of malaria with quinine.

Enclosures: Ship timetable for Australia-Papua-Solomon Islands.

SMITH, ORLANDO JAY. *Eternalism: A Theory of Infinite Justice.* Boston: Houghton, Mifflin and Company, 1902. viii, 321 pp., HL 336746

Contents: "It is usually assumed that the individual is created at his birth by a Divine Power, or by the processes of Nature. . . . If God or Nature has created a criminal, can we acquit the Creator of all accountability for the criminal? . . . Are those who are born vicious really the victims of the malice of Nature or of the wrath of God? I shall attempt herein to answer these and kindred questions and to prove that the Eternal Order can be and must be just and right." —Preface.

Inscription: "To Mr. Jack London, with regards of O. J. Smith[,] July, 1902[.]"

Marginalia: London provided a critique of this book for Smith, writing long commentary in the margins of over one hundred pages. At the end of the book, he summarized his findings: "Much of my criticism may seem capricious, but it is sincere and is delivered with the idea of causing you to reconsider some of your own propositions & to consider anew some of mine.

"I cannot insist too strongly that morality is a development formed only in man. There is no morality to natural processes: The force of gravitation is neither moral nor immoral, no more than the rule of three is moral or immoral. All nature is outside the realm of morals.

"Main argument for me.
"Attack.
"State evolutionary aspect of the ascent of life from lowest to highest—irritability the sole general characteristic. Lowest form—highest—where did conscience come in? Where sense of equity? Where freedom of will? This is for you to show.

"I cannot emphasize too much that the sense of justice is a development in man, & that man, in interrogating & measuring the universe, is prone to project this justice into the whole order of things: This is, of course, a vital mistake on his part.

"Your main weak point is the fallacy No. 2, page 28, in which confusing 'form' with 'substance,' you wrongly conclude that the individual is eternal. You make this fallacy a foundation stone for your theory of Eternalism. Therefore your theory is invalidated. To make your theory stand, you must make your foundation stone stand. You must demonstrate it. And you must 'induce' it, not 'deduce' it.

"If you accept evolution, then you must accept that man is a development from lower forms of life. I accept this, & am a materialist. If you say that the materialist believes in Creationism, then you also must believe in Creationism; for both you and I accept the same thing. In reality, considering the uses to which you have put to the word 'Creationism,' I think it a misuse of the word to apply it to the development theory of the materialist, which theory is also yours."

London's notes were followed by the score of a card-game.

As president of the American Press Association in New York, O. J. Smith started a magazine the summer of 1902. It was for this magazine that London was going to travel to South Africa that same year.

SMITH, STEPHEN. *Who Is Insane?* New York: The Macmillan Company, 1916. 285 pp., HL 336738

Contents: "This Book is a commentary on my experiences as an official visitor of the Institution for the Insane and the Charities and Reformatories of the State."—Foreword.

Marginalia: London marked paragraphs describing the fetishes of cleanliness, the proposition that both the sane and the insane recognize insanity, and the slender thread of destiny that locks some up for insanity, but lets others roam free. His notes at the end of the book include: "p. 17—good example of cleverness of insanity. 23— to 27—Dandy—who is insane."

SMITH, WALKER CONGER. *Sabotage: Its History, Philosophy and Function.* Spokane, Washington: Walker C. Smith, 1913. 32 pp., HL

Contents: "This little work is the essence of all available material collected on the subject of Sabotage for a period of more than two years."—Preface.

Marginalia: The six pages London marked discuss the unconscious advocacy of sabotage, and the potential of a worker's force armed with the knowledge of sabotage. London's notes on the cover include: "File 'Syndicalism'[.] Not a point on which I can disagree with you. A straight-from-the-shoulder, revolutionary statement of the meaning & significance of sabotage. Put on my desk. Walker C. Smith[.] Box 464 Spokane, Wash[.]"

SONNICHSEN, ALBERT. *Deep Sea Vagabonds.* New York: McClure, Phillips & Company, 1903. 336 pp., HL 332520

Contents: Fictionalized account of deep sea voyages.

Marginalia: London's interest in this book centered on a number of sea chanties, a description of a deep sea tyrant, the sailing ship *Calcutta,* the tale of a common sailor who educated himself with a trunk full of books, the sailor's spirit of unrest, striking sailors, and a cockney accent. At the end of the book, London wrote: "40— learning in fo'k'sle. reference to Wolf Larsen[.] 139—chanty—'on

the Banks of the Sacramento[.]' 146-7—chanties[.] 171—chanty[.]
320—to get the best of a captain without mutiny."

SPARGO, JOHN. *The Bitter Cry of the Children*. New York: The
Macmillan Company, 1906. xxiii, 337 pp., illus. HL 336790
Contents: "The purpose of this volume is to state the problem of
poverty as it affects childhood. . . . I have tried to visualize some of
the principal phases of the problem—the measure in which poverty
is responsible for excessive infantile disease and mortality; the tragedy and folly of attempting to educate the hungry ill-fed school
child; the terrible burdens borne by the working child in our modern industrial system."—Preface.
Marginalia: London used this book in his novel *The Iron Heel*. The
subjects of his annotations include the lack of nutrition among poor
children, infant death statistics, child slave trafficking, the abuse of
child workers (including the use of child "inmates" as a source of
cheap labor), malnutrition, and working in a mill.

Although Spargo's's own work and writings were quoted in *The
Iron Heel,* he did not accept the book with the praise one might
have expected. "It is impossible to deny the literary skill which
London displays in this ingenious and stirring romance," Spargo
wrote in *The International Socialist Review*. "He has written nothing
more powerful than this book. In some senses it is an unfortunate
book, and I am by no means disposed to join those of our comrades
who hail it as a great addition to the literature of Socialist propaganda. The picture he gives is well calculated, it seems to me, to
repel many whose addition to our forces is sorely needed; it gives a
new impetus to the old and generally discarded cataclysmic theory;
it tends to weaken the political Socialist movement by discrediting
the ballot and to encourage the chimerical and reactionary notion of
physical force, so alluring to a certain type or mind . . ." (Joan
London, *Jack London and His Times,* p. 310).

SPARGO, JOHN. *The Common Sense of Socialism: A Series of Letters
Addressed to Jonathan Edwards of Pittsburg*. Chicago: Charles H.
Kerr & Company, 1908. 184 pp., HL 336809
Contents: Socialist essays.
Marginalia: the miners' strike in Goldfield, Nevada, and general

discussions of socialism and anarchism were the subjects of interest to London in this book.

SPENCER, HERBERT. *An Autobiography*. New York: D. Appleton Company, 1904. 2 volumes, xv, 655, vii, 613 pp., illus. HL 334749

Contents: Autobiography.

Marginalia: London underlined Spencer's comments on the Greeks, epic poetry, Emerson, the opera, vegetarianism, love and Raphael's "Transfiguration."

Herbert Spencer's work was part of the bedrock of London's philosophy. In an early letter to Johns, London acknowledge this, and lauded the popular philosopher: "Spencer's *First Principles* alone, leaving out all the rest of his work, has done more for mankind, and through the ages will have done far more for mankind than a thousand books like *Nicholas Nickleby, Hard Cash, Book of Snobs, and Uncle Tom's Cabin*" (Charmian London, *The Book of Jack London*, 1: 304).

Spencer is mentioned, quoted, or alluded to in almost all London's novels, including *The Sea-Wolf, The Little Lady of the Big House, The Iron Heel,* and *Martin Eden*. In *Martin Eden* (pp. 106-8), London captures in fiction much of what he probably felt himself when he first came upon Herbert Spencer's *First Principles:* "Martin had heard Herbert Spencer quoted several times in the park, but one afternoon a disciple of Spencer's appeared, a seedy tramp with a dirty coat buttoned tightly at the throat to conceal the absence of a shirt. Battle royal was waged, amid the smoking of many cigarettes and the expectoration of much tobacco-juice, wherein the tramp successfully held his own, even when a socialist workman sneered, 'There is no god but the Unknowable, and Herbert Spencer is his prophet.' Martin was puzzled as to what the discussion was about, but when he rode on to the library he carried with him a new-born interest in Herbert Spencer, and because of the frequency with which the tramp had mentioned *First Principles,* Martin drew out that volume."

"Morning found him still reading. It was impossible for him to sleep. Nor did he write that day. He lay on the bed til his body grew tired, when he tried the hard floor, reading on his back, the book held in the air above him, or changing from side to side. He slept that night, and did his writing next morning, and then the book tempted him and he fell, reading all afternoon. . . . he was now learning from Spencer that he never had known, and that he never could have known had he continued his sailing and wandering forever. . . . And here was the man Spencer, organizing all knowledge for him, reducing everything to unity, elaborating ultimate realities, and presenting to his startled gaze a universe so concrete of realization that it was like the model of a ship such as sailors make and put into glass bottles."

SPENCER, HERBERT. *Facts and Comments.* New York: D. Appleton and Company, 1902. viii, 292 pp., HL 336724

Contents: Essays.
Marginalia: Light and its influence on health was the subject of a paragraph on page 118 that London marked. On the front endpaper, he wrote "74 miles away at 12 M. 12 M. Log. 95" referring to the progress the *Snark* made that day. Later on, possibly the same day, the rear endpapers served as a score card for a game of casino the Londons and Martin Johnson played. The result was "Oct 7 / 08[.] Mate owes Martin .30[.] I [owe Martin] .30[.]"

SPENCER, HERBERT. *The Principles of Psychology.* New York: D. Appleton and Company, 1896. Volume II: 1. viii, 302 pp., illus. HL 339184

Contents: Philosophical essays.
Bookseller: D. P. Elder and Morgan Shepard, San Francisco, California.
Marginalia: "Time & Space can respectively be thought of only in terms each of the other—pp[.] 207-208."

SPENCER HERBERT. *The Principles of Sociology.* New York: D. Appleton and Company, 1896. Volume II: 2. iv, 843 pp., HL 339184

Contents: Philosophical essays.
Bookseller: D. P. Elder and Morgan Shepard, San Francisco, California.

Marginalia: This set of Spencer's works in London's library un-doubtedly replaced earlier copies that he either lost, returned to the library, or gave away. Thus it is not terribly surprising that, in this, the second most important book by Spencer (to London), there is only one marking: On page 611, London marked a paragraph deal-ing with the regime of "status."

SPRADING, CHARLES T. *Liberty and the Great Libertarians.* Los An-geles: Published for the author, 1913. 540 pp., HL 261073
Contents: Essay on liberty and how it has been defined by famous people from different eras.
Inscription: "With Compliments of the Author. Charles T. Sprad-ing. To Jack London, a fellow Libertarian."

STARBUCK, ALEXANDER. *History of the American Whale Fishery from Its Earliest Inception to the Year 1876.* Waltham, Massa-chusetts: Published by the Author, 1878. 766 pp., illus. HL 339663
Contents: History of whaling.
Marginalia: London noted a list of whaling ships and their owners, etc., for the year 1839.

STEELE, RUFUS. *The Fall of Ug: A Masque of Fear.* San Francisco: The Bohemian Club, 1913. xv, 50 pp., illus. HL 339724 PF
Contents: A Bohemian Club Grove Play.
Enclosures: London inserted his notes for *The Acorn-Planter* (a play he wrote for the Bohemian Club's High Jinks): "Red Cloud—Bari-tone[.] White Man—Big Tenor[.] Quail Woman[,] White Woman[:] Light Tenors[.] Medicine Man—Bass[.] He sings dawn song.
    "*Acorn Song* enlarge these four lines, play any trick I please, in the enlargement—so that at least 4 stanzas.
    "Names. Indians[:] Red Cloud[,] Quail Woman[,] Medicine Man[,] Ishi[,] War Chief[.] Whites[:] White man[,] Sun Man[,] Mate Woman[,] Dreamer[,] Gunsmith[,] Gunner[.]
    "Introduction[.] The life made abundant. greater use of the earth[.] items, we should not regret the passing of the buffalo which permitted only thousands of lower-typed Indians to subsist

on the land (grass to meat, & meat to Indian) where today, where the buffalo grazed, millions of higher-typed subsist—higher in beauty, in sentiment, in fellowship & highest of all, in joy in the joy of life.

"Introduction[.] Quote Porter Garnett's end of Introduction at end of mine.

"Stewart[.] Send him 3 copies. Ask him, one copy fix for me with the music items inserted in the text wherever necessary.

"*Music Scheme*[.] Main scheme[.] 2 motifs, Indian & White[,] that are an apparent conflict, that is reconciled in the end. These two motifs are the same in impact, though one is phrased in terms & measures of European music, the other in terms & measures of Indian, primitive, barbaric music.

"The two motifs, which are one in impact, carry dominant motif of the play, namely fecundity, with its two divisions, acorn planters & love of woman.

"Argument[.] The soil & the world belongs to those who make the soil & the world most fruitful & thereby make possible a life more abundant.

"Argument (2)[.] In the morning of the world, while his tribe makes its hunting trip in the grove, Red Cloud, the first man of men, and the first man & leader of the Nishinam tribe, stresses the duty of life, which duty is to make life more abundant, and sings the song of fecundity, which is dual-being the song of the acorn-planting, the second the song of the love of woman.

"Act II[.] War Chiefs' song of triumph, joined in by tribe—at killing of Sun Men[.]"

STEFFENS, JOSEPH LINCOLN. *The Shame of the Cities.* New York: McClure, Phillips & Company, 1904. v, 306 pp., illus. HL 259464

Contents: "Introduction; and Some Conclusions," "Tweed Days in St. Louis," "The Shame of Minneapolis," "The Shamelessness of St. Louis," "Pittsburgh: A City Ashamed," "Philadelphia: Corrupt and Contented," "Chicago: Half Free and Fighting On," "New York: Good Government to the Test."

Marginalia: London's markings in Steffens's book concern the corruption of the businessman, an analysis of the profit motive, graft and the political machine, delegates and politicians, and control and corruption of the church. On the rear pastedown, he wrote: "5—7—8—10—11—14[—]142."

STERLING, GEORGE. *Beyond the Breakers and Other Poems.* San Francisco: A. M. Robertson, 1914. 141 pp., illus. HL 20333
Contents: Poems.
Inscription: "Dearest Wolf. Another book of verses, to you who has given me so many glorious books. My love to you, Wolf-man! Greek[.] Sag Harbor, N.Y. October 1st, 1914."
London's first meeting with George Sterling came some time after the turn of the century. Sterling, who worked as a secretary in his uncle's real estate firm, was a bohemian poet and protégé of Ambrose Bierce. When Sterling and London met, possibly at Coppa's restaurant in San Francisco, they immediately tried to impress one another: Sterling deluged London with the airs of the artful bohemian, and London bludgeoned Sterling with his knowledge of the Oakland abyss. The contest proved to be a stand-off, and the beginning of a long and deep friendship which would last the rest of London's life.

STERLING, GEORGE. *The Caged Eagle and Other Poems.* San Francisco: A. M. Robertson, 1916. 167 pp., HL 339654
Contents: Poems.
Inscription: "Dearest Wolf! Only a few more of my vain rhymes. But let us hope they'll pain the hyphenated! With my best love, Greek. San Francisco, June 27th, 1916."
Marginalia: London made check marks by two poems: "To Twilight" and "In Autumn."

STERLING, GEORGE. *The House of Orchids and Other Poems.* San Francisco: A. M. Robertson, 1911, 140 pp. HL 339667 PF
Contents: Poems.
Inscription: "Dearest Wolf: Another of my butterflies, destined to share for a while the same air as your own wide-winged eagles. My best love goes with the book, Wolf. Greek. San Francisco, April 11th, 1911."

> To our genius,
>
> Jack London :
>
> Here's my book, my
> heart you have already.
>
> George Sterling.
>
> Piedmont, Cal.,
> Dec. 24ᵗʰ, 1903.

On the half title page, Sterling wrote: "For Jack London from George Sterling."
Enclosure: "A Dream of Fear": Two-page manuscript poem, signed.

STERLING, GEORGE. *Ode on the Opening of the Panama-Pacific International Exposition.* San Francisco: A. M. Robertson, 1915. 16 pp. HL 253838

Contents: Poem.
Inscription: "Man of Men! This eupiptic ode of mine. Ever and always, Greek. San Francisco, Nov. 6th, 1915[.]" "For Jack London, from George Sterling."

STERLING, GEORGE. *The Testimony of the Suns and Other Poems.* San Francisco: W. E. Wood, 1903. 142 pp. HL 339655
Contents: Poems.
Inscription: "To our genius, Jack London: Here's my book, my heart you have already. George Sterling. Piedmont, Cal., Dec. 24th, 1903."

STEVENSON, PAUL EVE. *By Way of Cape Horn: Four Months in a Yankee Clipper.* Philadelphia: J. B. Lippincott Company, 1900. 410 pp., illus. HL 337224
Contents: A personal account of life aboard a merchant Yankee deep-water ship. London characterized the book as "The Cyrus Wakefield—Captain Henry[.]"
Marginalia: A description of a ship "in the doldrums," accounts of weathering gales and rough weather, sailors' speech patterns and a dialogue describing the setting of the ship's sails, rounding Cape Horn, a sea story, and the sighting of an albatross in a storm are the subjects London noted in Stevenson's book. Much of the book found its way into London's own sea fiction. On the rear endpaper, he wrote: "maneuver of wearing ship[—]103[.]"

STEVENSON, ROBERT LOUIS. *In the South Seas, Being an Account of Experiences and Observations in the Marquesas, Paumotus and Gilbert Islands in the Course of Two Cruises on the Yacht* Casco *(1888) and the Schooner* Equator *(1889).* New York: Charles Scribner's Sons, 1905. viii, 409 pp., illus. HL 338618
Contents: Travel guide and narrative.
Inscription: "Leigh H. Irvine, May, 1906. To Jack London, with Sincere regards, Leigh H. Irvine[,] 4/12/07[.] Oakland, Cal."
Marginalia: Most of the markings in this book appear to have been made by Charmian London. However, the marginal scorings on

pages 25 (a paragraph describing the beauty of Anaho in the Marquesas), 169, and 171 (paragraphs about trade winds) were probably made by Jack London.

London's reading of and admiration for Stevenson's work started early. Stevenson is mentioned at the very beginning of the London-Johns correspondence, for instance: "I do join with you, and heartily, in admiration of Robert Louis Stevenson. What an example he was of application and self development! As a storyteller there isn't his equal; the same might almost be said of his essays. While the fascination of his other works is simply irresistible, to me, the most powerful of all is his *Ebb Tide*. There is no comparison possible between him and that other wonderful countryman of his; there is no common norm by which we may judge them" (*Letters*, p. 20).

STEVENSON, ROBERT LOUIS. *The Letters of Robert Louis Stevenson.* New York: Charles Scribner's Sons, 1911. Two volumes, illus. HL 339381
Contents: Letters.
Marginalia: London wrote "314—unbelief in immortality" on an endpaper."

STODDARD, CHARLES WARREN. *For the Pleasure of His Company: An Affair of the Misty City Thrice Told.* San Francisco: A. M. Robertson, 1903. 257 pp., illus. HL 290758
Contents: Tales of San Francisco.
Inscription: "Dear Jack London. To you, the writer of brave and splendid Novels, I offer this poor story with all its imperfections—though there may be no pleasure in such company. Accept it for the love that goes with it. Chas. Warren Stoddard."

STODDARD, CHARLES WARREN. *The Island of Tranquil Delights: A South Sea Idyl and Others.* Boston: Herbert B. Turner & Company, 1904. 318 pp., illus. HL 28314
Contents: Short stories.
Inscription: "To Jack London with heaps of love—Chas. Warren Stoddard. Sept[.]—'04"

Dear Jack London.

To You, the writer
of brave or splen-
ded Novels, I offer
this poor story
with all its im
perfections — even
though there may
be no pleasure
in such company.
Accept it for the
love that goes with it.

Chas. Warren Stoddard.

STODDARD, CHARLES WARREN. *South-Sea Idyls.* New York: Charles Scribner's Sons, 1899. vi, 339 pp. HL 332467

Contents: Short stories.

Inscription: "To Jack London with the love of his friend Chas. Warren Stoddard."

STODDARD, CHARLES WARREN. *Summer Cruising in the South Seas: [South-Sea Idyls.]* London: Chatto & Windus, 1905. x, 319 pp., HL 333043

Contents: "The experiences recorded in this volume are the result of four summer cruises among the islands of the Pacific"—Preface.

Marginalia: London was interested in Fête-day in Tahiti and Pomotow Island currents.

There are many other annotations and markings throughout the book, made by Charmian London.

Poet and writer Charles Warren Stoddard traveled to the Hawaiian Islands and Tahiti during the early 1870s. Upon his return to the mainland in 1879, he met Robert Louis Stevenson in San Francisco. His tales of the idyllic island life probably encouraged the Scottish author to visit the South Seas. Stoddard's later years were spent in San Francisco and Carmel, where he met both Jack London and George Sterling.

STREETER, JOHN WILLIAMS. *The Fat of the Land: The Story of an American Farm.* New York: Grosset & Dunlap, 1904. xi, 406 pp., illus. HL

Contents: Novel depicting life on a rural farm.

Marginalia: London underlined passages about the best kind of chickens and building a hog pen, and noted the following farm hints on the rear endpapers: "112—Leghorns good summer layers[.] Wyandottes better winter [layers.] 134—brood-sow house[.] 168—Grease & house all tools when *not* in use. Don't keep pigs more than nine months—sell by then for the meat. 282—how to catch hens that will lay when eggs are high. 306—Cost per year of feeding cows, pigs, chickens, etc. see also p. 400."

The book also prompted a few notes for *The Valley of the Moon:* "Billy: After eating trout: 'Don't care if I never see a moving picture show again.' Cross-trees—from deck 99'—10" truck—[from deck—] 172' 10"[.]"

STROBRIDGE, IDAH MEACHAM. *Stories*. New York: Idah M. Strobridge, 1900. Various paginations, illus. HL

Contents: Short stories.

Inscription: "For *Jack London* with the sincere regards of *The Bibliopegish*[.] September[,] MCM."

Ida Meacham Strobridge was a native Oaklander who moved, possibly in 1900, to the Pasadena art colony of Arroyo Seco. London had evidently met her while they both lived in Oakland, and carried on a friendly correspondence with her.

STRONG, JOSIAH. *Expansion Under New World Conditions*. New York: The Baker and Taylor Company, 1900. 310 pp., illus. HL 337222

Contents: "The twentieth century is confronted by conditions which are new in the history of the world, which concern the nations in general and the United States in particular. In this book the subject of *Expansion* is discussed in the light of these new conditions." —Preface.

Bookseller: Smith Brothers, Oakland, California.

Marginalia: London marked paragraphs dealing with the output of U.S. steel mills, and also with the superiority of the Anglo-Saxon, races, and race-development.

SWIFT, LINDSAY. *Brook Farm: Its Members, Scholars, and Visitors*. New York: The Macmillan Company, 1900. x, 303 pp., HL 337233

Contents: "The Transcendental Club," "Brook Farm," "The School and Its Scholars," "The Members," "The Visitors," "The Closing Period."

Marginalia: The falling price of land prompted London to comment: "$50 an acre. Could be bought for $7.50 in 1911."

Brook Farm was an experimental community situated on a 192-acre farm in West Roxbury, Massachusetts. Founded on the premise that

To Jack London.
A Kingly man.
To. Charmian London;
A Queenly Woman,
Without the taint of Royalty.
Sincialy & Affectionately,
George W Galvin M.d
Boston. Nov 27, 16.

plain living and high thinking were beneficial to life, the community lasted only a few years.

SYMONS, ARTHUR. *Poems*. New York: John Lane, 1902. 2 volumes, illus. HL 334830

Contents: Poems.
Bookseller: Paul Elder and Morgan Shepard, San Francisco, California.
Inscription: "Dear Jack, Some hot coals to warm your Christmas evenings. 'Greek.' Christmas, 1902."

London quotes extensively from Symons's "The Daughters of Herodias" in *The Mutiny of the Elsinore*.

TABB, JOHN BANNISTER. *Poems.* Boston: Small Maynard & Company, 1900. xi, 172 pp., HL 338673
Contents: Poems.
Bookseller: Paul Elder and Morgan Shepard, San Francisco, California.
Inscription: "Jack from George [Sterling]. Jan. 12th, 1903."
This book was a birthday gift to London from Sterling.

TALMEY, BERNARD SIMON. *Love: A Treatise on the Science of Sex-Attraction, For the Use of Physicians and Students of Medical Jurisprudence.* New York: Practitioner's Publishing Company, 1915. viii, 438 pp., illus. HL 336715
Contents: A treatise on the emotions of feminine and masculine love.
Marginalia: "160—sperma permanently absorbed by woman—see 191—215[.] 173—tactile eroticism[.] 180—female has greater pleasure[.] 182—transfer of clitoris sexuality to cervix, etc. at puberty. 223—mixoscopy. 306—Woman's wail that men do not understand them[.] 307—woman [*sic*] more interested than men in woman's form[.]"

TALMEY, BERNARD SIMON. *Woman: A Treatise on the Normal and Pathological Emotions of Feminine Love.* New York: Practitioners' Publishing Company, 1912. xii, 262 pp., illus. HL 336764
Contents: "Medico-philosophical treatise . . . [on] feminine amatory emotions.
Marginalia: Among the subjects that London noted were the philosophy of Sappho on sex, Lesbianism among prostitutes, women's breasts, Eros and Libido, jealousy, and a form of vaginal masturbation. He wrote the following notes about the book: "3—10—the breasts[.] 118—the Japanese woman stunt[.] 145—Sappho's perishing of the race in the sterile embrace[.] 150—explanation of *Lesbianism* among prostitutes[.] 223—dandy[.]"

TAYLOR, FITCH WATERMAN. *A Voyage Round the World and Visits to Various Foreign Countries in the United States Frigate* Columbia. . . . New Haven: H. Mansfield, 1846. 2 volumes in one, 317, 331 pp., illus. HL 334845

Contents: Account of a visit to China during the Opium War, the bombing of the Malay coast, and general travel notes.
Bookseller: Dawson's Bookshop, Los Angeles, California.
Marginalia: London noted the following subjects on the front pastedown: "Hawaiian Islands. Vol. II[—]210[.] Picture of Valparaiso[.] [Vol. II—]278[.]"

TAYLOR, FITCH WATERMAN. *A Voyage Round the World and Visits to Various Foreign Countries in the United States Frigate* Columbia. . . . New Haven: H. Mansfield, 1850. 2 volumes in one, 317, 331 pp., illus. HL 334840

Contents: See preceding entry.
Marginalia: In this later edition of the above title, London found a description of burial at sea interesting: "26—sunset[.] 27–8–9— Burial at Sea[.]"

TEICHMANN, ERNST GUSTAV. *Life and Death: A Study in Biology.* Chicago: Charles H. Kerr & Company, 1906. 158 pp., HL336299

Contents: "How Life Appears," "How Life Is Maintained," "How Life Arose," "How Life Disappears."
Marginalia: The fertilization of the egg by the sperm was the subject of a paragraph on page 77 that London marked.

TERRY, T. PHILIP. *Terry's Mexico.* Mexico City: Sonora News Company, 1909. 595 pp., illus. HL 332719

Contents: Mexican travel guidebook.
Bookseller: Smith Brothers, Books, Kodaks, Oakland, California.
Marginalia: London marked passages describing cacti, theaters, beggars, and the Texas dispute of 1820.

THOMPSON, FLORENCE SEYLER. *A Thousand Faces.* Boston: Richard G. Badger, 1915. 308 pp., HL 330822

Contents: "It is hoped that *A Thousand Faces,* which gives a glimpse of our living hells, designated as asylums for the insane and private sanitariums, will stir every man and woman of red blood to immediate action in behalf of those who cannot speak for themselves." —Preface.

Inscription: "To Jack London. A Kingly Man. To Charmian London: A Queenly Woman, Without the taint of Royalty. Sincerely & Affectionately, George W[.] Galvin M.D. Boston. Nov. 22, [']16[.]"

Enclosure: Eight-page pamphlet entitled: "Trustees of Our Public Charitable Institutions in Consequence of Criminal Lack of Interest and Responsibility Are to Blame for the Shocking Conditions in Our Asylums for the Insane.

"One of our most interesting acquaintances in Boston was Dr. George W. Galvin, staunch Socialist and clever surgeon," Charmian wrote in her biography (*The Book of Jack London,* 2: 694). She went on to recount the events of that day with Galvin, which included witnessing two operations. Roughly eleven years later, Galvin sent the above book to the Londons—the day before Jack London died.

THOMSON, SIR BASIL HOME. *The Diversions of a Prime Minister.* London: William Blackwood and Sons, 1894. xiii, 407 pp., illus. HL 332655

Contents: Character sketch and sociological study of the Tongan chiefs inhabiting the Tonga Island Group, South Pacific Ocean.

Marginalia: Cricket matches and the legend of Mary Butako ("telling her soul" was London's comment) are two subjects that London found important enough to mark in this book. He also noted the following other subjects: "51–2–3–4–5—full ceremony of kava drinking[.] 79–80—Short humorous story—'When Mary Told Her Soul'[—]good[.] 81–82—the rival volcanoes[.] 85—kava. 187–8–9—church collections when copra is ripe. 293–94—the Highest of high chief greatness, ceremonial, etc. 297—cutting to pieces in the trough with bamboo knives[.] 298—preparing woman to be married[.] 347–48—Destroying idols[.]"

"When Alice Told Her Soul" was the story that resulted from London's notes in *The Diversions of a Prime Minister.* Completed 30 August 1916, the story was published in the March 1918 *Cosmopolitan,* and later collected in On the Makaloa Mat.

THOMSON, SIR BASIL HOME. *South Sea Yarns*. London: William Blackwood and Sons, 1894. xii, 326 pp., illus. HL 339681
Contents: Stories with a South Sea island setting.
Marginalia: Notes for navigation and a card game score were written on the back pages. London also marked paragraphs describing the last of the cannibal chiefs, and, on the rear endpaper, wrote: "Title & motif for a modern South Sea yarn: 'The Swell of the Reef.'"

THORPE, ROSE HARTWICK. *The Poetical Works of Rose Hartwick Thorpe*. New York: The Neale Publishing Company, 1912. 137 pp., illus. HL 337630
Contents: Poems.
Inscription: "To Mr. and Mrs. Jack London—Rose Hartwick Thorpe[.]"

TORREY, WILLIAM. *Torrey's Narrative: Or, The Life and Adventures of William Torrey*. Boston: A. J. Wright, 1848. xii, 300 pp., illus. HL 75387
Contents: Account of a shipwrecked sailor held captive by cannibals in the Marquesas.
Marginalia: A story of the retrieval of the bones of a missionary prompted London to write the following note: "152—South Sea Story[.]"
Enclosures: Numerous newspaper clippings laid in.

TRAUBEL, HORACE. *Chants Communal*. Boston: Small, Maynard & Company, 1904. 194 pp., HL 332425
Contents: Collection of chants.
Inscription: "This is the moment of the lapse of eros of force in loss of love. This is the bridegroom, this is the mysterious archway of the rainbow.
"To Jack London from Horace Traubel[.] 1905[.]"
Marginalia: London marked a line from the poem "Optimos."
Enclosure: "Chants Communal," a review printed in *The Papyrus*.

TRAUBEL, HORACE. *Optimos.* New York: B. W. Hueback, 1910.
viii, 371 pp., illus. HL 277588
Contents: Poems.
Inscription: "Camden[,] New Jersey. February 18th 1911. For Jack
London with loving feelings. Horace Traubel."

TRAUBEL, HORACE. *With Walt Whitman in Camden.* Boston:
Small, Maynard & Company, 1906. xiv, 473 pp., illus. HL
334791
Contents: Diary and journal of the author's visit with Walt Whitman.
Inscription: "To my dear brother rebel Jack London & with love &
all that goes with love. Horace Traubel[.] 1906[.]"
Enclosure: Note from Traubel dated 12 November 1906, Philadelphia: "I am sending you my book today. I hope it reaches you un-
violated and that you may reach out a glad hand to it when it arrives. Love to you both. Traubel[.]"

TREADWELL, SOPHIE. *An Outcast at the Christian Door.* San Francisco: The Bulletin, 1914. 614 pp., illus. HL
Contents: Religious pamphlet.
Marginalia: London wrote "Fiction data" on the cover of this small
pamphlet.

TRIDON, ANDRÉ. *The Fifth Gospel.* San Francisco: André Tri-
don, 1910. 4 pp., HL
Contents: Short stories.
Marginalia: "Stories to Read" written on front cover.

TRUMAN, BEN CUMMINGS. *The Field of Honor: Being a Complete
and Comprehensive History of Duelling in All Countries: Including the Judicial Duel of Europe, the Private Duel of the Civilized
World, and Specific Descriptions of All the Noted Hostile Meetings
in Europe and America.* New York: Fords, Howard, & Hulbert, 1884. 599 pp., HL 37632
Contents: History of dueling.
Inscription: "With Compliments of the Author. Ben L. Truman."

TURGENEV, IVAN SERGEEVICH. *On the Eve.* London: William Heinemann, 1903. xix, 289 pp., HL 331934

Contents: Story.

Inscription: "To Jack London from Leonard Abbott. Jan. 25/06."

On 27 February 1899 London confessed, in a letter to his friend Cloudesley Johns, that he knew little of Turgenev: "I appreciate, in a way, the high praise of being likened to Tourgenieff. Though aware of the high place he occupies in literature, we are as strangers. I think it was in Japan I read his *House of Gentlefolk*, but that is the only book of his I have ever seen—I do not even know if the title is correct. There is so much good stuff to read and so little time to do it in. It sometimes makes me sad to think of the many hours I have wasted over mediocre works, simply for want of better" (*Letters*, p. 18).

TURNBULL, JOHN. *A Voyage Round the World in the Years 1800, 1801, 1802, 1803, and 1804; in Which the Author Visited the Principal Islands in the Pacific Ocean and the English Settlements of Port Jackson and Norfolk Island.* Philadelphia: Published by Benjamin and Thomas Kite, 1810. 364 pp., HL 334787

Contents: Travel and descriptions, mostly of the Sandwich and Society islands.

Marginalia: London marked a sentence about the "God of Britain" on page 262 and, on the endpapers, wrote: "63–69—South Sea story ideas[.] 262[—]quaint religious observation[.]"

TURNER, GEORGE. *Samoa a Hundred Years Ago and Long Before, Together with Notes on the Cults and Customs of Twenty-three Other Islands in the Pacific.* London: Macmillan and Company, 1884. xvi, 395 pp., illus. HL 145468

Contents: "In the present volume I go back to other ages (prior to the introduction of Christianity into Samoa in 1830) and give the result of my archaeological researches for upwards of forty years." —Advertisement.

Marginalia: Both Jack and Charmian London read and marked passages in this book. Jack's markings include paragraphs about the spinning of a coconut, a village arrangement, the word for "Samoa," and Polynesian dialects. In a series of jottings which he labeled "Samoa Notes," London referred to "Turner's *Samoa*, p. 116 for Prayer on 'Ava.' p. 116 [for] Prayer of Flaming Fire[.] 'Papalagi' (Samoan for 'The White Country,'[)] 'The Dim Distant Place, from which whites came, and to which they went.'—Make title and motif for a story."

TURNER, JOHN KENNETH. *Barbarous Mexico.* Chicago: Charles H. Kerr & Company, 1911. 340 pp., HL 334755

Contents: Social history and description of Mexico.
Marginalia: London marked passages dealing with Vera Cruz, Mexican wages, and the cotton mill strike at Rio Blanco.

TWOMBLY, ALEXANDER STEVENSON. *Kelea: The Surf-Rider.* New York: Fords, Howard, & Hulbert, 1900. 400 pp., illus. HL 331865

Contents: Historical fiction.
Marginalia: London recorded the following notes on the rear endpapers: "The Wild Boar of Maui. *Maikola*—contemptible one. 'Down face!' When king orders, it means the man is to be slain. 169—a good trick, to take the place of an idol. Alii-nui—(big chief, big alii). Alii-kapu—sacred chief. p. 237—Kolon—prostration before a *sacred* chief."
"*Names*[.] Female[:] Mamahana[,] Hoko-lele (shooting star)[,] Kulianui (my Beauty)[,] Kaalumanu Feather Mantle[.] Male[:] Hookama[,] Numuku[,] Kahahana[,] Paao[,] Hewahewa[,] Kaluhaupio[.] *Gods*[:] Kuula God of the fisherman[.] Miscellaneous[:] Menetrune—is Brownie. 10—keeper of the chief's mouths[.] 11[—] 'dog of a pig[.]' *Thing*[.] p. 8—mu—assassin[.] Pau—short grass skirt p. 16[.] Hoko-lele shooting star[.] *Place*[:] Kapena[,] Waihee[,] Kahu—nurse[.] *Characters*[:] 6—the dwarf nicknames 'nenehume.' 168—dwarf giant—good character[.] 1—Pu'Hloba, is girl's name meaning 'flower of love.'"

TYLER, CHARLES MARION. *The Island World of the Pacific Ocean.* San Francisco: Samuel Carson & Company, 1887. viii, 337 pp., illus. HL 334798

Contents: "A journal . . . of the ups and downs of trade and adventures among the Pacific Islands."—Preface.
Marginalia: London marked pages describing Samoa and explaining the migration of Oceanian peoples.

UMBSTAETTER, HERMAN DANIEL. *The Red-Hot Dollar and Other Stories from* The Black Cat . . . *With an Introduction by Jack London.* Boston: L. C. Page & Company, 1911. ix, 239 pp., HL 12766
Contents: Short stories.
Inscription: "Dear Mr. London—If you need any $ I'd wish for a Million—less if you say so—but not of the Red Hot vintage. Sincerely, H. D. Umbstaetter. Boston, Mass., July 1911[.]"
Since H. D. Umbstaetter, editor of *The Black Cat,* was one of the early publishers of London's stories, London was delighted to write the introduction to this book. In it he praised Umbstaeter for accepting (and paying for) stories on their merits, and recalled his early days as a struggling writer.

UNITED FRUIT COMPANY. *Cruising the Caribbean in the Wake of Pirates.* New York: United Fruit Company, 1915. 32 pp., illus. HL
Contents: Short pamphlet giving brief biographical sketches of famous Caribbean pirates.
Marginalia: London made notes by the sketches of Captain Kidd, Sir Francis Drake, Blackbeard (Edward Teach), and the *Jolly Roger.* On the rear cover he wrote "Mexico."

UNITED STATES. COPYRIGHT OFFICE. *Report on Copyright Legislation by the Registrar of Copyrights.* Washington, D.C.: Government Printing Office, 1904. 159 pp. HL 336116
Contents: "A special report on the copyright legislation now in force in the United States."—Letter of Transmittal.
Inscription: "Jack London."
London was prominent among the many authors in the Authors' League who pressed for passage of a new copyright law.

UNITED STATES. DEPARTMENT OF COMMERCE AND LABOR. COAST AND GEODETIC SURVEY. *Tide Tables for the Pacific Coast of the United States, Together with a Number of Foreign Ports in the Pacific Ocean.* Washington, D.C.: Government Printing Office, 1910. 528 pp., HL

Contents: Daily tide charts for the western coast of the United States.

Marginalia: On the cover London wrote "p. 390 for place[.] p. 158[—]Golden gate." He also marked paragraphs discussing tide tables at Mare Island Light, San Diego Bar, San Francisco Bay (southern portion), and the Carquinez Strait. On page 158 he noted the details of a trip he was planning up Sonoma Creek: "Add to L.W. 2.05 at Mare Island Light[.] Start six A.M. on Thursday—Go up[.] [Start] 12 M. [on Thursday.] Go down[.] Start at 7 A.M. for Sonoma Creek." The trip was planned for 13 April 1911.

UNITED STATES NAVY. HYDROGRAPHIC OFFICE. *The International Code of Signals for the Use of All Nations.* Washington, D.C.: Government Printing Office, 1903. 546 pp., illus. HL 339158

Contents: Sailing signals.

Marginalia: London noted the following signals: "*Snark[.]* San Francisco[:] A U G F[.] Bound towards[:] H B Q[.] Sailed from [:] V E J[.] Yes[:] C[.] No[:] D[.] I want a pilot[:] S[.] What Ship is that: E. G[.] N. C.—Distress[.] Solomon Is[.] A Q W E[.] Reporting all Well: U C[.]"

London used this signal book occasionally aboard the *Snark*.

UNITED STATES. PUBLIC HEALTH SERVICE. *Studies upon Leprosy: Public Health Bulletin No. 61.* Washington, D.C.: Government Printing Office, 1913. 30 pp., illus. HL

Contents: Medical articles dealing with the lepers at Molokai.

Marginalia: London marked the article entitled "The Danger of Association with Lepers at the Molokai Settlement."

London's interest in leprosy came as a result of his visit in 1907 to the Molokai colony. This is but one of the many pamphlets that he read and filed about the disease during the course of his extensive study.

UNTERMANN, ERNEST. *Science and Revolution*. Chicago: Charles H. Kerr & Company, 1905. 195 pp., HL 336726

Contents: Historical outline of the evolution of science and revolution.

Marginalia: Historical materialism, the awakening of philosophy, Darwinian theory, Aristotle, the "metaphysical rubbish" of the Middle Ages, Bacon, Locke, Kant, and materialistic monism are a few of the subjects London noted in this slim volume.

Enclosure: Note written by Charmian London: "*Science: Philosophy: Cosmic: Inductive* and *analytical methods. Synthetic:* Kant (Nebular theory)[.] Demotivitos: (Atomic Theory) *Monism.*"

One of London's oldest friends, Ernest Untermann was a socialist, an author, a painter, and also a translator. It is probable that London read much of Karl Marx via the translations made by Untermann. It is also likely that both men discussed (at Wake Robin Lodge) many of the issues concerning the socialist party at the time. London modeled the character Ernest Everhard *(The Iron Heel)* after Untermann.

In her biography of London, Charmian recalled one of the annotations in Untermann's book: "In a little book of Ernest Untermann's, *Science and Revolution,* which Jack gave me to read at that time, I came upon a sentence underscored for my benefit: 'My method of investigation is historical materialism'" (*The Book of Jack London,* 2: 46).

VACARESCU, ELENA *The Bard of the Dimbovitza. Roumanian Folksongs Collected from the Peasants.* New York: Charles Scribner's Sons, 1904. xii, 274 pp., HL 338610

Contents: Folk songs.

Inscription: "To Jack *with my heart's best* wish, Nov. 1st, 1906[:]
His feet have trod the higher way
   Where the hills upstand in light.
His eyes have seen the greater Day
   Unroll from the shroud of Night.
"And all God hides among his Stars—
   The favour of worlds unseen—

The glory matting human wars
  The light of his soul hath been.
"Yet he, who brothered with the storm,
  And knew the heart of the sea,
Hath reached his hand to the sordid swarm
  Of men in their agony.
"Hath forged his path on downward grades
  Which lead to the pit of Despair;
Hath swung his lamp in its fouling shades
  To lighten his brethren there.
Tho' Art ascend her shining way,
  Her star-crowned peaks unveil, —
He seeks in the mound of human clay
  The light of his Holy Grail."
Marginalia: London made markings beside the following poems: "Hopeless," "The Maiden's Blood," "The Soldier," "Faithless," "Barren," "Dirge on the Death of a Child," and "Stillborn."

VANDERVELDE, EMILE. *Collectivism and Industrial Evolution.* Chicago: Charles H. Kerr & Company, 1901. 199 pp., illus. HL 336810
  Contents: "Capitalist Concentration," "The Decadence of Personal Property," "The Progress of Capitalist Property," "Objections," "The Socialization of the Means of Production and Exchange," "The Three Elements of Profit," "The Advantages of Social Property," "The Administration of Things," "The Formulas of Distribution," "The Means of Realization," "Objections."
  Marginalia: London was interested in the uprooting of the peasants and the transition to the factory system.

VERNON-HARCOURT, FREDERIC C. *Bolts and Bars.* London: Digby, Long & Company, 1905. 256 pp., illus. HL 331716
  Contents: Novel.
  Marginalia: A description of a prisoner swallowing belladonna boluses and becoming ill struck London as an exploitable fiction

Snark

San Francisco   A U G F

Bound towards.   H B Q
: Sailed from   V E J

Yes   C
No   D

I want a pilot S

What Ship is that E C

N.C. — Distress
Solomon Is A Q W E
Report me all well U C

episode, and he wrote "65—data for shamming & beating the doctors." on the rear pastedown.

Vɪᴛᴛᴜᴍ, Wɪʟʟɪꜱ Hᴀʟʟ. *Orpheus and Other Poems*. Boston: Richard C. Badger, the Gorham Press, 1911. 122 pp., HL 337664

Contents: Poems.
Inscription: "To Mr. Jack London, from the author's wife—Jessie Detchon Vittum[.] Feb. 16th, 1916."

Vᴏʏɴɪᴄʜ, Eᴛʜᴇʟ Lɪʟɪᴀɴ (Bᴏᴏʟᴇ). *Olive Latham*. Philadelphia: J. B. Lippincott Company, 1904. 337 pp., HL 31920

Contents: Novel.
Bookseller: Smith Brothers, Oakland, California.
Marginalia: London marked a sentence on page 32–33: "Olive had always been instinctively repelled by any forcing into speech of things which one can take for granted."

Wᴀʟᴋᴇʀ, H. Wɪʟꜰʀᴇᴅ. *Wandering Among South Sea Savages and in Borneo and the Philippines*. London: Witherby & Company, 1910. xvi, 254 pp., illus. HL 332606

Contents: "A few of the more interesting incidents, such as would give a *general impression* of life among savages. . . ."—Preface.
Marginalia: Cannabalism and a New Guinea native war were the two subjects of interest to London.

Wᴀʀᴅ, Lᴇꜱᴛᴇʀ F. *Dynamic Sociology*. New York: D. Appleton & Company, 1897. 320 pp., illus. HL

Contents: Sociology textbook.
Marginalia: London's comments, written during the fall of 1901 in "Books I Have Read," include the following: "For relation of man to the universe—pp. 2–3–4–5–6. Chap. I. Comparative summary of the three great schools of thought—Happiness the object of existence, & cleverly put—133–4–5–6–7[.]

"Differentiation sharply drawn between dynamic sociology & moral science, or, between direct & indirect methods of gaining

Jack London, Rex Beach, and Eddie Smith, ca 1914

ends, or between intellectuals & emotionals—pp. 159–68–etc."

"Explanation of empiricism, & of snivel, the latter being me-thodical empiricism. To show that material discovery & execution are the real progressive forces, & not political philosophies—pp[.] 308-[1]0. T[.]

"The struggle of desires in man—"Desire for thing or (2) opin-ion or judgement[.]"

WARE, LEWIS SHARPE. *Cattle Feeding.* Philadelphia: Philadelphia Book Company, 1902. xxiii, 389 pp., illus. HL

Contents: "The main object in view is to prevail upon farmers to use either sugar beets, sugar, or sugar beet residuum in its varied forms . . . [to feed their cattle]."—Preface.

Marginalia: In his attempt to turn the Beauty Ranch into a scientifically run, modern farm, London turned to the latest agricultural writings and methods. In this volume, he noted the effects of feeding molasses to cows and horses.

WARE, LEWIS SHARPE. *Cattle Feeding.* Philadelphia: Philadelphia Book Company, 1902. xxiii, 389 pp., illus. HL

Contents: See preceeding entry.

Marginalia: In this second copy of Ware's *Cattle Feeding,* London computed the cost of feeding twenty-five horses: "2 cts. a day for 25 horses = 50 cts. a day = $182.50 per yr."

WATT, AGNES C. P. *Twenty-Five Years' Mission Life on Tanna, New Hebrides.* Paisley: J. and R. Parlane, 1896. 385 pp., illus. HL 332739

Contents: Collection of letters.

Inscription: "To Mr[.] and Mrs[.] London[.] A momento of their visit to Port Resolution[,] Tanna[,] New Hebrides[.] W. Watt[.] 12.6.08[.]"

Marginalia: London used the front flyleaf for a bit of navigational data: "star N. 40 W. Corr. M. C. log 21.50—8 A.M. Tuesday June 16/08[.]"

WAUGH, WILLIAM FRANCIS. *The Practice of Medicine: With Especial Reference to the Use of Active Principles and Other Definite Methods.* Chicago: The Abbott Press, 1912. xxviii, 992 pp., HL 336113

Contents: Medical text.

Marginalia: London noted passages discussing dysentery and cancer of the stomach.

WEBSTER, HERBERT CAYLEY. *Through New Guinea and the Can-*

nibal Countries. London: T. Fisher Unwin, 1898. xvii, 387 pp., illus. HL 332732

Contents: Personal description of "the manners and customs of inhabitants of the various countries . . . visited and passed through, who are almost entirely unknown to the European."—Preface.

Marginalia: London marked passages on the solitude of the islands, a description of Banda harbor, and the account of a killing of white men by a head-hunting party.

WEININGER, OTTO. *Sex and Character.* New York: G. P. Putnam's Sons, 1906. xxii, 356 pp., HL 336713 PF

Contents: A treatise on "the special problem of sexuality[,] . . . the problems of individual talent, genius, aesthetics, memory, the ego, the Jewish race, and many others, rising finally to the ultimate logical and moral principles of judgments. From his most universal standpoint he succeeds in estimating woman as a part of humanity, and, above all, subjectively."—Publisher's Note.

Inscription: "To Jack London: 'The genius is he who is conscious of most, and of that most acutely.' Sincerely yours[,] Everett Lloyd[.] *The Vagabond*[.]"

Marginalia: London made markings throughout this entire book. He was interested in Weininger's definition of males and females, a discussion of sex organs, sexual attraction, homosexuality, the emancipated woman, male and female sexuality, talent and genius, talent and memory, logic and ethics, genius, male and female psychology, motherhood and prostitution, eroticism, the significance of woman, and Judaism. Charmian wrote on the rear endpaper: "The genius is he who is conscious of most, and of that most acutely. Genius is simply intensified, perfectly developed, universally conscious maleness."

Enclosures: Postcard addressed to Beatrice Barrangon Ragnour from Frederick O'Brien. Also publisher's flyer for *The Vagabond,* with a note by Everett Lloyd: "Marked just a bit! I let an old maid school teacher read it, and you see what she did."

Charmian remembers the day London received *Sex and Character* from Lloyd: "it was a day of rejoicing when one departed guest, Everett Lloyd, sent him Weininger's *Sex and Character,* with the author's definition of a genius: 'A genius is he who is conscious of most, and of that most acutely'"(*The Book of Jack London,* 2: 49).

London might have enjoyed Weininger's definition of "genius," but he fundamentally disagreed with much of Weininger's thesis, as he pointed out in a letter of 10 September 1914 to Bram Norsen (*Letters,* p. 428): "No, you will not find 'henidical' in the dictionary. The word henid was coined by a crazy German philosopher but I find no substitute for it in the English language. All persons possess henids. A henid is a vague thought which we think is a thought and which is no thought at all, in contradistinction to a real thought which on analysis proves to be a clear concept.

"Weininger is the name of the above mentioned German philosopher. He committed suicide when he was about twenty-five years old after writing a book that made quite a stir in the world, entitled *Sex and Character.* It was all about women and was very uncomplimentary to women. I think this man Weininger is the guilty party for whom you are searching."

WELLS, HERBERT GEORGE. *The Discovery of the Future.* New York: B. W. Heubsch, 1914. 61 pp., illus. HL 331912
Contents: Essay.
Marginalia: Charmian London wrote "His lovely belief that man has not reached the end of his development . . . ." on the title page. London marked pages 56, 57, 60, and 61, which deal with the twilight of man's existence.

WELLS, HERBERT GEORGE. *A Modern Utopia.* New York: Charles Scribner's Sons, 1905. xi, 392 pp., illus. HL 331913 PF
Contents: Novel.
Bookseller: Smith Brothers, Oakland, California.
Enclosure: Clipping from the *Independent:* "Socialism and the Family" by H. G. Wells.

London found use for this book in *The Mutiny of the Elsinore* (p. 77): "I have had a revelation to-day. I have discovered Captain West. He is a Samurai.—You remember the Samurai that H. G. Wells describes in his *Modern Utopia*—the superior breed of men who know things and are masters of life and of their fellow men in a super-benevolent, super-wise way? Well, that is what Captain West is."

WELLS, HERBERT GEORGE. *New Worlds For Old*. New York: The Macmillan Company, 1908. vii, 333 pp., HL 331962

Contents: Critique of modern socialism.

Inscription: "To dear Jack. Always yours, Fred. Sept., 1908."

Enclosure: Photograph of H. G. Wells pasted onto front pastedown.

London was quite ill when Bamford's gift reached him in Australia, and thus the thank-you note he wrote was brief: "Yours of April 13th just recently to hand. Too sick to answer till just now. Am some sure keeping cool and waiting for *Snark* to arrive in Sydney. When shall sell her and return home. Enclosure speaks for itself. In some way, tropics knocked me out. Wells's book came to hand. Just pulled through two more—with fever" (Georgia Bamford, *Mystery*, p. 221).

WELLS, HERBERT GEORGE. *The Research Magnificent*. New York: The Macmillan Company, 1915. 460 pp., HL 182022

Contents: Novel.

Marginalia: London marked pages 293–95 and 82–83, which deal with British politics and civilization and Trinity Hall. The book is also annotated by Charmian London.

WELLS, HERBERT GEORGE. *The Wife of Sir Isaac Harman*. New York: The Macmillan Company, 1915. v, 525 pp., HL 331945

Contents: Novel.

Marginalia: London marked a number of passages dealing with women. On page 242 he marked the following sentence: "So far he had either joked at her, talked 'silly' to her, made, as they say, 'remarks,' or vociferated. That had been the sum of their mental intercourse, as indeed it is the sum of the intercourse of most married couples." Beside the sentence, London wrote: "Not I, my Lord, not I."

Enclosures: Business card of Mrs. Rudolf Büchly, Waikiki, Hawaii, with the following message: "A thousand thanks for the books I've had from you, and apologies for not returning this one before you left. L.H.B." Also newspaper clipping from a San Francisco paper: "Burglars Make Off with Jewelry, Rug. Continental 'Hide and Seek' Brings Divorce."

She turned towards him. "Yes," she said. "I think — I think we can't go on like this."

"*I* can't," said Sir Isaac, "anyhow."

He too came and stared at the rose planting.

"If we were to go up there — among the pine woods" — he pointed with his head at the dark background of Euphemia's herbaceous borders — "we shouldn't hear quite so much of this hammering. . . ."

Husband and wife walked slowly in the afternoon sunlight across the still beautiful garden. Each was gravely aware of an embarrassed incapacity for the task they had set themselves. They were going to talk things over. Never in their lives had they really talked to each other clearly and honestly about anything. Indeed it is scarcely too much to say that neither had ever talked about anything to anyone. She was too young, her mind was now growing up in her and feeling its way to conscious expression, and he had never before wanted to express himself. He did now want to express himself. For behind his rant and fury Sir Isaac had been thinking very hard indeed during the last three weeks about his life and her life and their relations; he had never thought so much about anything except his business economics. So far he had either joked at her, talked "silly" to her, made, as they say, "remarks," or vociferated. That had been the sum of their mental intercourse, as indeed it is the sum of the intercourse of most married couples. His attempt to state his case to her had so far always flared into

WENDELL, BARRETT. *English Composition. Eight Lectures Given at the Lowell Institute.* New York: Charles Scribner's Sons, 1891. x, 316 pp., HL 336848

Contents: Essays.

Marginalia: London marked pages 162, 151, 192, 222, and 295.

This book is possibly one of the earliest additions to London's permanent library. Removed from the Oakland Free Library, it bears the numerous markings of that institution, and a number of penciled marks on the pages.

WENZ, PAUL. *Sous La Croix Du Sud.* Paris: Plot-Nourrit et Cie, 1910. 304 pp., HL 331984

Contents: Novel.

Inscription: "Aux l'our amis les Jacks qui nous espérons bien revoir un jour ou l'autre[,] Paul Wenz. Navima[,] Dec. 31, 1910[.]"

Enclosures: Pamphlet entitled *Chemin de Fer de Paris a Orléans, Pyrénées,* and a booklet: *Bulletin de la Librarie Plon.* Mars, 1910.

WESTERVELT, WILLIAM DRAKE. *Legends of Maui—A Demi-God of Polynesia and of His Mother, Hina.* Melbourne, Australia: George Robertson and Company, [190-]. HL 332602

Contents: Hawaiian legends.

Bookseller: Thrum's, Honolulu, Hawaii.

Marginalia: London noted paragraphs dealing with Mount Haleakala, Ra—the Sun God of Egypt, and made a number of notes on the rear pastedown: "p[.] 3—Genalogy [*sic*] *mele* of first Mauis,— the beginning of Liliuokalani's mele. 12[—] Chant of Maui's great fish hook[.] 40[—]Chant: Maui Snares the Sun[.] 44—Antiquities of Polynesia, names of gods, etc.[;] contact with those ˙of ancient Egypt. 56—Invocation to fire[.] 138—'But death is nothing new'— dandy quotation."

WEYL, WALTER E. *The New Democracy: An Essay on Certain Political and Economic Tendencies in the United States.* New York: The Macmillan Company, 1912. 370 pp., HL 336812

Contents: Political history of the United States.

Marginalia: London marked passages about the U.S. Declaration of

Independence, exclusions from political office, the passage of the Constitution, the Hague Convention, German atrocities, the success of small states in establishing independence, international arbitration, disarmament, and the creation of a humane code of war.

WHEELER, CANDACE (THURBER). *Principles of Home Decoration.* New York: Doubleday, Page & Company, 1903. 227 pp., illus. HL 337329

Contents: Do-it-yourself manual for home decoration, complete with examples.

Marginalia: London noted paragraphs dealing with oil-covered cloths, color with reference to light, buying only the best, and color schemes.

This book was possibly used as a source of ideas for decorating Wolf House.

WHITAKER, HERMAN. *The Mystery of the Barranca.* New York: Harper & Brothers, 1913. 280 pp., illus. HL 331987

Contents: Novel.

Inscription: "Dear Jack. You are living hard. This exchange is rank robbery. Nevertheless, I am absolutely unprincipled. Send on your *Barleycorn.* Jim. Piedmont Cal[.] Sept. 1913[.]"

Herman Whitaker, or "Jim" as he preferred to be called, was a struggling writer and self-elected member of the "Crowd." Whitaker often accepted London's assistance—financial and otherwise—but was unappreciative of London's help, and proved to be a somewhat treacherous friend.

WHITAKER, HERMAN. *The Planter: A Novel.* New York: Harper & Brothers Publishers, 1909. 535 pp., illus. HL 331986

Contents: Novel.

Inscription: "To Jack & Charmian London, with affection and esteem. Always your friend, Herman Whitaker. Piedmont, March, 1909."

"Jack, ye devil! I've gien ye buit for built the hou. Pingle up! Jim."

ENGLISH COMPOSITION

EIGHT LECTURES GIVEN AT THE LOWELL INSTITUTE

BY

BARRETT WENDELL

ASSISTANT PROFESSOR OF ENGLISH AT HARVARD COLLEGE

NEW YORK
CHARLES SCRIBNER'S SONS
1891

WHITAKER, HERMAN. *The Probationer and Other Stories.* New York: Harper & Brothers Publishers, 1905. 328 pp., illus. HL 332447

Contents: Novel.

Bookseller: Smith Brothers, Oakland, California.

Inscription: "To you, Dear Jack, who gave me my first lift over the stones; in memory of the good old days. As ever, Jim."

WHITAKER, HERMAN. *The Settler: A Novel.* New York: Harper & Brothers Publishers, 1907. v, 368 pp., illus. HL 297945

Contents: Novel.

Inscription: "To Jack and Charmian, where ever this may find you, with love, from Jim. Piedmont, Nov. 7—1907."

WHITE, STEWART EDWARD. *The Silent Places.* New York: Mc-Clure, Phillips & Company, 1904. 304 pp., illus. HL 332439

Contents: Northland novel.

Bookseller: Smith Brothers, Oakland, California.

Marginalia: London wrote his notes for *Scorn of Women* on the endpapers of this book: "Act II[.] Freda & Mrs. E. Freda: 'I have privileges you have not.' Mrs. E. '—Licenses.' Freda: '—Thank you, licenses.' Have Freda slur Mrs. E for having to deal with Vanderlip—'You have your husband.' Mrs. E.—'And you.' Freda, wearily—'Men, just men' (better, this as it stands is a bit too gross[)]."

"Act II between Freda & Mrs. E. Mrs. E. tries to meet in all fairness. Freda defiant, in revolt, from very sensitiveness. Make it a sharp tilt & ere she is done with it, have Mrs. E., at midship of scene, scath her unmercifully in clean-cut language—cold as steel, emotionless—then have Freda turn her blazing face on Vanderlip, master him, & command him to come with her. Have her not look behind to see if he is coming, & have him slink after her. Curtain with final sniff of Mrs. McFee (preceding page)."

WHYMPER, FREDERICK. *Travel and Adventure in the Territory of Alaska, Formerly Russian America—Now Ceded to the United States—and in Various Other Parts of the North Pacific.* New York: Harper & Brothers, Publishers, 1869. xviii, 353 pp., illus. HL 334816

Contents: "A large portion of these pages refers to a journey made in the Yukon region . . . The opening chapters contain some earlier reminiscences of British Columbia and Vancouver Island, while in the concluding pages I have attempted to sketch California of our own time. I have also briefly recorded some visits paid by me to the eastern coast of Siberia and Kamchatka."—Preface.

Marginalia: London underlined passages dealing with the town of Sitka, Kalosh Indian grave boxes, Siberian horses, and salmon.

WILDE, OSCAR. *Children in Prison and Other Cruelties of Prison Life.* London: Murdoch & Company, 1898. 16 pp. HL

Contents: An exposé of the treatment received by children imprisoned.

Marginalia: London marked two passages, on pages 8 and 9, which deal with the suffering and hunger children experience in prison.

WILDE, OSCAR. *De Profundis.* New York: G. P. Putnam's Sons, 1905. ix, 123 pp., illus. HL 338617

Contents: Reflective prose, written by Wilde while in prison.

Marginalia: Most of the markings were made by Charmian London.

Frederick Bamford gave this book to London in 1905, and although he made no markings in it, London did read the book, thanking Bamford for it 28 May 1905: "I was very much taken with *De Profundis,* but I'm not going to make you think any thoughts by telling you what I thought about it" (Georgia Bamford, *Mystery,* p. 187).

WILDE, OSCAR. *The Soul of Man under Socialism.* New York: The Humboldt Publishing Company, 1892. 48 pp., HL

Contents: Philosophical reflections on the merits of socialism.

Marginalia: London annotated this fragile pamphlet quite heavily. His markings concern the London East End, the selling of birthright by the poor, the necessity for agitators, the fact that only the poor think more about money than the rich, and an assertion that socialism will annihilate family life and free love will flourish. By the last concept, London wrote: "Socialism, scientific & up-to-date, does not endorse this[.]"

Evidently this pamphlet had been in London's library for some time. In a letter of 7 June 1899 to Cloudesley Johns (HL), London wrote: "I think I have the very thing for you, *The Soul of Man under Socialism,* by Oscar Wilde. I have not had a chance to read it myself, yet, but as soon as I do will forward it to you. Same volume contains in addition, *The Socialist Ideal—Art* by Wm. Morris, author of *Earthly Paradise,* etc., and *The Coming Solidarity,* by W. C. Owen."

WILLARD, JOSIAH FLYNT. *My Life.* New York: The Outing Publishing Company, 1908. xxv, 365 pp., illus. HL 332446

Contents: Autobiography.

Marginalia: Although London evidently read this book carefully, it is his own autobiographical notations that are important. On the rear endpapers he wrote: "The Fading Beyond—

"—passing through the world—sickness, without any sanction, many, by the metaphysics of religion, leap beyond the Beyond, and find a super-rational sanction for the world misery, & unfairness, etc.—a philosopher's yardstick, a [*sic*] scales, by which all unfairnesses & inequalities are squared & balanced.—so argues the white logic of mine. etc. etc.

"White logic is the truth. I sober, say it now. With its truths I now play—They are so serious that I refuse to take them seriously. They are sleeping dogs, at the back of my consciousness. I do but stir them, yet let them lie. I am too wise, too wicked wise, to wake them. But white logic wakes them. White logic is a hero, unafraid of all the monsters of the earthly dream.

"Why should I be sad? land, money, children, wife, health of body, brain, recognition from the world—everything.

"White logic on ranch—I pore over deeds from days of old Spanish grants, the men who toiled, & cleared, & planted, & gazed with labor-stiffened bodies on these same sunsets & sunrises, the autumn red of the grape, the fogs across Sonoma mountain. These men are gone.

"I too, ride & gaze on all this. And will I some day, too be gone. 'This dreary agitation of the dust.'

"I remembered the brave fellows that dined with death & wine, & passed out, the Dawsens, the Henrys, the Flynts—[.]

"World-sickness—my disintegrating body that has been dying since I was born. I am aware that I carry a skeleton inside this flesh.

a grinning, noseless, death's head. Ah, thou Noseless one, I'm not afraid of you.

"My smashed knees & ankles—ruptured tendons of my thumbs, scars & mars. arsenic slough on cheek from Australian hospital—; broken bone, never set, in hand from hitting horse—my missing teeth, dropped by from me, the jewels of youth etc.

"I return across the ranch[.] Twilight—the hunting animals, no morality in nature, only in man & man has created it. I look in gorgeous sunset sky for my evening star, & find it not. Then, in house, there it is—the Scotch. I perk up, go to dinner with guests, am serious, madly brilliant, or uprorious [sic] with bucolic boisterousness—& then to bed, bad tooth in mouth, & books—(annotations) and the magazines & the silly doings of the world's day. etc."

London's notes for a tramp series originally entitled "Leith Clay-Randolph" (HL) contained a few references to Willard's autobiography: "A kangaroo Court—full description, with a motive running through it all. For Kangaroo Court see Flynt p. 84. Judas. See Flynt pp. 22–23."

WILLIAMS, EDWARD HUNTINGTON. *The Walled City: A Story of the Criminal Insane.* New York: Funk & Wagnalls Company, 1913. 263 pp., illus. HL 336737

Contents: A study of insane asylums.
Marginalia: London wrote "p[.] 34—euchre player, & stupid beast in everything else—a character" on the rear free endpaper.

WILLIAMS, THOMAS. *Fiji and the Fijians: The Islands and Their Inhabitants; Mission History.* London: Alexander Heylin, 1860. 2 volumes in one, x, 266, 435 pp., illus. HL 332601

Contents: "The information contained in this volume is the result of the patient and intelligent research of the Reverend Thomas Williams, of Adelaide, during his thirteen years' residence as a Wesleyan Missionary in Fiji."—Preface.
Marginalia: This book was heavily marked by London. Some of the subjects of his annotations include: the formality of giving the aristocratic Malayan dialect, Fiji taxpaying, native ships, Fiji barter and trade, native proverbs, the story of Tambai-valu, a description of the interior of a Fijiian home, cooking, manners, and customs in

Fiji, cruelty to the aged, burying royalty, killing wives after the death of their husband, and a Fijiian fight and battle with white men. London also recorded the following notes for a South Seas story: "From the Eye of the Sun—title for story of the first white man in Fiji—He was an enigma, a god—who came from the eye of the sun. He was braver, more ferocious, a terrible fighter. They killed & ate his fellows. He, however, conquered them by his brass. Finally, sailed away, in a canoe."

"p. 183—p[.] 210 note—A Fiji Story for *When God Laughs*. p. 202—a story[.] 131-132—a story. Conceal from the reader the death of the king until the son's head is brought in. Maybe told in first person, by native, to me, a sailor, in our night watches. He is half Fiji, half Tongan. I had thought he was all Tongan. He looked Polynesian. His father had married Fiji mother. He fled, for Queen, through her son, proceeded to get away with all who had brought head of Fiji Son."

WILSHIRE, HENRY GAYLORD. *Wilshire Editorials*. New York: Wilshire Book Company, 1906. 416 pp., illus. HL 279941

Contents: "The contents of this volume consist almost exclusively of my editorials published within the past six years either in *Wilshire's Magazine* or in *The Challenge*, its predecessor."—Preface.
Inscription: "With my compliments[.] Gaylord Wilshire[.]"
Gaylord Wilshire came to California in 1884, where he dabbled in real estate development, orange and walnut growing, gold mining, and inventions. He made several fortunes through his endeavors, only to lose them again through faulty management. When his last venture failed (a real estate development in West Los Angeles, through which ran the boulevard he named after himself), Wilshire became a socialist, and began publishing a magazine. London may have met him in 1905.

WILSON, HARRY LEON. *The Boss of Little Arcady*. New York: Grosset & Dunlap, 1905. 371 pp., illus. HL 331957

Contents: Novel.
Inscription: "Dear Jack and Charmian London. Just a little story about the little town that most of us came from. Harry Leon Wilson[.] Ocean Home[,] Monterey[,] 1912[.]"

WINCHESTER, LYDIA. *A New System of Analysis.* London: Blackie and Son Limited, 1914. 56 pp., illus. HL 336920
Contents: Grammatical study.
Marginalia: London found a familiar sentence on page 48, and put a pencil mark in the margin beside it: "Deep in the forest a call was sounding, and as often as he heard this call, mysteriously thrilling and luring, he felt compelled to turn his back upon the fire and the beaten earth around it, and to plunge into the forest."

WINSLOW, KENELM. *The Home Medical Library. Volume II: The Eye and Ear, the Nose, Throat and Lungs, Skin Diseases, Tumors, Rheumatism, Headache, Sexual Hygiene.* New York: The Review of Reviews Company, 1907. 267 pp., illus. HL 338746
Contents: Medical encyclopedia.
Marginalia: London marked pages 206-10, which deal with the symptoms and diagnosis of syphilis.

WOLFE, THEODORE FRELINGHUYSEN. *A Literary Pilgrimage Among the Haunts of Famous British Authors.* Philadelphia: J. B. Lippincott Company, 1906. 260 pp., illus. HL 339868
Contents: Notes "of the writer's sojurns in the scenes hallowed by the presence of famous authors. . . ."—Preface.
Inscription: "Mr. Jack London, With all good wishes[.] Yours Sincerely, Theo. F. Wolfe. Succasuona. N. J., Nov. 10."

WOODFORD, CHARLES MORRIS. *A Naturalist Among the Head-Hunters: Being an Account of Three Visits to the Solomon Islands in the Years 1886, 1887, and 1888.* London: George Philip & Son, 1890. xii, 249 pp., illus. HL 332730
Contents: "The object of my visits to the island was neither political nor commercial, but the following pages, while giving some account of the islands, will enable the outside world to form an idea of the state of affairs now existing."—Preface.
Marginalia: London was interested in Woodford's description of the South Sea island labor trade.

WOODRUFF, CHARLES EDWARD. *The Effects of Tropical Light on*

White Men. New York: Rebman Company, 1905. vii, 358 pp., illus. HL 337220

Contents: "This work had its origin in an attempt to prove or disprove the theory announced by Von Schmaedel in a paper read before the Anthropological Society of Munich in 1895, that skin pigmentation of man was evolved for the purpose of excluding the dangerous actinic or short rays of light which destroy living protoplasm."—Preface.

Marginalia: London marked passages dealing with the zoological zones of the earth, the effects of ultraviolet light, and the destruction of parasites with light.

Enclosures: Medical Record, 18 December 1909, pages 1019–21: "The Physical Decay of Northern Europeans in our Northwest" by Charles E. Woodruff. Woodruff made a few marks around the title of this clipping, and wrote: "You should appreciate my enthusiasm for western Alaska! *Please return.*" in the top margin. Also enclosed were the galley proofs for *Science,* pages 82–83: "Does Excessive Light Limit Tropical Plankton" and "To the Editor of Science." Both articles were written by Charles Woodruff.

London was convinced that Woodruff's thesis was correct, and that the cause of his illness in the South Seas was a direct effect of the sun's rays on his fair skin. In *The Mutiny of the Elsinore* (pp. 148–49), he explained the thesis of Woodruff's book in detail: "I have made a discovery. Ninety per cent of our crew is brunette. Aft, with the exception of Wada and the steward who are our servants, we are all blondes. What let me to this discovery was Woodruff's *Effects of Tropical Light on White Man,* which I am just reading. Major Woodruff's thesis is that the white-skinned, blue-eyed Aryan, born to government and command, ever leaving his primeval, overcast and foggy home, ever commands and governs the rest of the world and ever perishes because of the too-white light he encounters. It is a very tenable hypothesis, and will bear looking into."

WOODRUFF, CHARLES EDWARD. *Expansion of Races.* New York: Rebman Company, 1909. xi, 495 pp., illus. HL 334777

Contents: An "anthropological study of one of the reasons for migration, war, famine, and pestilence, and why mankind, in obedience to natural law, is unconsciously organizing to prevent these disasters."—Preface.

Marginalia: London was interested in Woodruff's comments on Darwin and the population explosion, the evolution of disease germs, the beginnings of man, currents, migration, the use of war as a population control device, murder, infanticide, and the diminishing birthrate. On the rear pastedown, he glued a four-page review of the book: "Comments on Woodruff's *Expansion of Races.*" London mentions this book in "Account with Swithin Hall" *(A Son of the Sun),* thus giving indication that he read the book some time in 1911.

WOODRUFF, CHARLES EDWARD. *Medical Ethnology.* New York: Rebman Company, 1915. viii, 321 pp., illus. HL 336735

Contents: "This work was begun as a revision of the first edition of *The Effects of Tropical Light on White Men,* but it was necessary to change the title . . . because so many other factors beside pigmentation have entered into the discussion of the reasons for the differences between the present races and subraces of men."—Preface.

Marginalia: Pigmentation, sunstroke, the origin and distribution of blondness, and the results of insufficient pigmentation are the subjects that interested London in this revision of *The Effects of Tropical Light on White Men.* On the rear pastedown, he wrote: "p[.] 37— Why modern Greeks are not Aryans[.] 136–137—Sunstroke and actinic shock. 144–45—my own actinic eczema[.] 148—sun cocktails & drunks[.] 149—drinking in the tropics[.] 177—the Aryan Race[.]"

WORTH, CLAUD ALLEY. *Yacht Cruising.* London: J. D. Potter, 1910. 272 pp., illus. HL 336883

Contents: "This book consists partly of 'logs' of cruises and partly of articles and notes on various matters connected with cruising." —Preface.

Inscription: "For the *Roamer*[.] Aloha Nui[.] E[.] S[.] Goodhue[.]"

WRIGHT, CHARLES DANA. *Bits of Verse from Hawaii.* Honolulu: Privately printed, [19—]. 126 pp., illus. HL 332034

Contents: Poems.

Inscription: "Jack London from Mary E. Low[.]"

Mary Low was a friend of the Londons who lived in Honolulu. After Jack London's death in 1916, she visited Charmian at Glen Ellen.

YOUNG, ROSALIND AMELIA. *Mutiny of the Bounty and Story of Pitcairn Island 1790-1894.* Oakland, California: Pacific Press Publishing Company, 1894. xi, 266 pp., illus. HL 337100
Contents: History of the crew of *HMS Bounty.*
Marginalia: London wrote the following under the signature: "J. R. McCoy, January 10, 1908.": "The Governor of Pitcairn Island—the fourth generation from McCoy, the mutineer of the *Bounty.*"
London used this book in his short story, "The Seed of McCoy" (1909).

ZANGWILL, ISRAEL. *The Mantle of Elijah.* London: William Heinemann, 1900. viii, 424 pp., HL 331981
Contents: Novel.
Bookseller: Walderstruck, Maidstone, London.
Enclosure: Postcard picturing Maidstone.
London's reading of Zangwill spanned many years, but the influence of the author on him was greatest during London's early years. In 1899, for instance, on 29 July, he wrote to Cloudesley Johns: "Many thanks for short story collection. All of Zangwill's I had read before—isn't he wonderful in his way?" (*Letters,* p. 45).
    Mabel Applegarth and London also discussed Zangwill, 28 January 1900: "Speaking of marriage—the following is what Zangwill calls Spinoza's 'aphorism on marriage': 'It is plain that Marriage is in accordance with Reason, if the desire is engendered not merely by external form, but by a love of begetting children and wisely educating them; and if, in addition, the love both of husband and wife has for its cause not external form merely, but chiefly liberty of mind'" (*Letters,* p. 13).
    London also wrote to Anna Strunsky on 21 January 1899, citing Zangwill's influence: "Tell me what you think of Ms. It was the work of my golden youth. When I look upon it I feel very old. It has knocked from pillar to post and reposed in all manner of places. When my soul waxes riotous, I bring it forth, and lo! I am again a lamb. It cures all ills of the ego and is a sovereign remedy for self-

conceit. 'Mistake' is writ broad in fiery letters. The influences at work in me, from Zangwill to Marx, are obvious. I would have protrayed types and ideals of which I knew nothing, and so, trusted myself to false wings" (*Letters*, p. 85).

ZOLA, EMILE. *Truth*. New York: John Lane, 1903. ʿviii, 596 pp., HL 331989

Contents: Novel.

Enclosure: A small card upon which London wrote: "Remember me when this you see."

Notes

1. Celeste G. Murphy, "Library Collected by Jack London Reveals Thirst for Knowledge," *Overland Monthly and Out West Magazine,* 90 (May 1932): 111–12, 120.

2. Jack London to *The North American,* 30 March 1913, HL.

3. See especially Jack London to George Sterling, 7 March 1916, HL. For a more complete study of the friendship between London and Sterling see Robert Leitz and David Mike Hamilton, "Dear Greek: Dear Wolf: The Literary Correspondence between Jack London and George Sterling," HL.

4. Jack London, *Jack London, By Himself* (New York: The Macmillan Company, 1913), p. 3.

5. Ibid.

6. Jack London, *John Barleycorn* (New York: The Century Company, 1913), p. 41.

7. Clipping from the *Boston Evening Transcript,* 26 May 1900, found in "Jack London Scrapbook 1," p. 58, HL.

8. Franklin Walker, *Jack London and the Klondike* (San Marino: Huntington Library, 1966).

9. Jack London, *Martin Eden* (New York: The Macmillan Company, 1909).

10. Ibid., especially pp. 54–55 or 106–7.

11. James Hopper, "Jack London on the Campus," *California Alumni Fortnightly,* 9 (2 December 1916): 277.

12. See Earle Labor, Robert Leitz, and Milo Shepard, eds., *The Jack London Letters* (Stanford: Stanford University Press, in press).

13. Jack London " 'Christ Novel': Notes for a Novel," ca. 1900, HL.

14. Cloudesley Johns, "Who the Hell Is Cloudesley Johns?": Autobiography, Johns Collection, HL pp. 258–60.

15. Jack London to Frederick Irons Bamford, 21 February 1905, quoted in Georgia Loring Bamford, *The Mystery of Jack London* (Oakland: Georgia Bamford, 1931), p.184.

16. Joshua Slocum, *Sailing Alone Around the World* (New York: The Century Company, 1900), p. 11.

17. Martin Johnson, *Through the South Seas with Jack London* (New York: Dodd, Mead and Company, 1913), p. 40.

18. King Hendricks and Irving Shepard, eds., *Letters from Jack London: Containing an Unpublished Correspondence between London and Sinclair Lewis* (New York: Odyssey Press, 1965; London: MacKibbon and Gee, 1966), pp. 280-81. Hereafter cited as *Letters.*

19. "American Fiction Lacking in Courage," New York *Sun,* 2 March 1912, found in "Jack London Scrapbook 11," p. 72, HL.

20. Jack London, *A Son of the Sun* (New York: Doubleday, Page and Company, 1912), p. 184.

21. Henry Meade Bland, "Jack London's Literary Habits," *Writer's Monthly,* 6 (July 1915): 3.

22. James McClintock, *White Logic* (Cedar Rapids, Michigan: Wolf House Books, 1975).

23. Tokinosuke Sekine, "Man Who Knew Jack London Tells About Author's Life," *Tokyo Mainichi Daily News,* 26 January 1964.

24. Jack London, *The Little Lady of the Big House* (New York: The Macmillan Company, 1916), p. 4.

25. David Mike Hamilton, "Fifty-Three Years of Jack London at the Huntington," *Jack London Newsletter,* 11 (May-December 1978), p. 57.

26. Ibid.

27. Jack London, *War of the Classes* (New York: The Macmillan Company, 1905), p. 157.

28. Jack London, "That Pup: Notes for a Short Story," HL, probably evolved into "That Spot" published in *Sunset Magazine* in February 1908.

29. Jack London, *The Mutiny of the Elsinore* (New York: The Macmillan Company, 1914), p. 252.

30. Jack London, *The Star Rover* (New York: The Macmillan Company, 1915), p. 122.

31. Jack London, *The Iron Heel* (New York: The Macmillan Company, 1908), p. 97.

32. Jack London, *Jack London Reports* (Garden City, New York: Doubleday & Company, Inc., 1970), p. 5.

33. Cloudesley Johns, "Who the Hell Is Cloudesley Johns?" pp. 258–69.

34. Charmian Kittredge London, *The Book of Jack London* 2 vols. (New York: The Century Co., 1921), 2: 62–63.

35. Jack London, *A Daughter of the Snows* (New York: J. B. Lippincott Company, 1902), p. 78.

36. Jack London, *On the Makaloa Mat* (New York: The Macmillan Company, 1919), p. 185.

37. Joan London, *Jack London and His Times* (New York, 1939; reprint, Seattle and London: University of Washington Press, 1968), p. 304.

38. Franklin Walker, "Index File of Notes for a Biography of Jack London," Franklin Walker Collection, HL.

39. Jack London, *The House of Pride and Other Tales of Hawaii* (New York: The Macmillan Company, 1912), p. 116.

40. Jack London, *The Assassination Bureau, Ltd.* (New York: McGraw-Hill Book Company, Inc., 1963), pp. 58-59.

41. Jack London, "How We Die: Notes for a Short Story," HL.

42. Jack London, "A Dog Story," HL.

43. Jack London, *The Sea-Wolf* (New York: The Macmillan Company, 1904), pp. 107–8.

44. Jack London, *Smoke Bellew* (New York: The Century Company, 1912), p. 350.

Sailing San Francisco Bay

Appendix

Catalog for Books of Jack London
By Beatrice Barrangon Ragnour

Case 1:

Shakespeare, 40 books. *Sir Marrok*, French. *Tommy Remington's Battle*, Stevenson. *The Boy and the Baron*, Knapp. *The Cruise of the Dazzler*, London. *The Boys of the Rincon Ranch*, Canfield. *Eight Girls and a Dog*, Wells.

Case 2:

Bret Harte's Writings, 16 books. *Cashel Byron's Profession*, G. B. Shaw. Plays—3 books—Shaw. *An Unsocial Socialist*, Shaw. *The Perfect Wagnerite*, Shaw. *Love among the Artists*, Shaw.

Case 3:

Ruskin's Works, 13 books. F. G. Smith, 9 books.

Case 4:

Social Control, Ross. J. K. Bangs, 8 books.

Case 5:

The World's Great Masterpieces, 20 *books*.

Case 6:

The Works of Tennyson, 12 books. Putnam, 12 books. Roosevelt, 14 books.

Case 7:

Tolstoy and His Problems, Aylmer, Maude. *Foma Gordyieff*, Maxim Gorky. *Three Men*, Maxim Gorky. *Maxim Gorky*, E. T. Dillion. *Sea Urchins*, W. W. Jacobs. *Many Cargoes*, W. W. Jacobs. *The Lady of the Barge*, W. W. Jacobs. *Youth*, Joseph Conrad. *The Inheritors*, Conrad and Hueffer. *An Outcast of the Islands*, Conrad. *The Children of the Sea*, Conrad. *Typhoon*, Conrad. *Penal Servitude*, W. B. N. *Questions of Empire*,; Lord Rosebury. *The Battle with the Slum*, Riis. *America*, J. F. Muirhead. *The Unspeakable Scot*, Crosland. *The Egregious English*, McNeill. *The Economic Interpretation of History*, Seligman. *The Theology & Ethics of the Hebrews*, Duff.

The American Farmer, Simons. *The Social Unrest*, Brooks. *Dream of John Ball*, W. Morris. *Episcopo & Company*, D'Annunzio. *The Ballad of Reading Gaol*, Wilde. *Fables in Slang*, George Ade. *No. 5 John Street*, R. Whiteing. *The Forest Lovers*, M. Hewlett. *The Helmet of Navarre*, Berth Runkle. *The Right of Way*, G. Parker. *Lord Jim*, Conrad. *Essays of Mazzine*, Thomas Okey. *The Affirmative Intellect*, Ferguson. *Works*, Emile Zola. *Germinal*, Emile Zola. *The Transvaal from Within*, J. P. Fitzpatrick. *Notes of An Itinerant Policeman*, Josiah Flynt. *The Great Boer War*, A. C. Doyle. *The Story of a Bad Boy*, Aldrich. *The United States of Europe*, Stead. *The Great Battle of the World*, Crane. *Partisan Politics, The Evil and the Remedy*, Brown. *Outlines of Economics*, Ely.

Case 8:

Fabian Tracts, 1–112. *Capital*, Karl Marx. *Houdsditch Day by Day*, Pitcher. *The Annals of Toil*, J. M. Davidson. *The Heart of the Empire*, T. Fisher Unwin. *London in Shadow*, Bart Kennedy. *Problems of Poverty*, Hobson. *The Housing of the Working Classes*, Bowmaker. *Pictures and Problems from London Police Courts*, Holmes. *The Rural Exoduc*, Graham. *The Factory System*, Cooke-Taylor. *No Room to Live*, George Haw. *Cruelties of Civilization—Second Series, Cruelties of Civilization*, Henry S. Salt. *The Book of Lords*, J. M. Davidson. *New Book of Kings*, J. M. Davisdon. *Today's Work*, George Haw. *The Old Order and the New*, M. Davidson. *Karl Marx*, Liebknecht. *Jonathan and His Continent*, Max O'Rell and Jack Allum. *Anglo Saxons & Others*, Aline Corren. *Our Benevolent Feudalism*, Ghent. *Expansion*, Strong. *Our New Prosperity*, Baker. *Collectivism*, Vandervelde. *A Ken of Kipling*, Will M. Clemens. *American Whist Illustrated*, G. W. P. *The Riddle of the Universe*, Ernst Haeckel. *The Method of Evolution*, Conn.

Case 9:

Woman and Artist, Max O'Rell. *The Boasts of the Lord*, F. A. Steel. *Quisanté*, Anthony Hope. *Tristram of Blent*, Anthony Hope. *She Stands Alone*, Mark Ashton. *The Haunts of Men*, Robert Chambers. *Scarlet and Hyssop*, E. F. Benson. *Marietta*, Marion Crawford. *Babs the Impossible*, Sarah Grand. *The Conqueror*, Gertrude Atherton. *The Splendid Idle Forties*, Gertrude Atherton. *To London Town*, Arthur Morrison. *The Hound of the Baskervilles*, A. Conan Doyle. *The People of the Abyss*, Jack London. *The Call of the Wild*, Jack London. *Children of the Frost*, Jack London (3 books). *The Cruise of the Dazzler*, Jack London. *A Daughter of the Snows*, Jack London.

Case 10:

Annual Report of the Commissioner of Labor. Abstract of the Eleventh Census, 1890. Josephus's Complete Works. *Dr. Foote's Plain Home Talk*, Westland. *Anna Karenina*, Tolstoi. *Practical Authorship*, Reeve. *The Writer*. Vols. VII (1895), X (1899), XI (1898), X (1897), IX (1891).

Case 11:
Stories by American Authors, [volumes]: 1, 2, 3, 4, 5, 6, 7, 8, 9, 10. *Stories by Foreign Authors*: French (3 books), Italian, Scandinavian, Polish, Greek, Belgian, Hungarian, Russian, Spanish, [and] German (2 books). *Stories by English Authors: London, Scotland, Germany, Ireland, Africa, England, France, Italy, The Sea, [and] The Orient.*
Little Masterpieces by: Hawthorne, Carlyle, Franklin, Ruskin, Webster, Macaulay, Poe, Lincoln, Irving, Lamb, [and] Thackeray.

Case 12:
32 books by Abbott.

Case 13:
Nations of the World: Grote's Greece (Vols. I–XII), *Gibbon's Rome* (Vols. I–VI), *Guizot's France* (Vols. I–VIII), *Rambould's Russia* (Vols. I–II), *Scott's Scotland* (Vols. I–II).

Case 14:
Nations of the World: Green's England (Vols. I–IV), *Thebaud's Ireland, Menzel's Germany* (Vols. I–IV), *Nilsson's Sweden, Wilberforce's Spain, Sorensen's Norway, Grattan's Holland, Abbott's Austria, Abbott's Italy, Clarke's Turkey, Mccoan's Egypt, Kitto's Palestine, Wheeler's India* (Vols. I–III), *Boulger's China, Dickson's Japan, Hawthorne's United States* (Vols. I–II) *Hawthorne's Spanish America, Prescott's Peru* (Vols. I–II) *Prescott's Mexico* (Vols. I–II).

Case 15:
Encyclopaedia Britannica, Ninth Edition, Vols. I–XV.

Case 16:
Waverley Novels, 25 books.

Case 17:
Waverley Novels, 23 books, Thackeray's *Complete Works*.

Case 18:
Dickens's *Works*, 30 books.

Case 19:
The House with the Green Shutters, George Douglas. *The Gadfly*, Voynich. *The Leopard's Spots*, Thomas Dixon, Jr. *Jude the Obscure*, Thomas Hardy. *The Return of the*

Native, Hardy. *To Have and To Hold*, Johnston. *The Decameron of Boccaccio*, Leopold Flamey. *Dwellers in the Hills*, Post. *The Octopus*, Frank Norris. *In the Country God Forgot*, Frances Charles. *The Untilled Field*, George Moore. *Esther Waters*, George Moore. *Ijain*, Lady Florence Dixie. *Wolf-Ville Days*, Lewis. *Masters of Men*, Robertson. *The Maid at Arms*, R. W. Chambers. *Active Service*, Crane. *The Transfiguration of Miss Philura*, Florence Kingsley. *The Historical Novel*, Brander Matthews. *Paradoxes*, Nordau.

Case 20:

Encyclopaedia Britannica, Ninth Edition, Vols. XVI–XXIV, *Index, American Supplement*, Vols. I–V.

Case 21:

Works of James Whitcomb Riley (10 books), Works of Eugene Field (12 books), *Rubaiyat of Omar Khayyam*, Gladstone Edition. *The Light of Asia*, Arnold. Chaucer's Poetical Works. Shelley's Poetical Works. Burns's Poems.

Case 22:

10 books by J. M. Barrie. *The Decameron of Boccaccio*, Vols. I–II. *The Heptameron of Margaret of Navarre*, Vols. I–II. *The Confessions of J. Jacques Rousseau*, Vols. I–II. *The Works of Francis Rabelais*, Vols. I–II. *The Tales and Novels of J. De La Fontaine*, Vols, I–II. *The Novellino of Masuccio*, Vols. I–II.

Case 23:

George Eliot's Works, 8 books. Victor Hugo, 22 books.

Case 24:

The Voice of the People, Glasgow. *Trilby*, Du Maurier. *Hugh Wynne*, Vols. I–II. *An English Woman's Love Letters*. *The Etchingham Letters*, Pollock and Maitland. *Cecilia*, Crawdord. *The Splendid Idle Forties*, Atherton. *From Milton to Tennyson*, L. D. Syle. *Methods of Authors*, Ericksen. *The Damnation of Theron Ware*, Harold Frederick. *The Master Christian*, Marie Corelli. *The Story of Ab*, Stanley Waterloo. *The King's Mirror*, Hope. *The Greater Inclination*, Edith Wharton. *Fantastic Fables*, Bierce. *Five Years of My Life*, Alfred Dreyfus. *The Odd Number*, Maupassant. *The Jimmyjohn Boss*, Owen Wister. *Lin McLean*, Owen Wister. *The Grey Wig*, I. Zangwill. *The Little White Bird*, Barrie. *Captain Macklin*, R. H. Davies. *Little Novels of Italy*, Maurice Hewlett. *Richard Yea and Nay*, Maurice Hewlett.

Case 25:

Honoré De Balzac, 25 books. *A Sack of Shakings*, F. I. Bullen. *A Bunch of Rope Yarns*, King.

Case 26:
Robert Louis Stevenson, Vols. I–XXII.

Case 27:
Letters, Robert Louis Stevenson, Vols, I–II. *Works*, Rudyard Kipling, Vols. I–XVIII. *Poetical Works*, Burns. *Poetical Works*, John Keats. *Faust*, Goethe. *Poetical Works*, Byron.

Case 28:
The Book of the Thousand Nights, Vols. I–XV.
Robert Browning, 6 books.

Case 29:
Mark Twain's Works, Vols. I–XXII.

Case 30:
Poe's Complete Works, 11 books.

Case 31:
Principles of Biology, Spencer, 15 books. Darwin, 9 books.

Case 32:
Darwin, 5 books. Huxley, 9 books. *Descent & Darwinism*, Schmidt. *Man and the Glacial Period*, Wright. *Criminal Sociology*, Ferri. *The Evolution of Man*, Haechel, Vols. I–II. *Educational Reformers*, Quick. *Evolution*, Le Conte. *Other Worlds than Ours*, Proctor. *Education as a Science*, Bain. *Life and Growth of Language*, Whitney. *Ancient Life History*, Nicholson.

Case 33:
The Sun, Young. *Responsibility in Mental Disease*, Maudsley. *History of Education*, Painter. *Religion & Science*, Draper. *Hours of Exercise in the Alps*, Tyndall. *Forms of Water*, Tyndall. *Fragments of Science*, Tyndall, Vols. I–II. *New Fragments*, Tyndall. *Sound*, Tyndall. *Mythropology*, Tylor. *Bimetallism in the U.S.*, Laughlin. *Culture Demanded by Modern Life*, Youmans. *What Is Electricity?* Trowbridge. *A History of the Warfare of Science with Theology*, White, Vols. I–II. *History of European Morals*, Lecky, Vols. I–II. *Wages and Capital*, Taussig. *Money and the Mechanism of Exchange*, Jevons. *Recent Economic* Wells. *Juvenile Offenders*, Morrison. *Woman's Share in Primitive Culture*, Mason. *The Female Offender*, Lombroso. *The Beginnings of Art*, Grosse.

Index